Journey Into The Light

The Path to Enlightenment and Transformation: An Ascension Manual For Apprentice Earth Masters

Art Martin Ph.D.

Other Books by Art Martin

Mind/Body Medicine Connection:
Pscychoneuroimmunology in Practice
Your Body Is Talking; Are You Listening?
Becoming a Spiritual Being In a Physical Body
2011: The New Millennium Begins
Opening Communication with GOD Source
Recovering Your Lost Self

Journey Into The Light

The Path to Enlightenment and
Transformation: An Ascension Manual
For Apprentice Earth Masters

Art Martin Ph.D.

Personal Transformation Press
A Division of the Wellness Institute

Journey Into The Light
by Art Martin Ph.D.

Published by
Personal Transformation Press
8300 Rock Springs Road
Penryn, CA 95663
Phone: (916) 663-9178
Fax: (916) 663-0134
Orders only: (800) 655-3846

ISBN 1-891962-05-1

Printed in the United States

Table Of Contents

Let There Be Peace On Earth

Let there be peace on earth
And let it begin with me.
Let there be peace on earth,
The peace that was meant to be.

With God as our one source
United all are we,
Let us walk with each other
In perfect harmony.

Let peace begin with me,
Let this be the moment now
With every step I take,
Let this be my solemn vow:

To take each moment
And live each moment
In peace eternally.

Let there be peace on earth
And let it begin with me.

— Anon

Dedication

This book is dedicated to all those
who have committed to the Spiritual Path.

Acknowledgments

Lifetime after lifetime, we come to the Earth plane in the hope of finally figuring out what is to be learned here so that we don't have to come back. Of course, this is not a realistic hope. Or is it? Until about forty years ago, I believed firmly that we are hopelessly and helplessly mired in the cycle of return. As a child I was aware of another reality but I did not understand it—nor was my mother willing to acknowledge it—so it was blocked out my life. Then I met a man who changed all that, a man who was intimately aware of the metaphysical realms. Beginning with palm reading and astrology, we soon delved into many new disciplines, and I thank him with all my heart for introducing me to the world of metaphysics. And this was at a time when most people considered the occult as tantamount to devil worship, when all the word really means is "hidden."

When I graduated from college, I lost contact with transformation and relapsed into the physical world for about 20 years, trying to make a living and raise a family. In 1977, my world turned around and I reawakened, prompted oddly by the night manager of the restaurant I owned. He rekindled my interest and again I really appreciate the time he spent with me.

Of all the teachers who came and went in my life after I sold the restaurant, Paul Solomon stands head and shoulders above the rest. He reawakened my basic knowledge of the ancient mystery schools and, in studying with him, I finally got on with the path to ascension. In his lifetime, he imparted to us a staggering body of knowledge.

During workshops with Ronald Beasley, I came to my understanding of the spiritual realm. I met Gwyn Judge, with whom I did much work exploring the world of transformation. In fact, this book is named after *Journey Into The Light*, which she originally loaned to me in 1979, and with whose concepts we spent many hours working. Intrigued with the idea that you could actually leave the physical world and take your body with you, Gwyn brought the process of ascension to my attention and we both committed to stepping off the cycle of return. I thank her for the opportunity to explore the process of ascension.

I also want to thank Mary Best and my wife, Susie, for all the work they have done, proofreading and correcting the manuscripts of my books.

My transformation would not have been possible without all of the people who have worked with me and helped me rewrite my life scripts. Most recently, Bernard Eakes has provided much of the needed support in shifting my life pattern so that I had the courage and self-confidence to write, and could get over a serious case of "writer's block."

My root problem with writing was fear of failure based on the fact that I perceived myself as "not all right." My basic interpretation was, "Because I am not acceptable, no one will be interested in reading what I write." This degenerated into self-rejection. My best teachers have been the students of N/CR who provided the medium to remove all those false beliefs, and the accompanying programs and patterns. I really appreciate their help in doing the work with me.

The final editing and getting to the point of publishing would not have happened without the help of Tony Stubbs, who has provided the inspiration to publish my books. His knowledge and expertise have put my books in the professional category, and without his help, this book would not be the same.

Preface

I had heard a few people talking about *ascension* but paid little attention until Clara, a friend, told me in 1979 that she was going to India to meet an ascended earth plane master by the name of Hari-Kan-Baba. I simply couldn't see why she would spend over $2000 to meet this man, until she returned with amazing stories about her experiences with him.

"He limits the time anyone can study with him to just two weeks because he feels that he can impart all you need to know in that period if you're committed. I was at a discussion group when two people started to argue with him about a point he'd been discussing. He stood up and said, 'I do not argue. What I was describing was fact and you can accept or not. It makes no difference to me. It just is.' When they continued to try to argue with him, he turned, walked right through the wall behind him, and disappeared for the rest of the evening. This upset many people because they had limited time and wanted to get as much information as possible.

"The next day, as I was walking down the street with him, it was raining hard and I was soaked through yet he was quite dry. When I asked him, 'How can this be?' he said, 'If you are in a light body, you are not dense. Things will go right through you.'

"I was going to ask him how he'd walked through the wall the previous evening, but he picked up on the question before I even asked. 'The same applies,' he said. 'As an ascended being, you are able to dematerialize yourself at will, so it looked as if I walked through the wall as I left because I was going in that direction. Actually, I dematerialized before I reached the wall, so it appeared that I'd gone through it. I had to leave because the dense negative attack thoughts were pulling me down. It is hard to maintain a light body in a negative environment.' "

His descriptions of what one must do to attain the level of awareness to attain enlightenment and step onto the ascension path were greatly in line with what I had read in *Journey Into The Light*, and prompted me to reread it. However, Gwyn had loaned out her copy to a friend who had lost it. The local metaphysical bookstore people told us that it was out-of-print, so we called the publisher, who denied having even published it. I tried to locate the authors but to no avail. They were psychologists who had hosted ascension study groups and conducted small workshops at their home in Santa Rosa, California until they moved to Hawaii in 1978. They were interested in stepping out of the cycle of return and had been researching the process for many years. Finally, a person who had attended one of their workshops told us that they had disappeared in May, 1980 without trace.

According to an article in the local newspaper, a friend had not seen them for a few days and went to check on them. No one was home, and food was on the kitchen table as if someone had been just about to sit down for breakfast. The cars were in the garage with the keys in them. Nothing had been damaged or was visibly out of place. The police theorized that the couple had been kidnapped with no struggle, and issued an all-points bulletin. However no trace was ever found of them and over 20 years later, no information has ever surfaced as to their whereabouts. We can only assume that their years of studying ascension finally paid off.

Many times I have heard people state that *this* is their last lifetime on this planet or *this* is their last incarnation. I have heard people in the past claim to be ascended beings but I have yet to meet one who could move from the physical to a light body at will and dematerialize on demand as could Hari-Kan-Baba. I understand from what I have read— and what the White Brotherhood and the Brotherhood of The Light have told me—that this is something people must demonstrate if they claim to have actually ascended. However, in my experience, ascended beings have no need to prove anything, so they will not perform tricks or rituals just to prove to you who they are. One of them once told me, "Those with the eyes to see and the ears to hear will be able to perceive who we are."

One may ask why I use the term "Apprentice Earth Masters" It goes back to 1979 and a two-week live-in spiritual bootcamp style workshop with Paul Solomon, where he described us as apprentice earth masters working to be meta-humans. He told us, "We will not make it to earth mastership in this workshop as this is only an initiation on to the path to enlightenment. You will not become a meta-human until you go through the bootcamp and work through the internship to earth mastership."

My intention in this book is to describe the path in our spiritual journey that takes us from conventional third-dimensional humans through transformation and enlightenment to become spiritual beings in physical bodies. When we make it to that level in our life, we are then ready to begin our internship as apprentice earth masters. At that point, we enter the transfiguration that leads to our becoming meta-humans who have the choice of total freedom as light beings.

Over the years, I have talked with many people who describe them-selves as light workers but I do not see the results in their lives. We must keep up with the times and energy shifts that are coming as we approach the critical mass shift in 2012. (It could happen sooner or as late as 2015.) We can work to shift the consciousness of this planet to a higher frequency, but we must rise up and take responsibility by doing the work in our own life, too. Nobody will do it for us, so must walk our own talk. We can play out our illusion, but we cannot fool the White Brotherhood, as they watch our progress on the path to enlight-enment. It is not to say that we are marionettes because we do have free choice, but we must follow a strict path on our spiritual journey if we expect to reach our ultimate goal of ascension.

From my reading and discussions with people about enlighten-ment, transformation and ascension over the years, many people accept and follow the New Age metaphysical concepts about the sub-ject, which involves a demanding regimen of spiritual practice. How-ever, many other people assume they can jump over the hard work and the reasons they incarnated on this planet in the first place, and simply proclaim that they are light workers.

Other people believe that humanity is going to be given some spe-cial dispensation to have a mass release of karma, and that a fleet of space ships will take us off this planet and rescue us from the terrible plight we are in. Who created all this mess we are in the first place and why would some extraterrestrials deny our free will and rescue us? Who are these beings that would come down and rescue us? The extra-terrestrials I communicate with say that this is nothing more than a pipedream to avoid taking responsibility for our own actions, and path to enlightenment and transformation. The Sirians said they know of no ET species willing step in and save us from our downward spiral.

The path of the earth master is not easy. Many times, I have doubted whether I was on the right track. Many of the lessons that I assumed were simple little tests turned out to be major initiations. This is not a path for faint-hearted or the undisciplined; if you choose to take the path to the light, be ready to climb the mountain. And once you embark on the path, you cannot back out. If you procrastinate, fall into confusion, or cannot discipline yourself to follow through, the cost could be high. You must walk your talk or you will cash yourself out in this lifetime, leaving the work to be done in some other incarnation.

Via after-death communication, some teachers who have passed on have told me that while alive they *thought* they were walking their talk, but now realize that they weren't, or they did not teach all the material to which they had access to. For example, Ronald Beasley said, "There was a fear I was not aware of when I was in the physical. I was afraid to teach all I knew for fear that once I had exhausted my material, I would lose my following. The fallacy behind this is that we need followers to validate us. We must detach from this need and transcend the desire to have others follow our path. We must allow those we teach to learn all we know so they can spread the word of light, love and forgiveness. We must also detach from what our students do with the knowledge for it is none of our concern. Our only obligation is to share it without regard to the outcome. Detaching from any results frees us up to stride forward on our path in integrity, honesty and with ethical behavior. We cannot cling to what we *think* our truth is, as there is only *one* eternal truth. Our path must be to find and teach that truth."

This tells us that we must become aware of all the fears that may block us from the path to the light. Before you make the transition into a light being, you must become an Earth master. However, you cannot just declare your mastery without going through the steps to initiation. History reveals that we *must* follow a path and that all paths get closer towards the top, ultimately merging into the single path to ascension. The results from past masters have proven we must follow their teaching but use discernment, because many people have corrupted the teaching or watered it down with their own beliefs. I have seen programs set up by self-proclaimed mystery school teachers who don't understand what comprises a mystery school curriculum or the concepts behind the foundation of the course material.

The spiritual journey must be built on a good foundation, which means clearing all the life lessons listed in our flight plan. Most people currently on the ascension path focus their attention on the spiritual processes, hoping to skip over the difficult task of clearing their childhood trauma because of the time, commitment and discipline needed to deal with childhood trauma and past life karma. Fortunately (or unfortunately according to your outlook), gathering those experiences is why we incarnated in the first place. Before we begin the journey, we must find out what those lessons were. Karma is the stumbling block that most people face in enlightenment. We must find out what lessons and programs are hidden in our time line and denial files so that we can release them. When we incarnated, our Holographic Mind downloaded the files from our flight plan so that we could take care of them. Then, as long as we demonstrate an awareness of the lessons and clear as many of them as we can, we can get on with the journey. Once they are cleared, it is smooth sailing.

Discernment is crucial to our awareness of the path's direction because, without it, illusion and denial can set in. If you do not have the ability to self-assess, it's easy to assume you are on the path. Many of my clients have discovered that, even after much diligent, focused work on the spiritual path, they have not even rounded the first corner in their journey. It's as if they are trapped in a revolving door, running hard but getting nowhere. Following a spiritual path may not lead to the expected spiritual journey unless you build a solid foundation to begin your evolution. In fact, I have worked with many people who have been on the path for up to 30 years and think they've attained much knowledge and made great progress, only to discover that they have built no foundation. They may have learned and practiced many processes yet are still caught in the revolving door of the first initiation. Discovering that their many years of work have achieved very little progress is disheartening.

When I started this journey, I was studying with many teachers until I found two who provided me with the answers I needed to begin the spiritual journey. Many people criticized the personal behavior of one the teachers, commenting that he was not walking his own talk, and asked me why I was continuing to study with him. I replied, "Some lesson may wake him up in the future but, if it does not, it's not my problem. He's able to provide me with what I'm searching for at this time. And as long as he provides the material I need for my personal growth, I'm not interested in what he's doing in his personal life. He may be teaching what he needs to learn, but that's not my concern. I'm only interested in what he has to offer as a teacher."

Paul Solomon's teachings provided me with many of the steps in my enlightenment. Quite often, I noticed that he was not walking his talk, but that wasn't important to me. I knew that he would recognize when he was off the path at times and center himself, which he did often over the ten years I studied with him. The information and understanding I sought were more important to me than losing my focus on the goal and falling into the trap of judgment. I received more than I expected in my tenure with Paul. My relationship with him worked for me, but it didn't work for other students who became caught up in judgment or didn't want to do the work required.

One of our major lessons on the earth plane is the let go of the need to judge. One the major lessons in enlightenment, judgment will hold you back. If you judge another person's path or what they are working with, you may be creating karma for yourself. We all have the right to our own path, whether it's right or wrong in someone else's interpretation. If it's a detour, then it's *your* challenge to correct your path. If you're willing to accept others' interpretations, that too is your choice.

In my teaching work over the past few years, I have found this same lesson confronting me. Some people object to my views on such topics as attached spirit beings, alien intruders and negative thought forms. Granted this is a new concept for many people and may be threatening to them, but it does exist. Denial does not make these things go away. When my clients and I clear attached beings in my sessions, amazing changes take place, such as the release of schizophrenia and other forms of mental illness, hyperactivity and addictions. People are free to disagree with other people's viewpoints, and detachment is vital here as humans are quick to reject concepts that threaten them. Over time, a few people have judged me and claimed that I was not walking my talk on an issue because they couldn't accept my views on the topic. Again, are we going to throw out the teacher or the teaching because we do not accept one of its concepts?

As long as I can prove and document that a concept works, I will teach it. If I later discover that it does not work, I'll drop it and move on. As an eclectic, I study every form and concept I can, and try everything, as I am my own laboratory. I try all concepts on myself before I introduce them in my teaching or with my clients, and include in my training and practice only those concepts that work over time. I refuse to reject a concept out of fear because that forces us to give our power away. Some of the positions I have taken in my personal life may cause people to judge me as out of integrity or not walking my talk but I refrain from judging others by their actions. I may observe people's behavior based on spiritual principles but they have a right to their opinion and I will not condemn their viewpoints.

When people ask me, "When you say you're searching for the truth, what are you actually searching for?" I answer, "I'm looking for processes and information that work to help us on our spiritual journey. I want pragmatic evidence that the process works on the path. I'm not interested in beliefs, illusions or interpretations of something that someone is passing off as method or a training that doesn't get results. I'm looking for teachings and training that embodies forgiveness, uncon-ditional love, non-judgment, and are devoid of manipulation, control or authority."

In recent history, some of the trainings played games such as not allowing attendees to go to the restroom. And anyone who does is not allowed back in until the next break. Similarly, latecomers are not allowed in until the break. In other training, the staff verbally beat people up with foul language, something I find totally uncalled for and unacceptable. However, most of those programs have died out.

Other people who are looking for a path or group where they do not have to make decisions; I call this falling into the Guru Syndrome. Such followers trade their personal power and freedom for the security of the group, not caring that the primary goal of personal empower-ment is not being met.

As far as Ego is concerned, I differ completely from the Eastern phi-losophy. To me, Ego is essential for an orderly mind and is that part of our mind that files ideas and experiences in the mind's "data base." Enlightenment is a cooperative process that involves our whole being, because body, mind and spirit are one and must be in harmony if we are to move forward on the path. Trying to destroy any part of our being will put us in chaos and create dysfunctional behavior. Trying to deny any part of our mind will cause a breakdown in the whole, as the whole of the self is greater than the sum of its parts. Every part of the mind has to be functioning effectively for us to reach enlightenment.

I value my freedom as the ultimate level of being, but this requires responsibility, a commitment that that scares many people from the path as they would rather have someone else make their decisions for them. Directing your own path takes discipline and consistent effort. For some people, a structured environment is more comfortable since their path is already laid out for them. I do not want anyone telling me that I must practice a certain ritual, follow a certain path or how to run my life. This book honors personal freedom and free will by laying out a path that guides and suggests rather than dictate.

Before you incarnated, you filed a flight plan with the Lords of Karma that specified your goals for the upcoming lifetime and the lessons you intended to take on. The Akashic Record is the companion to that plan. Unless you sealed the records, your past and present accomplishments, including where you are on your journey in this life, are available for viewing. The Akashic goes by many names, such as the Collective Unconscious but I describe it as the "Akashic Internet" because it can be accessed in the same way that one would access the Internet with a computer. In this analogy, your mind is the computer, your Higher Self is the phone line, the individual records are the websites, and the Highest Source of Your Being is the search engine that actually locates the website you're looking for. Every person who has lived on this planet has a personal "website" on the Akashic Internet that is available for anyone to view.

The steps of initiation along the mystery school path laid out in this book are not simple processes that you can zip through once you decide that you want to begin your journey to transformation. The initiation on each of the steps takes you through each door when you have proven that you are ready for the specific initiation by learning the lessons and taking and passing the tests.

Each path has many concepts that hopefully will work for you, but do not feel that you must accept all of them in totality. This book is a compendium of what works for us, and I hope you can put this process to work for you. If you can understand and set in motion the right causes to overcome victim consciousness, and work with the totality of your being, then you're on the path to enlightenment and mastership. Claims do not hold water; only demonstrable results prove your ability and readiness to your White Brotherhood teachers. When you demonstrate non-attachment and complete masterful control over your life at every level, it's quite obvious to those who have eyes to see and ears to hear. Universal laws and spiritual principles exist independent from our physical plane reality. We cannot control or change them; they just are. We are evaluated by our acceptance of them, not by our own beliefs or interpretations of them.

In a lecture in 1992, a psychology instructor at U.C. Berkeley presented a lecture on Native American shamanism and psychology. She was a full blood Cherokee Indian but denied being a medicine woman even though her grandmother had taught her all she knew in the practice. She said, "I'm quite appalled at all the pseudo-shamans and medicine people running around claiming to be teachers of Native American tradition. I can't understand why people would want to steal others' practices and try to make them their own. It would be different if they'd actually been trained through internship, but very few have. Most are self-taught and simply decide to claim the path."

When asked about ritual, she said, "Ritual is for the uninitiated, because true shamans and medicine people can create with the power of heaven and earth. They have no need for ritual, because they can create miracles from their own power that comes through them from Source." She also described the coming of the true spiritual teachers, Shamans and medicine people who will arise in the new millennium. The year 2000 will be the turning point. The pseudo teachers will begin to be exposed and fall away as people discover who the real teachers are. Also many organizations will fail if they do not follow the universal law of integrity, honesty and ethics."

Someone in the audience asked, "Where the did the term 'shaman' come from. Did it originate in the native North or South American cultures?"

She replied, "The root of the term is Turko-Persian, and originated in the ancient mystery schools."

Paul Solomon once said, "In the coming age, all organizations and businesses must be organized according to the Cabalistic tree or they will eventually fail." What this means is that, in the new age we are entering, we must be more aware of how we conduct our life. As time speeds up, everything responds more quickly, including karma. There is no justification, rationalization or excuse for unethical behavior.

It's as if the universe has an invisible Internet antenna that broadcasts to people about which are the most impeccable businesses and which are the best events to attend. The events that are not based on universal law do not get the patronage and eventually fail.

A good example or organizational karma came when we recently participated in a New Age Expo held in Sacramento, California. We had paid well in advance for a corner booth in a prime location but were delayed by two hours in arriving to set the booth up. Many would-be exhibitors had just showed up, hoping to find a booth, and the Expo manager gave our booth to a friend of his. When we arrived, the manager refused to give us the booth we had paid for and, since the show was sold out, could not give us another, so we ended up with just a bare table in a poor location. When I asked for a refund, the manager refused, so I had to arrange for a charge back through the credit card company and did eventually receive my refund.

Around the same time, the Expo promoter listed her bookstore for sale. The store didn't sell, however, so she simply closed it, losing her sizable investment. When she'd bought it ten years earlier, the store had been a successful and profitable operation for two decades but, under her ownership, began losing business because she hired inexperienced employees who did not take care of the store and were indifferent to customers. The Expo I mentioned above was a financial failure and, within four months, they stopped publishing their metaphysical newspaper and filed bankruptcy, never to be heard from again. As predicted by the professor at U.C. in her lecture in 1992, this is happening increasingly to people who are not in integrity or less than impeccable.

We were also exhibitors in a Toronto show in October, 2001 that was poorly attended. I also offered sessions and asked my clients why they did not attend the show. Their replies were along the lines of: "I intended to go but something came up so I wasn't able to get there." Others said, "The organizers jammed too many unknown speakers into the schedule." Some even said, "There was bad energy about the show." This was curious, because two other Toronto shows in 2001 had been well-attended and very successful for both us and the show promoters.

We declined to participate in four major shows during 2001 that we have regularly spoken at and exhibited in for 18 years because the staff treated us with condescension, as if their show did not need our participation. And every show lost money. One show was such a disaster for the vendors and the speakers that the organizers had to cancel the remainder of the shows for the rest of the year. They tried to blame it on the September 11 terrorist attacks, yet earlier shows had also done poorly. Further, a show in Philadelphia in October was a great success for the organizers and the exhibitors.

What does this reveal to us? When selling products or services to the public, we must be in integrity and ethical in our activity. We must handle all our affairs impeccably, because the Akashic Internet will energetically broadcast whatever we do.

If we do not treat people honestly and responsibly, it will backfire on us. If we do not treat our potential customers ethically, the invisible broadcast system will send out a message to keep people from attending our event or business. We have seen this happen repeatedly and are becoming more discerning after losing a lot of money on shows that failed to attract the numbers of attendees promised by the promoters.

With today's events costing $50,000 to $100,000 to put on, it is important that the show producers recognize that it is a different playing field than it was ten years ago. These days, business and personal karma happens immediately and will impact every level of our lives.

Where does this put you on the path? Since I am presenting my theories in this book, should you follow them? Some people say that I have created my own school of psychology and spirituality. I feel that I have tapped into the original source of knowledge that functions from the wisdom of peace, happiness, harmony and joy, with unconditional love and forgiveness as the guiding wisdom. To quote Lesson 121 in *A Course In Miracles*, "Forgiveness is the way to happiness."

When people ask me if I am a Christian, what church I attend, or what philosophy I follow, I reply, "For fifty years, I searched for the truth and a God I could believe in but did not find God in the Christian churches."

My book *Opening Communication With The GOD Source* relates my search for God and you will get your answer there, and this book offers some quotes from that book.

I personally make no decision as to where clients are on their journey. I ask their bodies by using Kinesiology (muscle testing) or watch their progress during a guided imagery going through the second initiation. This will reveal exactly where they are on their path. Regarding something that you may or may not have accomplished, you can fool yourself but not the Akashic Record. Every step and every action is recorded, so there are no false reports in the Akashic Record. I am not responsible for finding clients' paths for them. I only report on what has worked for me and other clients.

Before reading this book and embarking on your spiritual journey to ascension, please read my earlier books or least have access to them as we will refer to them and we do not want to repeat the same material.

We are the movers and the shakers in our lives. Nobody will do it for us as we are responsible for all our actions and the results we create. We have plenty of help available on our spiritual journey, and all we need do is access it. Have a great flight into the light.

Art Martin, Penryn California
December 2001

Introduction

I have found that many processes of transformation have 12-Step programs to help those in transition reclaim their personal power. In some of them, you can avoid the lessons but you do not get the payoff or "Pass Go and collect $200" until you take responsibility and recognize that *you* are responsible for everything that happens to you. You set all of it up somewhere on your path. There are no denials or illusions in the 12-Step program in this book; the only person you can fool is you. You can make all the claims you want but teachers from the Brotherhood of Light perform the actual grading and measure your progress. If you are willing to face the lessons, take responsibility and be honest with yourself, you can make fast progress. But, if you delude yourself into thinking you are a high being, clear of the lessons of the earth plane, refusing to deal with them, you may find yourself up a creek without a paddle, and with no one to call on for help when this planet hits critic mass and takes a quantum leap in consciousness.

In the 12-step movements, people may need a support group to help them realize that they are not lone victims adrift in a dysfunctional world. But many of them give their personal power away to the group, restating their victim-ness each time they attend a meeting. Once they recognize that no one is going to pull them out of their dysfunctional pattern and that it's up to them and, when they forgive their perceived oppressors, their life gets on track.

Some people feel that they must have a teacher or a guru to show them the way and lead them on the path. As we've seen before, these people cannot discipline themselves to follow through, and need continual encouragement to stay on the path. I have also met many teachers who claim they can do the spiritual work for you, but they're not walking their talk. My feeling is this is a self-directed course but getting started does take some direction. You do need a teacher in the beginning to show you the requirements and how to get on the path to enlightenment. However, you must use your discernment to make the proper choice and avoid following a dead end road that leads to disillusionment. After the initial introduction, it is then your responsibility to follow the directions given. Teachers can help you along the path but they cannot do the work for you.

Is a teacher a must on the path to enlightenment? No, but it helps in the beginning so you do not take dead end roads. Also, in the beginning, few people can discipline themselves to follow the path without some guidance and support. However, I have found that courses of study fail when students give their power away to the teacher and follow blindly without empowering themselves. Many teachers get their validation and self-worth from having followers who give away their power to them, but ironically followers do not make the first step on the journey until they reclaim their personal power.

Codependency comes in many disguises, so often we do not recognize we have replaced our parents with a guru or teacher. To find a true teacher with pure motives who has no need to control is rare. On my journey, I found two of them who empowered me to take my power and reclaim my self-esteem, confidence and self-worth. Doing so was a valuable lesson for me.

In my journey and teaching work, I am against following a teacher or guru because followers may become locked into the guru's path and thereby relinquish their power of choice. I have sampled the offerings of many teachers and selected what I wanted for my journey. Granted, this takes discipline and discernment but I feel that it has been more effective because the eclectic path provides more options. There is only one truth and our task is to find it, but undergrowth can obscure the true path. If we expect a guru or teacher to show us a path and lead us on it, I think we are missing the boat.

Regarding enlightenment, transformation and ascension, I follow the concepts developed in ancient the mystery schools. When the mystery schools alluded to ascension, they described a difficult path on the way to self-mastery. Many people seem to think that ascension is a simple journey that they can begin with a few ritual blessings or a meditation process, but it is not. My research has revealed that almost all mystery schools defined the early steps of the ascension path to include training the mind to:

1. Heal the separation with self.
2. Overcome self-rejection and become all right with yourself.
3. Release the need for control, authority, judgment or outside validation.
4. Reclaim personal power.
5. Become a cause in your life where you create your own reality.
6. Reach the point of awareness and detachment that leads to enlightenment.
7. Begin your internship.

We must begin as an apprentice, just as carpenters or plumbers must serve four years before they can become journeymen. Do you think life is any different? Why are almost all families dysfunctional? People are raising children without any training whatsoever, and can't even deal with their own lives themselves. Even though their own lives don't work, they embark on raising children. How can anyone bring functional children into this world when they are dysfunctional role models who can't conduct their own lives in a functional manner?

The resulting breakdown in our society is a vicious downward spiral due to the illusion that we can run our life and teach others how to live without any proper training. Then we run into the ultimate illusion that we do not have to do anything because somebody else will take responsibility for us, as per the eastern belief that everything is the will of God and is a fatalistic destiny that we cannot change.

Once you reclaim your personal power and take responsibility for your life, you do not need outside validation or acceptance, and can begin rebuilding your self-esteem and self-worth. Reclaiming personal power may sound simple but, in fact, it takes great discipline, commitment and consistency to follow through and release all the sub-personalities and programs that drive our life.

Many people try to avoid this work by going into denial, renouncing the world and following a spiritual path in which they do not need to make any decisions or confront their lessons in life. The path is all laid out for them, and all they need do is follow the leader and honor his decisions. This spiritual path does not lead to enlightenment, and such followers put their life on hold until they take responsibility for why they incarnated on this planet in a body in the first place.

Many other people believe that they can simply meditate their way to ascension or that fasting will lead them there. But I have yet to hear of a person achieving ascension by meditation and/or fasting alone. It may seem redundant to ask this question, but we must remind ourselves over and over again; "Why *did* we come here to this planet in the first place?"

We came here because the earth plane is the only dimension that provides conditions in which we can learn certain things. One of the best and fastest ways to learn about love is through its absence, but since love abounds on the soul plane, we can't effectively learn about it there. So we incarnate into a dimension where love is not taken for granted. But to avoid the lessons of the earth plane is to waste an incarnation and guarantee that you will need to return here until you decide to deal with them. You came here to clear your karma, learn earth plane lessons and become an earth master, so why deny your purpose just because it looks difficult?

I contend that few gurus, shamans, medicine people, teachers or spirit guides have achieved the level of enlightenment to help you in this journey. Those capable enlightened ones here to help will seldom interact directly with you. However, they monitor you all the time and place lessons and temptations before you every day to see if you will recognize them. You must do the work yourself; no guru or guide can carry you on the path.

Many people are rightly concerned about dark force entities from all levels that seek to beguile and deceive us with thoughts that we are enlightened masters. Their intent is to mislead us and throw us off our path to enlightenment.

In my research, I have found that the information about the concepts of universal law and spiritual principles from before the time of Atlantis were transmitted down through many groups that survived the pole shifts and subsequent earth changes. A few of the groups that scattered across the planet retained all knowledge about the spiritual journey but most did not because their knowledge became watered down by the political and religious leaders, and the gurus and teachers who set themselves up as the authorities on the law and the path. In order to establish their authority, they set themselves up as interpreters of the information that was passed down. Because nothing was written down, their word became the truth. Unfortunately, their Machiavellian methods were not true to universal law and spiritual principles because they had degenerated into power plays, control and manipulation. In order to be the intermediaries between God or the gods, these unscrupulous manipulators had to control the populace, so they passed down their concepts in a way that gave them power over the people. Over the millennia, the corrupt information became the accepted rule of law and the spiritual principles on which many cultures based their society.

A few groups of people, such as the Hawaiian Kuhuna, were able to keep the records clear of control and preserve the truth of the original universal law and spiritual principles from the GOD Source. The Kahuna remained isolated from any other culture until American Christian missionaries tried to force Christianity on them and destroy the Kuhuna traditions and culture. This is just one example of what happened to countless other cultures over the past 2,000 years. Zealous religious missionaries move in and try to destroy the existing free spirit cultures and traditions, and force their methods and teachings on peoples they declare as "ignorant savages." As with Native American peoples, the Kuhuna followed the wisdom of their culture for almost 10,000 years, yet an upstart religion such as Christianity invades them, takes over their kingdom, kills their leaders and forces an alien way of life on them. The aboriginals are then banned from using their rituals, traditions and even language, as when Native American children were dragged from their villages and shipped off to Christian schools, miles away from home.

Some cultures use God to justify aggression and religious wars, claiming they are destroying the imperialist aggressors, as we see in the Middle East with religious wars between the various factions. The loss of spiritual principles such as "Treat your neighbor as yourself" has brought us to our current level of degeneration. Nowadays, people set themselves up as authorities and pass off their beliefs as the truth even though there is no way to validate their source. How can a terrorist leader claim that a suicide bomber will have a special place with Allah, or that Allah approves of this aggression because the West is trying to destroy them? And a whole generation has grown up being taught that martyrdom is a noble thing and brings high honor to one's family.

Many people contend that there are many paths to the truth and there are many truths. I disagree; there may be many paths to enlightenment but they all merge into one as the only path to ascension, and they all focus on the Golden Rule: "Treat everyone as you yourself would wish to be treated."

According to anthropologists and paleontologists, the Earth has seen four waves of humanity that degenerated and were ended by cleansing. Today, we have degenerated almost to the level of chaos of Atlantis at the time of its destruction.

Of course, many dedicated lightworkers strive to restore the original wisdom and the teachings of the mystery schools but it's an uphill battle as this planet is in the final ten to fifteen years of this cycle. If we can change the consciousness that pervades planet Earth, we may avoid a fifth cleansing. There are hopeful signs. For example, many prophets predicted that California would break up into a series of islands but, because consciousness is shifting very fast on the West Coast, such doom-laden predictions have been transfigured.

I view our current dilemma as one of recognizing the duality we are living in and then detaching from it by reprogramming our mind to let go of the need to be recognized, validated and accepted—the final key in non-attachment. As we approach enlightenment, we shall see that control sub-personalities are our greatest challenge to deal with. But when we recognize that no one can reject or abandon us, we can move into the knowingness that, "I am all right."

Two other major obstacles are "I need to be someone" and "I need to be needed by someone." When we overcome our needs to be acknowledged, validated, needed and in control, we are on the path to enlightenment.

Most people have to go through a *dark night of the soul* to get to the level of awareness where they can detach from codependent victim consciousness. When suffering or pain rears its ugly head, many people run from it and never get through the valley of the snakes. However, we must hold our head high and not look down, knowing that we will get through without falling or getting lost. You can only lose your way and get pulled down when you doubt your ability to make it through this lesson. We can postpone the dark night of the soul for a while but must go through it sometime. However, the longer we wait, the more complex it gets. Our intent, discipline, and commitment determine its intensity.

I have noticed a phenomenon among baby boomers and their children that triggers dark night of the soul experiences. They attend workshops and seminars to collect concepts and information on spiritual growth and transformation, yet they do not apply the processes to their own lives. If you begin the spiritual journey and give up or drop out, assuming you can resume later, you will be surprised to find that your mind has allowed autopilot to take over, and that you will need to reclaim your personal power all over again. If this happens too often, you'll have a battle on your hands to wrest control from Middle Self.

Gaining enlightenment does not involve enduring emotional or physical pain and suffering. When we become aware that this is all a dream, we can break out of the illusion and transcend emotions because they are an illusion that we use to protect and defend ourselves. Then we pass to first step in enlightenment.

About five percent of the population does not have to go through the dark night of the soul. From childhood, these persistent "survivors" have disciplined themselves to take responsibility, to not let circumstances pull them down, and to not give up or let other people control them.

What Is Enlightenment?

The word enlightenment is bandied about by many people who desire to get on the spiritual path without knowing what the term really means and what is required to embark on this spiritual journey. Quite often, people will describe their spiritual awakening as a situation where they experience a vision or an opening in their awareness which puts them in contact with a new reality. Becoming aware of a new reality is an opening to a new way of viewing our life path, but is it enlightenment? The experience may show you what you could be if only you would commit yourself to a new concept and set your intention to discipline yourself to follow through on your commitment.

Desire and wanting will not produce the result. Intention and discipline are 80 percent of the requirement; knowledge is only 20 percent of what you need to reach enlightenment. You can know all the methods, spiritual principles, and the universal laws needed to meet the requirements, yet not be on a spiritual journey. Knowledge alone will not provide the results without the intention and discipline to follow through and walk the talk.

What is enlightenment then? It is an opening process wherein the mind changes its view of reality. This is not an instant process whereby you're suddenly a different person. It's becoming aware that you can move to a different reality and see life from a different viewpoint. When you get to the point where you can recognize that you are not treading along the same old rut of life, you come to a new reality. You begin to detach from the need to follow a set path. Detachment allows you to be flexible, so that you can take a new path without needing to remain in control. As you climb the path of transformation, the result is enlightenment. Detachment and forgiveness are the keys.

Some devotees of eastern disciplines describe enlightenment as "detachment and demise of the Ego." Others feel that if you renounce the world and go into seclusion, you can find it. I disagree totally. All my books stress that Ego is our friend, not our enemy. Some believe that you can find enlightenment through Tantra and sex. I disagree with this concept also and ask, "How can sex, which is a function controlled by the limbic, or lowest, level of the brain, ever provide the path to enlightenment?"

Many western teachers see sex as meditation to make contact with ascended masters. But how is one going to make contact with the spiritual self when the personality self is blocking the path? If you're on autopilot and not taking responsibility for your life, how are you going to make contact with the spiritual self? Separation at the level of the personality self blocks your ability to make the shift to contact High Self. If you don't have a telephone operator, how do you get a phone line into the Source of information that can guide you on your spiritual journey?

We can set as many goals as we want but they are all as hollow as New Year's resolutions if we don't discipline ourselves to follow through. Many people have attended the same workshops and seminars that I have over the past 25 years, yet I find when I meet them today that they're still in the same place in their lives that they were back then. Typically, they say, "I just was not in position to follow through," "I didn't have the time," or, "I got sidetracked and didn't recognize that I was in a rut."

Others said, "It was too much work," or, "I studied the materials but it didn't seem to produce results. I didn't experience any change in my life. Without a teacher to work with, I feel off the path."

These comments reveal why you must commit yourself to the path, and discipline yourself to follow through. Enlightenment doesn't just happen through awareness, which explains why many people make very little progress on their spiritual journey.

A specific spiritual path doesn't always lead to enlightenment. You must reach the level in your awareness of spiritual principles where transformation takes you into the enlightenment process. Not all cultures on this planet acknowledge this viewpoint, however. In fact, very few people know anything at all about this process of enlightenment. Most eastern cultures, philosophies and religions teach that we need an intermediary to provide the teaching and the path to enlightenment. The guru, or enlightened master, provides the direction based on teachings of Buddha, the various sects of Zen, Vipassana, Tibetan and Taoist traditions, or Hindu practices such as Vedanta and Adurveya.

The West is divided into many different sects and viewpoints. Conservative Christian dogma believes that they teach the only path to God through Jesus Christ as savior. Some New Age-style churches have developed a new brand of spirituality, an eclectic mixture of many concepts that fit their beliefs. These people question the nature of enlightenment and the right path to spiritual transformation. Some people criticize this "Boomerism," in which babyboomers take a little of this program, a little of that religion, and some of that spiritual discipline, in effect, becoming collectors of concepts without ever getting serious about applying any of them. As a result, they make little progress on the path to enlightenment and transformation.

Orthodox or traditional western psychology has separated from the spiritual path, triggering a major split on the role of the mind in transformation and enlightenment. Psychologists have reached their limits in being able to help us resolve the issues of value and meaning. At least an emerging group in the field of psychology acknowledges and incorporates spiritual principles in its work and teaching. There is an attempt in western psychology to bring spiritual principles back into the field of psychotherapy, which has its roots in the human potential movement of the sixties. In fact, Transpersonal Psychology and Humanistic Psychology have established themselves as authoritative voices on contemporary spirituality. However, I see them as being only on the periphery of true spiritual practice.

Defining spirituality is difficult, because religious people claim to be spiritual yet, in actual practice, they do not practice what I would describe as "spirituality." Some in the psychology field are asking, "Is spirituality, as the synthesis of the emotional, intuitive and inner realms, an important compass for orienting us in our lives and relationships?" I applaud psychologists for asking in-depth questions about our reality. Their research reveals that people become increasingly interested in spirituality as they pass the age of forty, and peak in their sixties. It seems that younger people are looking for a path in which they do not have to take responsibility, whereas those in the older group want more control over their lives. As they work through their search, they discover what spirituality is, and few describe it as "religion."

A study group polled by Psycho-Matrix through *New Age Magazine* found the profile of those who responded to the survey to be: 83 % female, 85% college graduates with 45% with advanced degrees. The survey also noted that spirituality was extending into business and personal relationships where it made it easier for people to relate to each other.

There seems to be a wide gap between what people think spirituality is and what the spiritual path is. God Source clarified this for me when I was writing my book *Opening Communication With God Source*. They define *spirituality* as: "The result of learning the lessons that are presented to you and letting go of the emotional attachments that hold you back from evolving." On the other hand, they define the *spiritual path* as: "The specific practice undertaken in one's learning," the *spiritual journey* as: "The journey of soul and spirit to heal the separation from self," and *enlightenment* as: "The result of awareness as you learn the lessons on the journey."

Many of eastern thought describe the mind and the Ego as the enemy of enlightenment, while others such as the Dalai Lama, describe it in this way: "Merely increasing the capacity of knowing is a level of enlightenment, but is limited. So the term *'enlightenment'* could refer to knowing something that you had not realized what you could be. When we speak about enlightenment at the state of Buddha-hood, we are speaking about a fully awakened state. That is why all our efforts should go to training or shaping our minds. Emotions such as hatred, resentment or strong attachments are destructive and harmful. We call them negative emotions. So how can we reduce these negative emotions? Not through prayer or physical exercise, but through train-ing of the mind. We try to increase the opposite qualities of compas-sion. Unbiased compassion will increase awareness. All the destructive emotions are based on ignorance. The antidote is enlightenment. That is why it is very important to analyze the world of the mind and find out what its basic nature is: what are the categories of the mind, and which are destructive and which are constructive. Some modern schol-ars have described true Buddhism as a *science of the mind.*"

Throughout my research, teachings that ring true to me all point to disciplining the mind. My contention has always been that, when we can control our mind and our thoughts, we will be on the most effec-tive track to enlightenment. Our mind can create illusions, delusions, misconceptions and misinterpretations that we may interpret as real-ity. What then is reality? That which we see? Is there one truth that we will not perceive until, as the Dalai Lama said, "We are enlightened when we arrive at the fully awakened state." But when do we reach that state of mind? Again the Dalai Lama said, "When we reach the point of emptiness and detachment, we are approaching enlightenment."

The many varied philosophies, cultures and religions on this planet all have a different interpretation of what is the state of enlightenment. Some see it as renouncing the world and separating from its conflicts. Others view it as following a spiritual path that focuses on acknowl-edging the world's conflicts but not letting them affect you.

Joseph Goldstein, a modern American Buddhist teacher, says that: "Real transcendence is a function of wisdom, not a function of some altered state or getting to some other reality. Spiritual practice, even in the most orthodox traditions, is about freeing the mind from attachment. It is not indifference. It is not pulling back. It's about how we relate in the world. Do we relate from a place of freedom or from a place of non-freedom?"

Eckart Tolle, a German-born Buddhist teacher, expands on the same concept: "Transcending the world does not mean to withdraw from the world, to no longer take action or to stop interacting with people. Transcendence of the world is to act and interact without any self-seeking, to enhance one's sense of self through one's actions and interactions with people. Ultimately, it means not needing the future anymore for one's fulfillment or one's sense of self or being. There is no seeking through doing, seeking an enhanced or greater sense of self in the world. When seeking is not there anymore, then you can be in the world, but not of the world. You are not seeking for anything to identify with out there. The purpose of the world is for you to be lost in it, to create the suffering that you needed for the awakening to happen. Once the awakening happens, with it comes the realization that suffering is unnecessary. You have reached the end of suffering because you have transcended the world."

Mind Control

My book *2011: The New Millennium Begins* explores the battle for your mind and how mind control is used at every level our world. On our journey, we have run into aliens who are much more technologically advanced than we are. Their desire to control drives them to use insidious mind control techniques to take over and possess people without their knowledge. Fourth-dimensional, or astral plane, resident, demonic and inter-dimensional beings proliferate and more people are being controlled and channeling the dark side than the light side.

Many people deny the subject of ET control, yet such denial actually supports and promotes the alien agenda. Denying the existence of something does not make it go away but merely allows it to operate unimpeded. I have been dealing with the dark forces for 20 years and, when people tell me, "I don't believe that dark forces are affecting people, therefore they don't exist," I simply shake my head at this ultimate and dangerous denial.

Problems with possession, curses, hexes and spells often go back to past lives when we were involved with the dark forces. During the

Inquisition (1200 – 1600 AD), dark forces often took refuge in the Roman Catholic Church, and *many* of my clients find they took vows, oaths and allegiances with the Church at that time. And most of those vows are still are in force today. I have worked with Catholic priests who have left the Church, only to find that their vows, oaths and allegiances are still in full force. Not only that, but the Church has placed curses, hexes and spells on them in current time in *this* life for leaving the order.

For example, a former priest contacted me. He had been transferred from a small town to the San Francisco diocese and was appalled at the sexual misconduct, dishonest financial dealings and other unethical practices of the people he had to work with. After he'd left the Roman Catholic order in protest, he started to notice that he was losing the feeling in the left side of his body. Thinking he may have suffered a minor stroke, he went to his doctor, who found nothing wrong with him. The condition became progressively worse, to the point that he lost control of the left side of his body. A friend referred him to me but he was skeptical because the medical field couldn't help him. In one session, we cleared all the symptoms and, in a second, we removed the curses, hexes and spells that the church put on him after he left.

I personally have had many troubled dealings with various churches in my past lives. When I confronted the conflicts from the past, all hell broke loose. Unwinding my connections with organized religion and the dark forces took more than a year. When I tried to break free of my dark force connections, all the dark force inter-dimensional beings and aliens bombarded me relentlessly, trying to stop me from breaking free of their control. After I cleared all the lessons and connections, all conflict dropped away and my life became much smoother and free of interference.

The battle for control of the so-called New World Order has been going on for over 12,000 years. The Roman Catholic Church took the reins in 300 AD and held them until 1954, when the leaders of the most powerful nations of this planet signed a historic agreement with dark force aliens. Under this agreement, the aliens provided advanced technology such as the transistor and fiber optics and many other advances in science. In return, the governments agreed to look the other way regarding alien bases, animal mutilation, and human abduction, etc. This has now gotten out-of-hand to the point that the dark forces are using mind control to work with terrorists.

Terrorist bombings and the recent World Trade Center destruction are not new and will continue until we pull out of our downward spiral. As the Pogo the cartoon character said, "I have found the enemy and he is us." Our apathetic behavior as a culture has brought all this on. Nobody can do anything to you unless you set up the situation and refuse to take responsibility. All the out-of-integrity and unethical behavior of the last ten years has just been pushed under the carpet. The downward spiral must stop, and we are the only ones who are going to stop it, yet we try to explain away and cover up anything we do not want to deal with.

Governments throughout the world are always looking for a patsy or fall guy to take the blame for a bombing or act of terrorism. These are worldwide groups bent on taking control and making money from their terrorism. The cover-up is so obvious now that mind control is not only working on the people who create these terrorist acts but also on people in general, who are buying the line that just a small group is responsible. People seem to have their heads in the sand, so that they do not have to take responsibility for the results of their inaction. The degeneration of our society is out-pictured in daily news headlines. People appear unwilling to be concerned with events outside of their own little life circle. The World Trade Center bombing in 1993 did not wake us up, so the lesson came back again, only much more intensely. What will it take to wake people up?

The American people may wake up to what is happening now but why did it take such an appalling disaster? Unfortunately, however, the situation may backfire and provoke a knee-jerk reaction of anger and revenge that would show that we have still not learned the lesson. It will therefore reoccur, only of an even more disastrous nature until we learn that we cannot act out in anger, resentment and revenge.

The cancer enveloping this planet began 2,000 years ago with the murder of a teacher sent by the White Brotherhood to show us the way. We seem to be "playing tag" with the universal principles that are supposed to guide us. Major social cancers escalate into wars and we suffer the consequences, eventually finding peace for a short while. Then the cycle repeats. In the last ten years, the cancer in the Middle East has metastasized. We no longer have one person leading a movement as in the past, but a network of loosely knit Muslim groups unified by the same objective—to create as much fear and damage as they can as they die in their suicide terrorist acts. In their minds, they are engaged in a religious war against western imperialism, and anything goes.

Christians are not blameless, either. They seem to think that they alone bear the Word of God and are justified in sending missionaries into non-Christian countries and destroying the native cultures and religions so that they can preach the "Word" and have the locals accept Jesus as their savior. And as for needing "forgiveness of their sins," the natives have no idea that they have even sinned. For millennia, females among the indigenous population of a country may have gone topless or even without clothing, and the first thing missionaries may do is to introduce body shame and require the people to "cover up."

A recent example of interference was when two young American women went to Afghanistan as "aid workers" with the covert intent of preaching Christianity in a Muslim country that despises Christianity. Western religions do not seem to get the lesson very well. Such blind intent has caused religious wars such as the Crusades that have claimed countless thousands of lives for millennia. Why can't we live and let live? To go into a country already inflamed with a religious war and pour gasoline on the situation is the height of irresponsibility.

Love, compassion and forgiveness in their pure forms can reach most groups and cultures and cause changes in behavior but, unfortunately in the Middle East, anger and resentment have existed between Jews, Muslims and Christians for two millennia, so there is little possibility that we can reach them now. I never expected to hear the God Source admit that we probably cannot halt this downward spiral until these cancers are eradicated, but that is what I was told as this book was in final draft.

Where Are We Going on this Journey?

Many people claim that ascended masters and benevolent ETs are going to lead us out of the mire of the physical plane by lifting karma from humanity so that we can better make our ascension or transfiguration. Others claim that a fleet of ships will "beam us up" if things get too bad, and one author insisted that ETs would land *en masse* in 1997, take over and change the whole planet for the good. It did not happen nor do I feel that it ever would happen as this would directly conflict with humanity's free will to determine its own future.

Events of mass destruction, both natural and manmade, are a clearing of mass karma. Some New Age prophets have predicted traumatic mass releasing of karma for humanity in the new millennium, but not how. At some level, we each choose the time, place, and means of our own demise. On September 11, 2001, why were fewer than 10,000 people in the World Trade Center towers when normally they are packed with over 50,000 people? Why were the four aircraft only one quarter full, when normally those flights are sold out? To me, those souls conspired in a mass release of karma.

Why should GOD Source or any master in the White Brotherhood give humanity a special dispensation by overriding our karma and free will when we as a species have lessons to learn? It hasn't happened in the past, or we wouldn't be in the mess we're currently in. The Higher Forces are not concerned with how many lifetimes it takes us to resolve our lessons. Their only concern is with our thoughtless, uninformed ways that cause massive destruction on this planet. Humanity has wiped itself out before and the hierarchy sees no need to intercede in today's rampant codependent/autopilot behavior patterns. Also, the amassed ET fleets are currently monitoring our responses to world events to determine whether we are mature enough for admission to their galactic federation. The key ingredient they look for in this is our level of compassion; I think it will be a while ....

Are You Ready For Ascension Now?

Admittedly our consciousness is shifting very quickly (witness the global moratorium on whaling), but not quickly enough to avoid many of the catastrophic events that are currently unfolding. For example, humans encroaching on delicate habitats wipe out about 200 species *every day*, many of them disappearing before we've even had a chance to study them.

Many people claim that this is a special time, that miracles can and do happen, and that we will be given special dispensation to avert the many looming catastrophes—pollution, acid rain, global warming, ozone layer depletion to name a few. It is true, however, that the planet seems to undergo sudden energy shifts. In recent times, it began with the Harmonic Convergence in August 1987, when many people "woke up." Then, with the conjunction of Neptune and Uranus in February 1993, conditions shifted again, signaling the beginning of a Cultural Revolution in which more people began to wake up to spiritual principles and universal laws. However, I question whether they are applying them in their daily lives and walking their talk. Only time will tell whether this new awareness will yield results before it's too late. Another shift took place in August 1999 that further opened the doors to transfiguration and increased the pressure to see the truth. The pressure is building, however, for us *all* to wake up and see reality (see my book *2011: The New Millennium Begins*).

It seems that many people *do* want to take responsibility for their own actions, but that many others want someone else to do it for them, remove the barriers, and make it easy. However, the journey is not a struggle when you're willing to take responsibility. You came here from the Source to create, learn and grow, and then ultimately return to the Source. To do that, you must move out of denial, and *see the path.*

I do know that we will get help, but not until we demonstrate our ability to handle the responsibility of the lessons: peace, harmony, love, joy, happiness and abundance on the one hand, and fear, anger, rejection, need to control, submission to outside authority and manipulation on the other. We also need to work with the cluster qualities of being "all right," i.e., self-esteem, self-worth, self-confidence, self-acceptance, self-approval, self-validation and inner peace. Until these qualities are working in your life, you will not pass the first six initiations—you can visualize going through the doors of ascension but it will only be a vision.

On the Path to Ascension are 12 doors you must go through, each with specific lessons to be clearly understood. (Each door, or major initiation, has 12 minor initiations. Each minor initiation has 12 lessons that will be revealed to you as they come up.)

This path is not of my school but of the school of the masters. I am just a physical extension who can guide you to the material you will need in working through the lessons along your journey. Your teachers will give you the lessons at whatever pacing you can handle.

In this school of life, we have a "triple-entry bookkeeping system." Everything you do or think about doing is recorded at three levels:

   1. *Subconscious Mind*, which is "on" 24 hours a day, seven days a week, and records all the actions you take and think. The entries that Middle Self (program manager) passes to your Ego to place in the Subconscious Mind's computer (without your knowledge of their content) are only recorded if they cause a program/pattern to be acted out. Remember your Ego has no agenda, nor any need to control your behavior. It's just a "file clerk" for the material that

it's given to file in the database. (Behavior such as the need to control or manipulate anyone is erroneously ascribed to Ego. Its only function is to file and retrieve information from your mind. It cannot and does not affect you or anyone else in any manner, which contradicts traditional descriptions of Ego, but ten years of research have shown that Ego is a record-keeper, librarian, secretary, and file manager for the Subconscious Mind, and nothing more.)

2. *Akashic Record in the Subconscious Mind* is your personal database, which contains only what you actually do in your daily life.

3. *Lords of Karma Akashic Record* that records the lessons placed before you and how you handled them. It is a record of all your lifetimes and the lessons that have not been learned. It also records all your flight plans, along with the lessons you completed in each one. You carry over any lessons not completed to the flight plan for the next lifetime. Each time you incarnate, the Lords of Karma present you with a list of the lessons you have agreed to undertake. They "grade" you on your ability to take responsibility and become a master in your life. Each door you go through, signifying completion of a major initiation, brings a new knowingness.

The major initiations are relatively simple accumulations of all the minor initiations and, when you pass all the lessons for a particular door, it will open for you. The minor initiations are the true challenges and some can be very tough indeed. Your teachers in the White Brotherhood are aware of each time you avoid the lesson and record it in the "future file" so that it will come up again, only each time it comes up, avoiding it will be more difficult, and dealing with it more challenging.

The first time a lesson comes up, it will drop a subtle hint or clue into your reality. The second time it comes up, it will cause something to catch your attention. The third time, you will find yourself in an unmistakable confrontation but can still call "time out." Next time, the lesson will get your attention maybe with a physical threat to your health. By the fifth encounter, it's too late to call time out, as you will experience a life-threatening disease or something that brings your life to a crashing halt, possibly even death.

You came to this planet for a specific reason. If you set a cause in motion, there is an effect. You came here to be a master, but you must set the *right causes* in motion to get the appropriate results. Then you are on the path to mastery. Claims are worthless; demonstrable results not only prove your ability, but they are also validated by your teachers on inner planes. When you demonstrate non-attachment and masterful control in your life, it is quite obvious to those who have eyes to see and ears to hear. Universal laws and spiritual principles govern, but exist separate from, our reality. We cannot control, alter or change them; they just are. We are evaluated against *them*, not against our own beliefs or interpretations.

The Recovery Process

The recovery process is not looked upon by people in the meta/spiritual movements as a program that is relevant to them. Recovery is not for the spiritually aware, is it? The twelve step programs are for the emotionally codependent, aren't they?

Many people in meta/spiritual movements seem to eschew the recovery movement, preferring to focus on the esoteric. You cannot build a house without a foundation, but some people try to build a spiritual "house" without the solid foundation created by addressing the emotional earth plane lessons that they incarnated to learn. This is akin to rearranging the chairs on the deck of the Titanic—a bustle of activity, but ultimately a waste of time. Recovery is the only way, and the first step is taking responsibility.

If we have not built a foundation for our spiritual journey, then regardless of where we are in our spiritual path, we need to get into a recovery program. One could describe this as a "spiritual 12-step program" since this book presents the 12 steps to Ascension. This is not a voluntary program because it can be spread across as many lifetimes as the soul and teacher decide and we are never able to escape this process as it is with us each lifetime. We must acknowledge it to get off the detour and back on the path. Many people traverse life after life, unaware that there is a 12-step process that will help them spiral upward out the mire they're in. Many seem to think they are becoming enlightened, so they try different spiritual paths which appear to lead nowhere, going through the cycle of return, lifetime after lifetime, searching the spiritual maze for the way out. The path is quite obvious but we must have the eyes to see and the ears to hear.

On the path through the 12 doors, it's vital to remember that the first challenge is *illusion*. The next is to understand love, compassion and forgiveness, putting them to work in your life. You can delude yourself into conditional love, and believe you are doing it, but the real test of whether you have mastered your emotions is whether you can extend your love to others unconditionally. It makes no difference whether others see it and validate it.

If unconditional love is not happening in your life, you need to take a good look at the illusions under which you're living. Who is setting the programs in motion? You can't stop doing anything of which you're unaware. You cannot recognize the illusion if you're in denial-of-denial. If you refuse to accept, justify or control the illusion, you're not in reality. *Reality just is.* It is all the same for all people. *Ultimate truth just is.* When you recognize that you're in a school and the lessons are before you each day, then metamorphosis can begin. There are no gray areas; it's black and white, either/or.

When you can demonstrate control over your body/mind, you have taken a major step. This happens during the fifth initiation when you realize that you can control your environment. People will respond in a loving, accepting manner when you overcome the fear of rejection. Everyone reacts according to the stimuli that they feel in their environment, and you are part of their environment. If you create a loving, supportive place, you can control everything around you. People will recognize your energy when you walk in a room, even if you try to remain unnoticed.

The most difficult challenge you have before you is allowing yourself to be *all right* at all times, under all circumstances. I have found that not feeling all right is the main stumbling block in life. In every lesson and initiation, feeling all right is the core issue. When you do not feel all right with yourself, you will attempt to project judgmental behavior on people, even if they have no intention of judging you. As a defense mechanism, many people practice self-deprecation to prove their unworthiness (lack of self-worth and self-esteem) before someone else does. We must master the cluster qualities of "alrightness" (self-worth, self-esteem, self-confidence, and self-validation/approval) before we can enter any form of mastery.

One of hardest lessons for most people involves money. When I hear people extolling the fact that they have given up their attachment to money, I ask, "Then why do you not have abundance in your life?" Abundance is not just money; it encompasses everything. When I check them with Kinesiology, I find that most people do not feel they are entitled to money and do not deserve it. Along with this goes the belief that, "Having money is not spiritual." Money is not "the root of all evil"; it is the worship of, addiction to, and obsessive compulsion about money that's the problem. Spiritually evolved people know that we are entitled to abundance and can demonstrate it, but it seems that most people are caught in the lesson on money, so they deny themselves abundance, offering every excuse in the world yet never going through the lesson of releasing attachment.

The fastest way to manifest anything is to drop the need for it and then know that you already have it. All you are doing is reaching out, knowing that you already possess it in principle. We must face this paradox because it seems prevalent in our lives, so study the paradox until you get it: *You will never get enough of what you do not want in your life.* Understanding the paradox will change your viewpoint about life. You will keep trying or become addicted to getting objects, situations, or relationships that give you the *appearance* of escape, control, happiness, love, acceptance, validation or bliss that you want in your life. Yet, you never get it. The best example are alcoholics who continue to abuse alcohol while despising what it does to them. They never get what they want from the alcohol but continue drinking to escape themselves.

Relationship addicts claim to be seeking love yet consistently choose relationships with people who reject, abuse or batter them. They hate, reject and despise their abuser yet they keep bringing into their life the same person with a different name and face but the same abusive behavior. Being addicted to love is impossible; you cannot be addicted to something that you can have as much of as you wish. It is also impossible because you cannot be addicted to something that is positive. Addiction means you're not getting enough of something you need in order to achieve the bliss you want. If you had all the love you wanted or needed, you would not be addicted to it. You would be satisfied, not needy. What's actually happening is that the person is codependent and needs *acceptance, and validation*, which results in relationship addiction.

We must learn all the "self-lessons" before we can be all right: love, worth, esteem, validation, approval, acceptance, and confidence. When these lessons are learned, we feel all right, and abundance of everything is on the way. Only one more lesson remains: detachment from everything we think we need.

The good news is that you will have everything you desire; all you need do is reach out and claim it. The bad news is that you must be willing give it all up. In actuality, you don't have to give it all away but just be *willing* to give up your attachments and know that you could get along without if you had to. Do not make this claim, however, unless you are willing to do without, for it may be taken away if you are still attached. This is Universal Law. You may *claim* that you are detached from everything, but the proof is always evident in your daily life.

In 1991, I attended an Adult Children Of Alcoholics (ACOA) conference and was surprised with some of the attendees' responses when I said, "All addictions are in your mind." Many times, they would interpret my remark to mean that someone had to be at fault. I replied by mentioning a workshop called "Recovery for Therapists" led by Wayne Gurtzburg in which he asked attendees to answer 35 questions so that he could gauge whether they understood what his workshop was about. Wayne later said, "This was a 'damned if you do and damned if you don't' questionnaire. You cannot deceive the questions as they showed me where you are in your recovery, assuming you answer the questions honestly. I received the results I expected because most of you are not in recovery nor have worked on your own issues."

He went on to describe the experience that launched him into recovery, which really opened some eyes. "I had begun leading group therapy discussion groups, and went to a psychodrama workshop in order to learn some useful tools. I discovered that most of the workshop participants were lay people, not practitioners, which surprised me so I kept quiet about being a psychologist to avoid making people feel uncomfortable. At lunch, I talked with a woman who revealed all her problems to me, but still I held myself back. I suggested that she volunteer for one of the demonstrations that afternoon. She did and asked for me to be her partner. I was uncomfortable about being in the demonstration but felt that I could help her. During the session, I became upset and began to perspire so badly that my clothing became visibly damp. Afterwards, I just wanted to crawl under the nearest stone, afraid of everyone finding out that I was a psychologist.

"When the facilitators asked me what was wrong, I became agitated and abruptly said in a loud voice, "Nothing." I knew I was caught but didn't know what to do about it. About 20 minutes later, I started crying and couldn't stop. It took about twenty minutes to clear the issue so that I could calm down. Then I recognized that I needed to get into recovery and made an appointment the next day. I realize now that for fourteen years, I'd been pushing people in other directions when one of my own issues came up in a session. We may not recognize this but we all do it. It makes no difference whether we're lay people or practitioners; we have all put our childhood in denial and it's about time to clear it out. We cannot be effective therapists when our own issues are not clear."

Wayne's words really shifted my reality at that point because, when working with people and owning my issues, they came out like a landslide.

The 12-Step Ascension Process

Using Kinesiology, I have found that I can check to see where clients are on the path. By asking the right questions, I can get clients' Holographic Mind or the soul level of their Subconscious Mind to reveal what doors they have gone through and the lessons they have passed. My Sources tell me that the Akashic Record logs each door we pass through, even though we may be unaware that we have passed that initiation.

Some people may feel that I'm making the following process too complex, but it has been compiled from many sources over a 20-year study. Many people on this path will attest to the concepts and theories. It really boils down to your choice in life. Nobody, including the Presence of GOD, is asking, demanding or forcing you to do anything. By virtue of your free choice, you have the right to continue in any way you wish. Nobody is controlling you, and you can go any direction you wish. There is no timeframe on enlightenment, evolution and ascension.

Throughout the steps, many issues such as unconditional love and temptation keep recurring as you go progressively more deeply into them. Removing blocks to loving yourself and others is similar to peeling away the layers of an onion (and often brings as many tears). Simply learning a spiritual principle in step 3 is only the beginning; your proficiency in applying it in your life will be tested in most of the later steps.

The steps are carefully calibrated to progressively unhook you from average consciousness and move you into ever-higher orbits. Some of the initiations are painful and difficult, some less so, but each one puts you more in touch with your Spirit and embodies more of its energy. Thus your fields contain ever more Light, until you are so Light-filled that you exist mostly in the fifth dimension. Then, being on the third or fifth is a matter of choice. Any pain along the path merely shows you what needs to be healed, so thank it and get on with your healing.

The First Initiation: New Life

The first initiation involves becoming aware that there is another way and stepping out of victim consciousness. If we are affected by others' projections, rejections, externalization, control or authority, then we are in *victim consciousness*. Most people do not recognize the illusions in which they live, and exist in "average consciousness." However, there will come a point when you see a glimmer of hope that there might be a better way to live. You also become aware of how the "great myths" in our culture limit you, and cast them aside, preferring to define your own picture of "how it is" rather than accept the "off-the-shelf, one-size-fits-all" dogma of religion. (The second edition of my book *2011: The New Millennium Begins* explores two of these—the God-myth and the Jesus-myth—and shows how fallacious they are.)

You begin to recognize that you have the right of self-determination and start to take responsibility for your life. You become aware that you create your own reality and begin with the most difficult step—mastering your emotions. You live in either love or fear; those are your only two choices. When you master fear, you move into mastership.

When you recognize that there is another path, you realize that you need not suffer, live in pain or struggle in survival, and that you can have unconditional love and abundance in your life.

The Second Initiation: Death and Rebirth

The second initiation is the hardest and you will not get through the second door until you discipline yourself to take full responsibility for, and take control of, everything in your life. In this step, you let go of the old, dogmatic controlling self and allow it to die. This opens the way for rebirth, not in the Christian tradition, but to let go of old patterns. Jesus Christ or the ETs are not going to "rescue" you. The old personality self lies within your Middle Self, and taking control of your life involves getting Middle Self to recognize *you* as the authority from now on. If you have given away your personal power to Middle Self, you can reclaim it, but you must get off autopilot. Again, this could be a real illusion of which you may not be aware. The personality self operates from Middle Self and has many disguises; it can masquerade as anything it chooses with which to delude you. It has no morals or need to act ethically or with integrity. It just wants to maintain control.

If you do not threaten the control sub-personalities it operates from, it will not defend itself.

This will be the first battle with self to let go of fear. Middle Self will not want to let go of control until you take full responsibility. You must make peace with Middle Self and affirm that Ego is the file manager and not the enemy. Taking responsibility is the most difficult lesson for many people. Removing all programs from the past and beginning a new life are daunting tasks but you have help by calling on your teacher from the White Brotherhood. The process is described in my books *Opening Communication with GOD Source* and *Becoming a Spiritual Being in a Physical body*.

The main lesson in this initiation is to reclaim your personal power and take responsibility. This is where evolvement begins. The ultimate delusion is to convince yourself that you do not need any help because you are in control and already a highly enlightened being.

The Third Initiation: Understanding Spiritual Principles and Universal Laws

The third door is a relatively easy initiation but it creates a challenge that you will have to deal with for the balance of your life. It is easy to get through the door once you understand universal laws and spiritual principles, which we will explore in Chapter 3.

You must also understand and begin to practice unconditional love even though you might not be able to live in that state for long periods. It is also important to overcome procrastination and indecision, confusion, frustration and stop denying your emotions and justifying situations.

The Fourth Initiation: Temptation

The fourth door is the challenge where the lessons become intense. When you proclaim to the Universe that you understand universal laws and spiritual principles, you will be tested. In this initiation, the tests are with temptations. Each time you're confronted with a situation, you're being tested to see whether you can recognize the lesson and how you handle it. Many times, the temptation will throw you back into acting out of personality self. You will not pass this initiation until you demonstrate that you can recognize the lesson when it is before you.

You may not pass all the tests, but you must recognize the lesson otherwise it will be brought before you again during steps 5 through 8. You cannot complete step 8 until you totally master the lessons. Before you can continue to the next step, you must demonstrate mastery of the following:

- Detachment. Are you attached, detached or non-attached? If you are attached, the situation will cause some form of emotional reaction. Detachment allows you to experience the situation with little emotional response. Non-attachment will not cause any reaction and possibly no response also.
- Being the *cause* of your outer world rather than its result.
- Being a co-creator with spirit and/or GOD Source of all your actions.
- Emotional mastery. Does a situation cause anger, fear, hurt, rejection, or emotional upset? In order to protect the vulnerable personality self, do you need to claim or regain control and authority, or use manipulation to maintain security?
- Releasing victim consciousness to build your "alrightness." To leave this step, you must attain inner serenity, self-esteem and self-worth.

The tests will recycle, getting progressively more intense during each initiation until the eighth. Lessons will involve unconditional love, rejection, abandonment, fear, anger and all of the 20-plus other emotions that can cause you fall back into victim consciousness where personality self takes over. Then, you must start over again until you can detach yourself from the payoff of emotional experiences. This does not mean that you will be able avoid emotional situations, but you must recognize that the payoff does not get you anywhere other than victim consciousness. When you can transcend the emotion, you will recognize what the effect of emotion does to you. This is the first step in detachment. You can then move to the next initiation.

The Fifth Initiation: Understanding the Power of Your Mind

The fifth initiation deepens your control over your life. You are now becoming the possible human and a master-in-training to demonstrate many feats that the average human considers out of his realm. You must also detach further from your emotions. During this initiation, you move between a human being having spiritual experiences to a spiritual being have human experiences. To move through this initiation, you must let go of the personality self, and move into your spiritual self.

In exploring the use of the power of your mind, the lessons on the temptations continue, only more intensely. The following must be mastered in this step before the fifth door opens:

- Mastery of your emotions, which are goal-oriented behaviors that have a payoff. This does not mean gaining total control, but you must at least take responsibility for all your actions.

- Unconditional forgiveness of self and others, demonstrating unconditional love in all situations, choosing the action that responds with love, acceptance and forgiveness. You must understand judgment for what it is, even though you don't have to master it at this level.

- Mastery of the Law of Cause-and-Effect. We create and are responsible for all reactions and responses. Nobody does anything to us; we allow it to happen. If we choose to impact someone negatively, we will reap the same in return.

- Recognizing fear and anger for what they are. (Fear creates illness and disease, and is False Evidence Appearing Real.) This includes letting go of the fear of death.

- Complete the elimination of irrational victim patterns from your repertoire.

- Self-confidence from recognizing and knowing your "alrightness" in the world.

- Asking for and receiving healing for all past wounds and hurts.

- Lucid living, so that you recognize lessons as they happen and release fear as soon as it arises. (Remember, all negative emotions are fear-based.)

- Releasing all AKA cords and attachments from self and others, both past and present. Demonstrating control over your environment at all levels. This means mastering stressful and emotional situations, knowing how to respond to physical conditions, and listening to guidance as to how to act.

- Releasing the need for control and authority of others.

- Understanding the Law of Communication.

The Sixth Initiation: Transmutation

Going through the sixth door involves the ability to claim and demonstrate power over your mind and body. This is another difficult transition, as you can no longer base your self-worth on who you think you are as a human or on what others think or feel about you.

You continue taking total control of your life. As a master-in-training, you can choose to experience pain if you wish but you can also choose control over every facet of your life, too, although you may occasionally stumble. The temptations of emotion and sickness will come up but, because you have total control over your body/mind, they will not have any long-term effects.

Other aspects of your life in this initiation are:

- Abundance as a way of life in all areas. (You may not have totally mastered lack and limitation but at least you understand them and begin to release them.)

- Understanding your soul level lessons, transmuting and beginning self-mastery. You become aware of the contents of your flight plan and can follow the lessons that you choose to handle in this incarnation. The focus of this lesson is clearing as much karma as possible. More will come up as you move up the path.

- Moving from faith and belief to *knowing*. Faith and belief are fear-based because you are assuming that something exists without knowing that it does.

- Self-aggrandizement, self-righteousness and arrogance are no longer issues. Freedom from the need to demonstrate spiritual power, as in, "See how great I am. I am an enlightened being."

- Becoming one with the Presence of God. Unconditional love is your will. Demonstrating miracles begins.

The Seventh Initiation: Moving Into Your True Place in Life, Locating Your Mission in Life

At the seventh door, you begin to demonstrate miracles on demand as the Presence of God is installed in your body, mind and spirit. The most difficult challenge in this initiation is to step above the Instinctual/Survival Mind and continue building the control over your body/mind that you started in the fifth step. Many people falter at this point due to their inability to overcome lower physical/mental temptations such as sex, alcohol, control, judgment, anger/fear and addiction. The transition through the lower nature is being able to rise above the desire state of control, need, addiction, conditional acceptance and rise to unconditional acceptance and love that leads to non-attachment.

Other hallmarks of this step include:

- Recognizing your mission in life and beginning the path to world service.

- Recognizing the true place of your three inner Selves as supporters and getting them to work with you.

- Mastery of unconditional love and forgiveness. You will be presented with lessons that will determine whether you're ready to continue on the path to ascension.

The Eighth Initiation: The First Step Into Earth Mastery

The eighth door will not open until you have overcome the lower nature temptations of the previous step. In this initiation, we are entering the level of the *meta-human*, or one who lives by spiritual principles.

On the third dimension, it seems that the feats that are being demonstrated by meta-humans are miraculous but, when we enter the fifth dimension and release ourselves from 3-D duality, everything will become an accepted result. We know that we can put the appropriate causes in motion and what the effect will be before it happens.

Other characteristics of the eighth initiation are:

- You knowingly allow the universe and Christ Consciousness to express through you. You do not have to be aware of it; you just *are* it.

- You do not need to be in a special place, dress in special clothes or demonstrate your powers. You are just who you are, with no need to impress people with who you are and what you can do, although your personal power and enthusiasm are obvious to observers.

- As the final door of temptation, this step presents final "tests" on releasing. By this stage, you are beyond the limited human notion of "tests" because who is testing whom? Every lesson will recur so that you can experience your level of inner peace, joy, happiness, self-worth, "all right-ness," abundance, self-love, self-approval, and self-esteem, and the absence of fear and all negative emotions. Earth Masters who have not mastered all the

emotions or the need for control, judgment, justification, unconditional love and forgiveness will remain in this initiation. Outside validation is not required.

• Miracles are mechanical effects that happen without concentration. Everything in your life begins to fall into place with very
little effort.

When you complete the eighth initiation, you, the *meta-human*, emerges.

The Ninth Initiation: Transfiguration

Your teachers control the ninth through the twelfth doors and coach
you at each step of the way, monitor progress, and admonish you to not
show off your abilities. Once you pass through this first real door to
ascension, you will never backslide. Source Self now directs your life,
as there is no separation from GOD Source. As a result, you are now in
a place where you control your life path. Your abilities are obvious to
observers, who are attracted to you for what you radiate.

As a manifest meta-human, you easily perform feats that normal
people would consider miraculous. However, you do not advertise or
demonstrate your skills just to impress or be recognized. You have no
need for another's acceptance or validation. Other qualities are:

• Mastery of all body functions and emotional repose.

• Unity of spirit within, as the spiritual self is totally integrated.

• High Self, Middle Self and Low self begin to merge into one.

• Personality self becomes one with the spiritual self.

• Body, mind and spirit act in unison now, without separation.

• You are supported at the level of abundance you choose.

The Tenth Initiation: Crucifixion

It seems as if you are going through the final temptation, as everyone
seems to be leaving you alone, isolated in a vast wasteland, deserted in
your quest. You will go through the same initiations that all other masters have done in their ascent into Earth mastery. You recognize that
you need no one to validate you and you are tested to ensure that you
can be a true teacher who can stand on your knowledge and experience. Other aspects include:

- Personal consciousness disappears as you let the physical/personality self (who you have been) die.
- The Low Self, Middle Self and High Self completely unify.
- Spiritual self now directs your life as your God Self emerges.

The Eleventh Initiation: Resurrection

Your spirit becomes the risen Christ as you recognize that this final initiation was to test your ability to handle all the initiations that you have passed through. You become an Earth Master with the choice of Ascension.

You live in the knowing that "God and I are one." The Presence of GOD becomes your moment-by-moment reality as you reach out for the final initiation. The next step in the journey is the most difficult because you recognize who you really are. You have no need for followers or supporters, although people naturally support you without you having to ask for anything.

The Twelfth Initiation: Ascension

There are no initiations at this door, as you have accomplished all of the initiations by the time you enter. When you pass the twelfth initiation, you enter the Brotherhood of Light, where you and your life records are reviewed in an interview with members of the White Brotherhood. They will meet with you and your teacher to discuss where you go from here.

If you have passed all your tests in each initiation, they will test you to see if you have mastered fear. They will assign you to a third-dimensional person on the earth plane to protect and provide support in their spiritual journey as a test to see how you respond to the lessons you had to deal with in your journey to light. If fail any of the tests or you have not mastered and are unable to deal with fear at all levels, you will be enrolled in the Earth Master Remedial School. You will not be allowed to return to earth as a teacher until you graduate to the Apprentice Ascended Master Mystery School. When you have become an initiate in this school, you can become a teacher anywhere you choose. You can then dematerialize your physical body to a light body and rematerialize at will. Gender differences disappear totally.

By the time you reach this door, you will have no need or desire to tell others of your accomplishment; it will just be evident by your actions and behavior. Some people will recognize who you are, and others will resent you because they see the acceptance you receive. It may seem as if you are in the eye of a hurricane. Those who cannot accept who are and what you represent will be unable to see the peace at your center and the energy will whirl them right out back into their illusions. Those who can see the peace will go right to the center as they recognize who you are and what you are teaching.

As a final note, do not be fooled into believing that this book is about you and your path; it is actually about you in service to humanity. Along the way to ascension, you will have opportunities to help countless people—a kind word here, a thoughtful gesture there, a listening ear with no criticism. DO NOT MISS A SINGLE OPPORTUNITY! Never be too busy in your growth to stop and help others.

In a book written in 1965 entitled *It's All Right*, Isobel Hickey described what she called a "karmic bank account" where, when you take positive action, you add to your bank balance. When you participate in negative actions, you draw from it. If you overdraw your account, you will create a landslide of karmic impact on yourself. Filling our account with positive points can mitigate some negative events that might cause us trouble in the future.

Finally, during Betty Eadie's famous near-death experience, reported in *Embraced by the Light*, she was shown the "ripple effect" and how, whenever she had been kind to another person, that person passed the good deed on to several others, who in turn passed it on yet others. Thus one kind deed impacted hundreds of lives.

1

The First Initiation: Enlightenment, A New Life and New Awareness

The first initiation involves becoming aware of a new path in life. This new path is not running away from the past or suppressing it so that we can avoid it. It involves becoming aware that we do not have to suffer from past situations. If we are affected by others' projections, rejections, externalization, control, manipulation or authority, holding resentments and blaming others for our predicaments, then we are in *victim consciousness*.

Most people do not recognize the illusions in which they live and exist in "average consciousness." However, there will come a point when they see a glimmer of hope and realize that there might be a better way to live. Beginning the path to enlightenment involves coming to this new awareness. It may be a *déjà vu* experience, a dream or an awakening to the fact that your life is just not working anymore. Whatever experience wakes you up is not important, but the recognition that there is another way is *crucial*.

You begin to understand that you have been living by other people's rules and beliefs, and recognize that you have the freedom to change your beliefs and the right of self-determination in situations. However, be careful. Don't rush out, checkbook in hand, looking for a guru or teacher. In the spiritual jungle, many scam artists out there will tell you what you want to hear, such as, "We have the easy way out. In the upcoming mass ascension, all your karma will be lifted. I have the formula for your enlightenment if you follow my path." Or, "I have ascended and have come back to show you the way ... for a fee."

Those who want to avoid taking responsibility for their paths in life will find this off-the-shelf spirituality inviting but rarely cheap. Some teachers charge outrageous prices for their seminars and workshops. Unsuspecting people will pay the price, only to find out later they've been scammed to the tune of $500 – $2,000 for a weekend workshop and up to $5,000 for a five- to seven-day retreat. Some scam artists even guarantee that their mystery schools are run by the ascended masters whom they claim to channel. Many naive people have followed teachers who claimed to have *the* truth, only to find out that the teacher was not walking his or her talk. Many of my clients report being relieved of their money by these false teachers, and all they really got out of the experience was a lesson in discernment.

People who are unable or do not want to take responsibility for their own decisions may place validity on information they receive from others' guidance without checking whether the guidance is accurate. A good example of this in my own life was when I was driving along a road and a sign announced: ROAD NOT MAINTAINED BEYOND THIS POINT DURING WINTER. Further along, another sign read: ROAD AHEAD CLOSED IN WINTER. My guidance was that the road was passable so I continued, only to almost get stuck in a snowdrift. After turning round in a very precarious place, my shortcut became a nerve-wracking wild goose chase that cost me about two hours of my time because I had to retrace my tracks and then take the long way round to my destination. I was puzzled because all the way along, I had kept checking my guidance, which said that I would be able to get through. I checked to see if I was clear and I was not. How many people even check whether they are clear or that the person they are receiving guidance from is clear? In my experience, not many.

Most people today are on autopilot, their actions and daily life controlled by sub-personalities. In fact, less than five percent have control over their lives. In the absence of your conscious control, autopilot sub-personalities will run your life. In fact, they would rather *not* have you involved and confusing the issue because, in their opinion, they do very well without your interference.

The problem is that your Middle Self sets up many programs and runs the one of its choice even though you may not consciously want to react in that way. Even if you can resist the sub-personalities' behavior pattern, you must still be on guard all the time. If you use your willpower to keep yourself on track, you will set up a double-bind when you have to go against your programming. Willing yourself through life each day takes enormous energy, and fighting your internal programming and Middle Self.can wear you down.

Each time you set aside your conscious control and allow autopilot to react for you, autopilot sets up a series of sub-personalities. Also, if you fail to complete an action you begin, Middle Self will assume that you no longer want to take that action, so it will cause you to avoid future situations that contain that same imprint. It locks it up in a denial file so you do not have to deal with it at the present time. But, as you transition through lessons, a crisis will activate a catalyst that brings the program up from denial files. You repress the emotion or feeling because you do not want to deal with it again but, this time, your program manager (Middle Self) instructs file manager (Ego) to put the file in denial-of-denial, and the file is locked up and lost so that you don't even know it exists.

When we are confronted by a person with whom we do not want to deal, such as a survival, trauma or insecurity, the situation will push us into shut down, or a flight or fight response. Middle Self sets up time line programs that become locked into denial in the Subconscious Mind's operating system. Programs that have a heavy emotional charge also have a time line file set up that is date-stamped with the original cause recorded exactly as it happened.

Around August 2001, I began to find Instinctual Mind files activated in people who did not have life-threatening diseases. When I tracked these files to their inception, I found that the phenomenon started in the first few months of 2001. Because this happened to everyone across the board, there had to be some common cause. I theorize that somehow our Higher Self downloaded information to the operating system in our mind's database, which means that we must be more vigilant and impeccable in our behavior from now on.

For example, I was able track the situation with one client named Jack. He was in conflict with his supervisor who blamed him for a problem that was not caused by his work group. Jack did not defend himself, which would have put him into a victim position, but neither did he correct the situation by standing up for himself. So by not taking responsibility, he gave his power away. By not saying anything, his Middle Self assumed that he accepted that he was wrong and called on the frustration, indecision, resentment programs he already had on file. This activated Instinctual Mind, which resulted in "I am not all right."

In another example, Jolene, a client, inadvertently slipped into rescuer/savior mode by trying to do something right and help another person. Jolene helped out Bill, her brother-in-law, by taking his children on a vacation with her. Bill's wife had passed on and he'd remarried. His new wife, the children's stepmother, didn't get along with the kids very well, but Jolene did, so they had a great vacation. The new wife resented Jolene, who did not feel validated or accepted for her kindness. Jolene's mind set up a "feeling of futility" program which ran frustration, judgment, resentment and anger at not being accepted, which mutated into "I'm not all right." Being concerned about the welfare of Bill's children and therefore attached to the situation, she felt there was nothing she could do. So her lack of detachment pulled her down.

Another client, whose fulltime job had been downsized into part time knew that she was equally as or more effective than other employees whose jobs were unscathed. She ran many behavior programs such as anger at having been rejected, which resulted in "I'm not all right." When we cleared all those programs from the past that put her into victim consciousness, she recovered her personal power and was reinstated to fulltime a week later. She had failed to recognize the lesson that had been placed before her.

These examples show what can happen when you lose your center and give your power away in a conflict. The key here is detachment. No one can do anything to you unless you let them. When anyone attacks you verbally or you begin to feel rejected, you have only 30 seconds to take your power back and take control of the situation. If you do not, your Middle Self will activate Instinctual Mind files that put you in survival mode and shut down all other files. As a result, you operate on autopilot and those essential files needed to function but, if you run in this mode for very long, your mind will activate "I want to die" and "fear of dying" programs that in turn will activate Alzheimer programs. Realizing that no one else can do anything to us and that we do it all to ourselves is one of the major initiations in beginning the enlightenment process.

Throughout this 12-step ascension program, you will tested to see if you understand the lesson. People and situations will come into your life to test you all the time. (People may not know that they are your teachers and possibly would act differently if they did. Your teachers are set up to teach the lessons even if they don't know it. As you go through the lessons, you must avoid judgment and resentment of those who are teaching the lessons.)

The Subconscious Mind and the Middle Self continually back up all their files so, even if we clear a program from the online file, the program will be retrieved and rerun when the situation recurs. That means that we must clear all the files in the operating systems of all the minds, including past and future time line files, too.

First, we must remove all the sub-personalities and the programs that drive them from Conscious Rational Mind's operating files, Middle Self's operating files, back-up files, time line files, denial files and denial-of-denial files. Before we can even get on our journey, we must clear, delete and destroy some 35 sub-personalities and go through our life, year-by-year, back to birth, clearing the time line programs and sub-personalities. We may find critical years when many traumatic experiences occurred. In working with clients, I have encountered anywhere from 100,000 to 3.2 million sub-personalities filed in each operating system, mainly involving control, justification, indecision, responsibility evasion and procrastination. We can clearly see the pattern in these programs. And the type of programs will indicate the personality type a person operates from.

The *first step*, then, is to reclaim your power and take responsibility for your life. Reclaiming your power sets up a new protocol in your internal operating system. When you get your Middle Self to recognize that you are going to take responsibility, it will relinquish its control. You must also make friends with your Ego and let it know that you are aware that you made a mistake by labeling it as the villain and enemy. Acknowledge your misinterpretation and forgive yourself for any trauma you caused Ego. Then, it can take its rightful role as your file manager, secretary and librarian for Subconscious Mind (see the affirmation in Appendix). Because this work is the basis for our spiritual journey, all my books stress this point repeatedly. We are not going anywhere on this ascension path without taking our power back. Surrender does not work, as our mind considers that giving up our personal power.

As stated before, enlightenment begins with the awareness that there is another way to exist in this world. We did not come here to live in pain and suffering, working our way through life in the hope that we will get to a place somewhere along the path where we can find peace, happiness, harmony and joy. These qualities are available to us right now, but the enlightenment path is not an easy one that you just jump on with some visionary experience that changes your life overnight. Many people would like to believe that you become enlightened when you have a sudden awakening to new awareness, but it's not that easy.

Enlightenment is more than just choosing to change your path in life; changing a lifetime's basic behavior takes work and, the deeper the rut you've walked in, the longer it takes. Granted, a few people do have overnight *déjà vu* experiences that shift their life path but they are a small minority and were already willing to let go of any future outcomes, so detachment came easily. If you're willing to set your intention, and discipline yourself to be consistent and to follow through without fail, you can shift your awareness but, if you falter at any point, you will not make the shift.

Enlightenment is a mind game. It is not about something outside of yourself changing, even though it may appear that you are seeing your external reality differently. The environment and the people in it are still the same; they didn't change in any way. It's your *perception* of external reality that changes. Once you no longer blame the world for your problems, you will respond in a new way. And once you change your viewpoint of the externals, you transmit a different signature to the outside world. Thus people will treat you with more acceptance, validation and recognition.

Studs Terkel's book *Working* is a sad commentary on the state of the population the United States. He asked people if they were happy with their lot in life, and the survey results indicate why our culture is in the garbage dump we're sitting in. He found four main groups:

- 65 percent of Americans are unhappy with their life as it is. They don't know how to change it, and see themselves as victims, unable to find a way out of the mire. As a result, they're not interested in doing anything about either.

- 20 percent are vaguely unhappy with their lot in life and would change it if they knew how but have not yet found the way.

- 10 percent know there's a better way, are committed to changing their life, and are actively doing so.

- 5 percent are happy with their life and wouldn't change a thing.

The 10 percent who know there's another way to live do not necessarily understand what "taking your power back" means, and some members of this group are giving their power away to a guru, leader or teacher. So where does this leave us? Very few people are committed to become earth masters and really take control of their life.

On this subject, my book *2011: The New Millennium Begins* presents my dialogue with the Sirian Council and how they view our grand experiment in human relations, and offers insights as to where we stand in relation to the balance of the universe. My experience is that the ET visitors with whom I have had contact are much older species than we are, and have superior powers, understanding and technology. They can, therefore, give us an enormous input about what's happening now on Earth and what's likely to happen in the future. Most of them are light beings who have mastered the physical universe. In fact, some of them are the original life forms that inhabited this planet in the beginning. The Mayans, Incas, Egyptians, Maoris, Hebrews, Polynesians, and Aborigines are descendants of the Sirians, Pleiadians, and Andromedans. However, the main forces of these groups left Earth to continue to advance their knowledge and evolve, leaving offshoots behind to explore whether the people of this planet could actually get along and work their differences out. The fact that at any one time on this planet, there are upwards of 30 points of conflict, from border skirmishes to full blown wars, speaks for itself. We have not received the message of love and forgiveness yet.

Throughout history, the Presence of God, ascended masters, the White Brotherhood, and many other groups, working with the evolved light beings who left this planet, have sent master teachers to wake us up. However, political factions invariably corrupt the pure teachings for their own ends, usually to divide and control the population, so very few people have access to the real teachings. As a result, we as a people continued to devolve to ever lower levels, preferring to *descend* rather than *ascend*.

We must recognize that enlightenment is the path to self-mastery. However, western spirituality and eastern philosophies view this path totally differently. The West sees self-mastery as positive, in the sense of the self being in control of one's personal power, being physically fit, being in the world but not of it, realizing that the externals do not control your reality, being financially abundant, and living in acceptance, with unconditional love. The East holds the I AM as part of the unconditional acceptance, but sees the self as surrendering to a no-self that transcends the world, and believes that everything is destiny, over which we have no control.

I consider enlightenment and spirituality to be an all-encompassing process that we work through on our path to ascension, surmounting the obstacles that block us from finding out who we truly are. With the capacity to meet the challenges that face us each day, we can work our way through our spiritual journey. Self-mastery leads to a life filled with peace, happiness, harmony, joy, unconditional love and acceptance.

Spirituality is the goal, and enlightenment is the path to it. In my view, eastern philosophy is missing many of the basic steps. We were not intended to live in poverty as self-effacing nomads. Abundance is our rightful path and, when we get to the point of accepting our abundance, then it will be offered to us without conditions. It's as if the universe opens up the path for us as we accept our entitlement to it. (When my wife, Susie, and I became detached from the *need to have*, we became aware of this effect as it opened up in our life. I consider abundance and opening up to it as part of self-mastery. When you become aware that you are entitled to abundance and can accept it, it opens up for you.)

Self-mastery is an ongoing process in which you meet the challenges of life knowing that you can accomplish each step. It is not a goal, however, but the tool box of methods and processes. The first step is knowing that *"I can."* When you recognize that "I can," you proceed to *"I am."*

When you know you're in the flow, everything opens up to you. It did for me when I recognized that "I have abundance now." When everything opens up for you and just comes to you without any effort on your part and without having to work through it, it's a wonderful feeling. People are happy to help and provide the way for you without you even having to ask them.

At first, when people volunteered their support, I wasn't sure why they were doing it, and often felt that I was taking advantage or imposing on them. Today, I finally feel comfortable with accepting support and help. Self-mastery involves knowing when to act supportively and when to accept support.

I often hear people say, "This is my last lifetime on this Earth." To many other people, planet Earth is the totality of being; you live once and that's it. Many fundamentalist Christians believe that the planet is only 6,000 years old because that's what the Bible says, and "the Bible is the absolute word of God." They ignore that it has been translated through many languages before ending up in English, or has been periodically modified to enforce the Church's political agenda.

Christianity was conceived by powerful factions in the Middle East as a Machiavellian way to control populations by dividing them into warring factions and pouring fuel on their hatred. Their tool, the Bible, was created by man purely to mislead the ignorant masses who couldn't read Latin, so they relied on the priesthood to read it to them, further removing them from any truth in it. I suggest that those who believe such dogma get a reality check.

Don't believe me? Let's take a brief look at one of the greatest scams in history ever pulled off—the God Myth (the second edition of my book *2011: The New Millennium Begins* goes into much more detail of the God Myth and also discusses its complement, the Jesus Myth).

The God Myth

This myth tells us that there is a separate God up there or out there who created all we see around us and watches and judges us, giving us a cosmic thumbs up or down once we reach the afterlife. Then it's an eternity of either stoking the fires or glorious salvation. How did this myth come about? It did not originate in the Bible, but was already an ancient misunderstanding long before the books making up the Old Testament were even contemplated. We need to go back *much* further back in time.

According to Darwin's Theory of Evolution, whenever conception occurs, there is a slight chance of a birth defect, a deviation from the norm for that species. Some deviations will give that creature a survival advantage when a situation arises that threatens existence. That creature then has a better chance of mating and passing its abnormality along, which eventually becomes the norm for that species. (This is often confused with "survival of the fittest.")

Species evolve, therefore, slowly and randomly over untold millions of years. Qualities that promote survival remain; those that hinder survival die out quickly. However, something occurred 300,000 – 500,000 years ago that signaled a complete discontinuity in evolution. A new species emerged almost overnight: *Homo sapiens*. Then about 30,000 years ago, it happened again, to form a new subspecies—*Homo sapiens sapiens.* Where did they come from? It happened so quickly that it obviously was not evolution.

Ancient Sumerian clay tablets record that a group of ETs who had colonized Earth needed a workforce of intelligent slave labor, so they used genetic engineering to create one, i.e., human beings, who referred to their ET overlords as Yahweh. The ETs lived for millennia, were telepathic and possessed amazing technology so, to their primitive human creations, they appeared capable of miracles. When the ETs finally left, the humans passed stories of the miraculous Yahwehs down through the generations, and storytellers compressed them into one all-powerful Yahweh that eventually became the God worshipped in ancient times. Hence the origin of the external God myth.

Where does this leave us in the process of enlightenment and evolution that some of us are seeking? This question has been asked for many years. The ancient mystery schools that taught this knowledge and information all but died out but, today, we are finally seeing a few people willing to ask the question and actively seek the answers. It could be that the downward spiral of devolution is beginning to turn around.

So the question before you is: are you ready to take your power back and take responsibility for everything in your life? This is the question you must face with every issue that comes up with each lesson.

As you move through this door to the next step on your spiritual journey, you will be asked to address the question: "Are you willing to let go of the past and take responsibility for creating all the lessons you face in life? Are you willing to forgive your parents and all the teachers who have come into your life to teach you the lessons that you filed in your fight plan?"

Joining this mystery school puts you in control of the speed at which the curriculum is presented to you but, once you get on the path, you cannot get off. If you *do* choose to drop out, you will still be on the cycle of return. The difference between what's happening now and the days of the ancient mystery schools is that today we are moving toward a critical mass. When we reach that point, a sudden shift in planetary energy will occur and those who have chosen not to take responsibility will be unable to handle the frequnecy, and will depart the planet.

The final question before you in this step is, therefore: "Are you going to let go of the past and stop playing the soap opera star who gets into situations that stop you from be who you want to be?" This is where self-mastery begins. Transformation, freedom and enlightenment mean letting go of limitation. How long are you going to dabble on a spiritual path that does not lead to what this whole chapter is about? How long are you going to play games in your head such as, "If I could only get this right or get that process down, I would reach the goal?"

There's no need to go through any pain and suffering to get to enlightenment. You just have to build the foundation day-by-day, knowing that the path is before you and that you can meet all the challenges as they come up.

2

The Second Initiation: Death and Rebirth

In the previous step, you realized that there is an alternative to pain, struggle and limitation, and decided to step on the path to enlightenment. There is another way to approach life. We must let go of who we have been up until now and step into a new path. Making this shift can be very threatening to some people since you are being asked to trust that you're making the right decision with no proof that it will work. Just because others have done it proves that it *can* be done, but does it mean that *you* can do it? The more your mind is caught up in the need for control or if you have autopilot running, Middle self will try to stop you until the programs that block your path are removed.

We will be repeating over and over that, "You can step on to the path to enlightenment but you will not be able to travel very far on your spiritual journey until build a foundation and complete it." After you complete the foundation, you must set your intention and commit yourself to staying on the path and following through. You can't look at someone such as Hari-Kan-Baba whom we met in the Introduction and say, "I want to be like him, so I think I will begin the ascension path." Copying someone else would be the wrong motivation. Because you have no personal experience of being ascended, you cannot use that as motivation, but you have *plenty* of experience of being a limited human having occasional spiritual experiences, so it's perfectly okay to let your desire to cease being limited motivate your transformation. You will still get to the top of the mountain, but you cannot hide in a spiritual pursuit without taking responsibility for self.

Where do you fit into the four statistical groups that Studs Terkel identified? The five percent who are happy with their present station in life? Let's narrow it down further. Only one in five of that group are really in control of their life and have taken total responsibility, which means one percent of the population. The other 99 percent are on auto-pilot, their actions and daily life controlled by sub-personalities that run their lives without their conscious awareness. If they're following a path where they give their power away to a teacher, guru or shaman, they are not taking responsibility in their life. They may be on the path to enlightenment but the journey will be long and arduous until they recognize that someone else cannot make their decisions for them or provide the path for their spiritual journey.

The Identity Myth

The eternal questions are: Who am I and why did I choose my life to be the way it's turned out? Why am I here and what am I supposed to be doing? If I'm not on the path that I'm supposed to be on, how can I change my direction?

Most people say, "I didn't choose my lot in life. My life happened to me." But if they didn't choose it, then who did? Surely not their parents, even though they were affected by their parents' behavior. It all comes back us. Before we incarnate, *we* lay it all out, and then *we* create everything that happens after that.

As children, many things are happening. We soon make the "me/not me" distinction, and we allow others to program our database by accepting their beliefs, interpretations and values about who we are. When our needs are not met, we tell ourselves that "me" is not accept-able because "not me" would not treat me this way if I were all right. "Not me" would not do this to "me" if they accepted me and loved me. So where does this leave you? With a major identity challenge. You are a vast divine spiritual being, here to explore, express, and grow via human experiences, yet you're told that you're an unworthy speck of human protoplasm. That's hard for five-year-olds to sort it out for them-selves. Can many of us do it? Judging by today's society, not many.

Can therapists do it for us? Highly unlikely because most of them are as confused as their clients. Most of us will have to tackle the chal-lenge alone, albeit with the help of the huge volume of teachings in bookstores, libraries and the Internet. But to follow through takes enor-mous desire, intention, commitment and willingness. It is easier for survivors than victims, but we *all* can do it if we set up the intention and refuse to give up.

In this step, you begin to realize that you are not who you think you are. Since childhood, you've been sold the illusion that you're a limited human being, synonymous with your physical body. What your caretakers told you about your identity and how you interpreted your treatment by them formed your basic structure of who you think you are. As a child, religions and cultural conditioning so greatly corrupt what limited exposure you have to your vast spiritual self as to be downright harmful. In most cases, it's highly unlikely you have made contact with your spiritual self since your personality self has run your life until now, and it knows nothing about your spiritual self.

There are exceptions, of course, as some children (often called "Indigo children") are aware and arrange to be born to aware parents who do not "dumb them down." Thus they retain the ability to use their intuitive senses. These are survivors but I often find that even these people have picked up such an emotional load growing up that their lives will not function well until they address their childhood issues. If you grew up in a dysfunctional family, who your parents were or what status they had makes no difference. No amount of money can buy health, happiness, peace, harmony, joy or love.

Dealing with these issues builds a good foundation for your spiritual journey. The first step is releasing the fear that drives our lives. Embracing fear drags us down but, when we rewrite the programs and embrace love, we begin evolving. We cannot begin enlightenment or go through this initiation until we allow unconditional love to guide us and, to do so, we must work out our lack of love issues. Hardly any of my clients have their love issues taken care of before I work with them, and very few people have even experienced real love in their life. Most relationships are really so that the parties can exchange attention or at best, practice conditional love. Most people look for love in the wrong places. It's not outside of us at all, and we cannot get it from somebody else until we first look inside and activate our own love.

In this step, then, we wake up to the fact that the limited self-image we've bought into is simply untrue. Because we knew no better, as children, we accepted the false belief that we were infinitely less than the glorious truth, and ended up with low self-worth. Maybe, just maybe, you *are* more than the authority figures in your life told you.

When you were a child, an indigenous program was installed in your mind so that you would follow your parents' guidance, but it has no value when you are an adult so, if the authority figure program has not been removed deleted, erased and destroyed, you must do that now (see appendix for affirmation).

Why and how has this massive illusion been perpetrated? My book, *2011: The New Millennium Begins* details how, for thousands of years, a small group of people has practiced Machiavellian "divide and conquer" techniques on the rest of us purely to strip us of our power and control us. But this and the next few steps are about waking up to the truth. Then, from step 7 onward, you begin to practice what you've learned.

Like a snake, you've been living in a skin that's gotten too tight, and it's time to shed that skin and grow a new one that gives you room to expand. The old skin was not "wrong," however, and the snake did not need "fixing." It just needs space to grow, as do you. So do not worry about self-*improvement* for there's nothing to improve; you just need a little more self-*awareness* about your true identity. YOU ARE PERFECT AS YOU ARE! Your challenge is to discover the perfection of your real identity. The perfect you is still there. All you need do is remove all the layers of dysfunctional programs that were written over the true you. Fortunately, no one can erase the database in your Subconscious Mind. All the original programs and blueprints for a perfect body/mind are still there. So the next step is to become aware of who you are, erase the dysfunctional programs and insert new programs in the files to support the original operating system files. In the process, you must forgive the people who put their values and beliefs into your database and forgive yourself for your misinterpretation of who you really are.

The Dalai Lama described the process as "a mind game" in which we must reprogram and train the mind so it can run on *functional* programs that support our spiritual journey.

Once you have taken responsibility for your life, your two challenges are:

- Seeing through the illusion that you are separate from All That Is and the Creator.
- Letting go of the illusion that you are flawed and need fixing. All you need is reprogramming to uncover the original programs. You have nothing to beat yourself up about once you uncover your true self.

To heal the separation, you must let go of the past and allow your true self to emerge. Your self-esteem, self-worth and self-confidence were shut off and written over by your program manager when your primary imprinters and caregivers and the influence of societal programming caused your personality self to accept the programs that were fed to you. Your mind is totally literal and will accept anything that an authority figure tells you. When you take your personal power back and assume responsibility for who you are, you can rewrite the programs that made you believe you were separate and had no self-worth.

If you have bought into Christian dogma, you have been told that because you're a descendent of Adam and Eve, you were created in original sin and are therefore not acceptable in God's eyes unless you accept Christ as your savior. Interestingly, the word "sin" was originally an archery term meaning "to miss the mark" but was construed as a religious term because it fit the intent of making you feel guilty. Guilt is a brilliant means to control people because they become self-policing. If you tell them that a behavior is sinful, their conscience bugs them and they feel guilty if they transgress.

If, however, you accept that Jesus Christ absolved of your sins, then you can be "saved." This is one of history's greatest con games because it lets you relax into a false sense of security. You may believe this illusion but it doesn't change your reality on an *inner* level. The Akashic Record lists all the mistakes you've made in the past and all the karma you've created. No amount of illusion can clear the slate; *you* have to do it. But, how can you do *it* when you don't know what *it* is?

First you must find out who you are and get begin bringing peace, happiness, harmony, joy, and unconditional love and acceptance into your life now. You may have made decisions in the absence of full knowledge and understanding of the outcome but that's called "being human." However, in this step, as you discover more about who you *really* are, you will "miss the mark" less and less often as honesty, ethics and integrity become your way of life. That is the intent of this 12-step ascension process.

Interestingly, only about a quarter of the planet's population is Christian, so what about the billions who do not accept Jesus Christ as their savior or share the Christian way to God. Will hell be large enough to contain them all?

Almost all religious sects (Buddhism is the notable exception) have some form of dogma to control their people. All the major teachers who have appeared over the past 3,000 years have advocated that the most important quality we can develop in ourselves is love and forgiveness and to treat others as we want to be treated. Either we no longer believe that or have swept it under the carpet in this fiercely competitive world. However, if we wish to enter enlightenment and transform ourselves on our spiritual journey, *we must honor and live by that concept.*

I also reject the concept of "no-self" as a cop-out. To give up your identity as a separate individual makes no sense to me. Many consider this the ultimate attainment in enlightenment but it's really just exchanging one lack of identity for another. In this faceless world we live in, few people know who they are and run away from reality so they can avoid the responsibility of finding out. If we are a "no-self," we are dead as far as our mind is concerned, so why not just die? Nothing in the universal laws or spiritual principles supports this concept and, according to the GOD Source, we are expected to develop a strong sense of self and take responsibility for who we are.

This is another example of the distortions perpetrated on the truth over thousands of years so that people could be controlled by destroying their true identity. The uniqueness of an individual is an important facet of who we are, and the eastern teachers fall into a paradox. On the one hand, they say that they have achieved enlightenment through attaining no-self yet they have set themselves up as unique individuals with a special identity. Therefore, the "no-self" is an illusion that no one can really achieve.

Hari-Kan Baba has reached the level where he knows who he is and what he stands for, but does not claim to have achieved no-self, or total "at-one-ness with GOD Source. I also feel that the Dalai Lama has also achieved a level of enlightenment that shows us the way.

Enlightenment is an ongoing process that happens over time, just as transformation happens over time. Few can shift their entire worldview overnight (with the possible exception of someone who has a Near-Death Experience, or NDE). Most people take years to come to a place of peace, happiness, harmony and joy in their lives.

Being an ongoing process, enlightenment encompasses the totality of our being, but most people do not know who they are, so identity crisis is the most rampant challenge we must confront on our spiritual journey. The question facing you is: Who are you and what do you stand for in your life?

As you integrate your life path on your spiritual journey, you are increasing your level of enlightenment until you reach the point where you transcend the body and become a light being. Even then, you have a unique identity as your spirit and soul direct your life. Being a strong individual is very important, so long as you do not separate yourself from the greater good by judging yourself as "better than." Getting caught up in self-righteousness becomes an identity crisis, too.

Many western people have achieved a place of fame in their life yet do not see themselves as masters of anything but themselves. They see their freedom of thinking, movement and eliminating stress as the most important facets in their life. When we see how they live, we know that love and forgiveness are basic concepts in their lives. They are physically fit, successful speakers, enjoy healthy relationships that work, and are abundant at all levels. They recognize the achievements of other people and do not put them down for following their life-path even if it diverges from theirs. Tony Robbins, Wayne Dyer, Jack Lalane, Michael Murphy, Jean Huston, Andrew Weil and Deepak Chopra are excellent examples.

Journaling

An important part of this process in getting on the path is keeping a journal. Many people feel that it takes too much time, but I have found it invaluable for tracking the issues and emotional programs that would reoccur in my life so that I could focus on them and deal with once and for all. When recognized, I could take care of the pattern and learn the lesson so I didn't have to repeat it. As part of this step, try a self-appreciation exercise in which you list everything you like or admire about yourself. Make it a *long* list, so have plenty of paper on hand. When you're done, put it aside but add to it frequently.

About 25 years ago, Mark Victor Hansen, the well-known author of the *Chicken Soup* series of books, developed what he described as a "future diary." As he would think of activities he would like to partake in, items he wanted or people he wanted to spend time with, he recorded them along with a timeline for its accomplishment. He said, "As I reviewed the items, I set in motion energy that would draw these people, things and situations to me, as I accepted that anything is possible if you allow the universal energies to work for you."

I have found Hansen's views to be true with only one catch: you must be clear enough to know that you are entitled to that outcome happening, and believe that it *can* happen. To be in this space, you must have let go of all limitations that block you from receiving. This may seem simple but, in my experience with my own awareness and people I have worked with, so many glitches block us from receiving abundance that it's amazing we're able to have anything.

Self-nurturing

We can become addicted to any practice that makes us feel better, but we must ask whether it provides what we need to reach our goals. Exercise, proper diet and nutrition are acceptable addictions. While on the path, taking rest breaks along the way is important. Use them to meditate, update your journal, or just gaze at a sunset, but be sure to tell yourself that the time spent is a "reward" for being who you are. You will be releasing thought-forms and toxins at great rates from now on, and "playtime" will be vital to your well-being.

Most people do not love themselves, so acknowledge that you are lovable by others and that you love yourself. If you do not love yourself, you may have been rejected by your parents at birth or soon after, and your self-worth and self-esteem were written over, so that you feel as if you're not all right and not acceptable. Many people have this program in denial so that they *think* they're all right yet exhibit needy behavior. People in this situation will continually look for people to validate them. You must released these programs before you can lock in the love program (see description and affirmation in appendix).

Self-love is quite evident in people who exhibit this quality in their life. They smile all the time and see life as an adventure. Happy people are easy to be with as they have no need to be constantly validated.

Living by Your Own Rules

For most of our life, we have lived by other people's rules. Society and religion have certain rules that we must follow in order to be accepted and validated. Until we reclaim our personal power, acceptance and validation are two highly sought after attitudes. When you become your own person and let go of group identity, what other people think about you makes no difference. You can then direct your life based on what *you* desire rather than on what society dictates to you what is acceptable behavior.

Once you have gone through the second door, your life will change dramatically. For many people, the challenge is taking responsibility for continuing on the spiritual journey. Many will fall back into their old behavior patterns and slide back through the door. Just going through a door does not make it a done deal. You must permanently change specific behavior patterns, take responsibility *and* follow through consistently. The whole process is a definitive life pattern shift, and you will be able to recognize the change when it happens. If you do not have the First Initiation lessons handled so that they work in your life, you will slide back until you do finally handle them.

Stepping on the path means living by your own rules, using your will, being patient or assertive as appropriate, and maybe undergoing some emotional pain. No matter how limiting they are, your current beliefs are comfortable and supportive. In fact, even the limitations you place on who you think you are feel comfortable. The weaknesses and faults you perceive in yourself prevent you from moving into new and scary areas, so now you begin to face them and explore them. Are you willing to come out of your cozy little shell and become the master you *really* are?

The "letting go" battle will seem like a great sacrifice. You will lose most, of not all, of your limited identity. Only afterwards, when you are free of the chains and burdens of these limiting beliefs, will you realize that it was *no* sacrifice at all and that you lost *nothing of value*. In fact, you will gain the most important thing imaginable— knowing who you really are. But until you go through it, it will *seem* like a sacrifice—this is deliberate. Until the Middle Self lets go of control, it can covertly slip in and set up autopilot. Since Middle Self is an operating system, we simply rewrite its programs and then function in whatever way we wish.

At the same time, you must make peace and become friends with your Ego. Most people see the Ego as the enemy since the psychological field, eastern and western religions and most people in the spiritual field have pushed this interpretation for hundreds of years. Ego is an operating system in the Subconscious Mind. (My other books describe what Ego is and how to reprogram the operating system. Higher Self will provide the entry to guidance from your soul and Source, but you have to open the door.)

As long as you run from personality self, you will not be able to go through the second door and make the transition to the third door. You must let go of personality self without thought or fear of the consequences, but it cannot happen until you relinquish control. In other words, you must release control *totally*, in complete faith that you will be provided for. Don't worry about what the remaining initiations hold for you. Focus on total change.

Over the years, I have observed many people who want to go through this door but can't because of fear. I have also seen many go through the door but then fall back into personality self by giving their power away and letting emotions take over, which pulls them back through the door because they do not stand up for themselves. (This can be tracked by which sub-personalities are recreated after they are all cleared.)

To step on the path, you must commit. When you can say, "I want this change more than anything else in my life, one hundred percent," you have taken the most difficult and important step. You will immediately feel a new strength within you, a purpose, and a direction.

When you make this shift, enlightenment goes into high gear. You must be ready for the temptations that the lessons bring because they will come at you when you go through the third door. Ask for help from your Higher Self or Source. As personality self is allowed to die out, spirit becomes activated. Find an open space and voice your yearning for assistance out to the Universe. Making this request is a formal and necessary part of the path, and must come from deep in your heart rather than just a vague wish that your life might be a little better. Do you *really* want it? Any reservations or conditions you want to stipulate will undermine your intent.

Denial

Many uncomfortable emotions and realizations will come up from now on and you may be tempted to defer dealing with them or even deny their existence. Both would be unwise. First they will reoccur until you face them and, each time a lesson comes up, its intensity will increase. Secondly you will not be able to go through or you will slide back through the door if you give your power away. While you don't go around looking for pain, when it finds you, it's best to deal with it head on because when it recurs, it will come back under more difficult circumstances. A few hours of discomfort are a small price to pay for the healing they will buy.

The ultimate level of this syndrome is denial-of-denial. When you deny something that exists in your life, your Ego will file it into an area of your mind that locks it up until some catalyst activates it. When it does come up, it usually rises in the form of intense pain, a life-threatening illness or an emotional breakdown. Do not let anything push you into victimhood if you can recognize the issue. You will often be tempted to fall back into the old pattern. If you're in denial because stuffing or suppressing the emotions of guilt for something you've done or shame over something you are, tell yourself, "I am human. I can clear this feeling and the program. I am loving myself and forgive myself for giving my power away." Then get back on the path. Pick up the pieces and carry on

Letting Go

Now that you're on the path, your life will be full of many new activities, such as meditation, journaling, reading, meetings, attending conventions, seminars and expos. Assuming your life was already busy before, you will need to curtail or even drop some of those activities. Let go of whatever doesn't serve Spirit unless, of course, it's for your playtime. This may cost you a few friends but you will find new ones on the path with whom you better resonate. When I made this shift to a new reality, I found myself in a vast wasteland. Most of my old friends found me odd and I found myself being excluded from their activities. I could no longer talk their language and they did not want to talk about what interested me. Developing new interests and new friends took a while but was well rewarded.

The past is just a bunch of dead ghosts, so you're free to reinvent yourself in the Now moment. The present is only time you've got, so let go of the past. No matter how you try, you can't heal or fix it. The past is a series of "canceled checks" you can't unwrite, so let your personal history go, without regret. (In the Carlos Castenada books, Don Juan goes to great lengths to have Carlos erase his history in order to become an impeccable warrior.)

Simplify your life in order to prevent your possessions from actually possessing you. A shiny new car needs washing; who cares with an older car? A large house requires care and upkeep; who cares with a rustic cabin in the woods? Masters run their lives; others let their lives run them. This is not to say that you should completely abandon your old way of life but undertake a reassessment as to what's important in your new life.

A friend of mine decided he was going to change his whole life because he felt he had to make a complete shift and go in another life direction. In doing so, he left his family and his children, claiming, "I am not the same person who entered into this marriage agreement and no longer feel bound by the vows." He believed this illusion so completely that he justified his action as acceptable. In my view, he was creating some serious karma with his family, but he didn't see it that way. Well, over the years, the karma has played out in his life in many ways.

When you go through this reassessment, you must look at what you have created in the past and how you can work with the consequences of that in your new path, so that the decisions you make in your new awareness do not create more karma. If we could be aware of steps we take from childhood on up, we could have peace, happiness, harmony and joy at every juncture in our life. The challenge is to remember our direction and the lessons we brought into this life as recorded in our flight plan. Few of us can tap into this memory so we easily become lost and make decisions that are not in line with our flight plan, and thus get further off track. Once we recognize that we're on a detour or dead end, we must change course. We may have chosen a dysfunctional partner in our travels but there is even a lesson in this, of which we must become aware of so that we do not repeat the same mistake. Few people recognize this lesson and, instead, drop the dysfunctional partner to look for another relationship that they hope will be a better match. If the lesson underlying the first "mistake" is not cleared and erased from the file, such people find themselves trapped in the same dysfunctional pattern again and again until they recognize what's happening. And the lesson? That finding love is not a matter of finding the right person but of *being* the right person, and that's what these steps are all about.

Early on in your search for enlightenment comes an "Aha, I have found the path." Then you can actually get on the path. People in the eastern traditions accuse the western "human potential movement" of self-mastery of using conditioning to delete limiting behavior by stating that: "Until we transcend conditioning altogether we will never truly be free."

Unfortunately, there is nothing in eastern wisdom to avoid this pitfall. The eastern traditions ask their students to practice the exact same thing: "Use this meditation, say that mantra over and over again, sit in this position, practice these postures, breathe in this way, etc."

Eastern wisdom claims to be a way of life rather than conditioning, and thus transcends conditioning. But if we must continue to use certain practices to stay on track, then we have not transcended the process of reconditioning. We should not have to use any particular practice to stay on the path.

When we pass each initiation, the lessons learned become an inherent part of our life. Our path to enlightenment should allow us to make the ultimate connection with the GOD Source and, when we do, there are no limitations as this is not a conditioning process. We need not follow any routine to continue in this level of awareness because we have transcended any needs that could create a barrier to oneness with the Godhead. Of course, this is the ultimate level enlightenment and takes time to achieve but there are no limitations to its attainment. Eastern traditions keep looking for a way to achieve profound surrender that allows access to a force greater than oneself in order to control one's life. This sounds suspiciously like the 12-step tradition where people give their power to a source higher than themselves to control their life so that they can overcome their addictions.

I have no intention of giving my power away to anyone, because the path is about *not* giving our power away, so that we can be our own person and take charge of our lives.

According to what little of universal laws has survived the ravages of the ages, we are part of All That Is/Creator/GOD Source, but have forgotten and devolved into a lower level of awareness. But we are working our way back up to the Godhead, and are guided to break through to Its guidance. However, we seldom hear it because we forgot that it even existed. (I just trust that my guidance is accurate, yet remain aware that it can be distorted if I am not clear. I constantly check myself to ensure that I am not attached to an outcome.)

I am not trying to control outcomes, and I know that everything will turn out perfectly even if I do not find an outcome acceptable. When things do not turn out the way I feel they should have done, I look for the lesson so I can turn the situation around. We must play a conscious part in our life and make decisions as to the course of our life. In fact, GOD Source specifically said that they expect us to do our part in this cooperative venture called the universe. In all my dialogues with Source, not once have they used the word "surrender." Quite the reverse; they want us to make our own decisions and will guide us in getting though our ascension process.

The Love Myth

Key to this step is reevaluating "love." Now, we're told since child-hood that being selfish is wrong, and giving to others is right. And that the greatest form of giving is love. Of course, you would like to love others as much as possible but feel unable to, so you wonder if you're at fault in some way. Maybe you even feel guilty about not "loving your neighbor as yourself." But how do you actually love? How can you learn to love?

Our major challenge is detaching from needs. Most people do good deeds for other people in order to win acceptance and hopefully love. But you can gain nothing from conditional love because it's not really love. True love has no strings attached, and fulfills no needs. It just is, but if you have programs that tell you that you are not entitled to it, you will never get it.

This may surprise you, but you cannot learn *how* to love; in fact, you've spent your entire life learning how *not* to love, how to block love for survival purposes. The love you want to give to others is not something you go out and find, and then bring into you for "recycling" out to others. The love is *already within you*, but covered by layers and layers of Middle Self's survival blocks that prevent it from shining out. These layers are your fears, and block you from expressing that love already in you.

So you cannot learn to love but you *can* remove the blocks, and then love will just flow on its own—you don't have to do a thing. When you discover that your awareness of love was taken away from you, we can take it back. Who took it from you? You did! You accepted that what people did to you made you unlovable. As you grew up, you made interpretations about how you were treated by your primary caregivers, which resulted in feeling "I am not all right, I do not fit in, I am not acceptable." And, of course, "If they loved me, they would not treat me this way." Worse, if you were rejected before you were born, the rejection was locked into your cellular memory.

Love is what happens naturally in the absence of guilt for what you've done in the past and fear of what will happen in the future. But how do you banish these twin monsters? The way is both easy and difficult—you *choose* to. You set your intent and exercise your free will to redefine your reality. You turn your mind in on itself, objec-tively analyze your beliefs, and declare, "This is not who I want to be," and "This is not what I want to believe."

Of course, redefining your beliefs won't happen overnight and you will have relapses, but eventually being fear-free will become a habit, just as being fearful currently is. Begin by forgiving yourself for having the guilt, shame and fear in the first place, for they just come with being human, part of the package called life. Your parents, educators and other imprinters drilled them into you as a child, and your job, beginning in this step, is see them for what they—just other people's *opinions* about reality—and pull them up by the roots like weeds.

Your beliefs are yours by choice, not some Universal Law that says, "This is how things are." Therefore, you can simply *choose* to have other beliefs. But before you do, you must figure out what you currently believe, so get into the habit of watching your thinking and your words during conversation, looking for fear-based, limited thinking such as, "Oh, I could never do that." Then, gently push it aside to make room for more loving, expansive thinking.

The Survival Self

Another key is letting go of your survival self. Your Middle Self strives to hide what you perceive as your faults, shortcomings, and weaknesses from others because you think that if others see them, they'll withhold respect, admiration, validation and love from you. So you push your "faults" into denial and strive to impress other people by holding up a cardboard cut-out of excellence rather than be your authentic self. You can will yourself through life in this manner but it will eventually take its toll when this façade collapses.

Because everyone else feels as insecure as you do, what happens if you strive to impress them with your brilliant cardboard cut-out? You make them feel even more insecure! They will look at your perfection and berate themselves further for not being as good. Their self-hate and despair will deepen and they will withdraw a little more behind *their* cardboard cut-out to further separate themselves from your shining example. They'll strengthen their attempts to polish the image they in turn present to you, and so the game goes on, with no one really knowing who anyone else is. Are we having fun yet? The only winner is Middle Self, which gets to be in control and creates the sub-personalities you need to present this façade.

In this initiation, you break the cycle and give of yourself as you *truly* are, admitting your weaknesses. Then you appear *vulnerable* to others and they will see that you are no threat to them. This gives them a lift, they feel less lonely, and more able to relate to you because of your vulnerability and *humanness*. And then what? You end up getting *exactly* what you wanted in the first place—their love in response to yours. And you got it because you stopped manipulating them for it!

Then, you rewrite your love program and let go of your idealized cardboard cut-out, allowing your true self to emerge. Since this is not threatening, people can accept you as you are. As we'll see in Chapter 3, a spiritual law states: "You must first give up attachment to what you want. To gain admiration, you must stop trying to be admirable. To gain love, you must first give up trying to be lovable. Instead, you must first *give* love by showing others your vulnerability and letting them in."

In the old way, you watch other people with suspicion, wondering if they are noticing *your* "faults." At the same time, you're cataloging *theirs* in the hopes that you will score fewer black marks than they do. So you're both trying to present the best cardboard cut-out you can, meanwhile losing your authentic self, even from yourself.

If you relate directly, without the polished survival shell, you give the greatest gift that one human being can give to another—yourself— and the Universal Law of Resonance will ensure that the gift is returned. At first, exposing your vulnerability may seem difficult and scary. After all, you've worked hard polishing and refining that image all your life. And now, to give it up! If you have not made peace with it, Middle Self will hit the panic button and your friends and relatives who are not on the path will suggest a vacation in a padded room. But try it. See if being authentic works, but be careful not to overcompensate and go around debasing yourself or putting yourself down. Parading your own unworthiness is either a plea for reassurances from others or a defense mechanism to preempt anticipated criticism. Simply take off your survival suit and be yourself. You will save an enormous amount of energy. And if you stumble and catch yourself acting out your "I am perfect" role, gently stop and just be *you*.

Where did this concoction of manipulative tricks and sub-personalities come from? As children, we soon realized that our parents and others rewarded us for being "good" and punished us by withholding affection or giving us time-outs when we were "bad." So, we quickly learned that being "good" led to acceptance and happiness, and being "bad" led to rejection and unhappiness.

You created the survival self to manipulate the world and those around you to meet your needs. It's a "political self" that is constantly dodging and weaving to get what it wants from others but, because everyone else is doing this, it's also the target of their manipulation. Thus interpersonal dealings become a series of barters as everyone strives to get their needs met.

Most of us also figure out that we could never be as "good" as the world expects us to be, so we learn to make this false survival self a "good" self designed to win the approval, affection, and love that we crave. Over the years, we forget that this is just a false self, a cardboard cut-out, built to win whatever signifies approval to us. And, over the years, we strive to *become* this survival self in the hope that, one day, we will. But we are always plagued by a nasty, nagging, underlying guilt about being an "imposter" and live in fear of being found out. "Would people really love me if they knew who I was?" is the drive behind those dreams in which you're naked in a room full of clothed people.

The problem is that trying to become your survival self is no recipe for real happiness or inner peace. In fact, it completely obscures your only chance of success—your *real* self—and consumes tremendous energy.

Your survival self *seems* so valid and worthy. It has all the right responses and makes all the right politically correct moves to win approval. It strives to be "nice," to understand others, to love, to avoid anger, to overcome its faults, and generally get "good grades" in life. And it goes to great lengths to deny its own imperfections and short-comings, fueled by a horror of "being found out."

It strives for self-development, but only because of the fear of being thought "not good enough." The high standards it sets for itself make it proud, ambitious, aggressive and competitive, but these traits can be channeled into politically correct enterprises for appearances' sake. They miss the fact that nothing makes you more vulnerable than pride because you've more to lose.

Most of us are in conflict because we cannot meet our Critical Parent sub-personality's needs for high standards but neither can we stop trying. Therefore, we beat ourselves up for failing, because one of our goals is to always achieve our goals, so we're a double failure. Of course, to ease the pain, many of us project blame on to others. Critical Parent will shut up when it sees that you are trying to become who you really are.

If you're from an abusive family, you have another one of your Middle Self's committee to deal with. Whenever you felt fearful about being abused, you escaped into the Magical Child sub-personality, where you did not have to feel the pain.

So, what's the alternative? First, stop beating yourself up and accept that you grew up in an imperfect world. To survive that world as a child, you *had* to build your survival self. Then, objectively accept responsibility for it, and work through it. Ironically, you created your survival self to build your self-confidence, but the stronger the survival self is, the lower your self-confidence. You created it as your "good guy" public persona, designed to win approval, but now you cannot meet its high standards, so you lose *its* approval. The public persona has become a cardboard cutout of a human being that you hold up in front of you. The more energy you give to fuel it, the less you have for the real self who is hiding behind it. This hidden part is the *only* part that can grow. It is flexible, intuitive, guided from within, and can know *real* truth and love. But the cardboard cutout eclipses it. So you're estranged from your real inner self and, without nourishment, it may become weak and impoverished.

In this initiation, you begin to ask, "Who am I *really*?" and "Where is that free, spontaneous, intuitive self I was as a young child before I began to worry about what people thought of me? Where did he or she go?" At some point, you will realize, in a flash, that your authentic self can only step forward once you do away with your cardboard cut-out survival self.

When that happens, you realize that you no longer need that self. After all, it was supposed to win love and approval from others but ended up distancing others and withholding love from yourself. As you reflect on friendships, marriage and jobs, you will see that trying to live up to your ideal of being the perfect mate, lover, worker, and friend has done more to separate than to bring together.

As you reflect on your survival self, you will see its worthy aspirations being fueled by pride, its competitiveness being fueled by a belief in separateness, its striving to be first, as in: "Do unto others before they do unto you," and so on. *Do this with self-love and acceptance* because realizing that you've been living a lie all your life can be very distressing. If you become angry or depressed at all the wasted years, own the emotion and thank it for being a great teacher. Do not blame or look outside for the cause. Let go of all these false selves and let your old self die.

You will soon feel a great sense of having been born again. You can now relax into your *real* self rather than fuel the old, false self. You're free to change, to grow, to be authentic. You will begin to react very differently to other people and to outside events and situations.

You will no longer ask, "How should I act?" You will just act, spontaneously and in touch with your inner impulses and hunches, saying just the right thing, without needing to check with what your survival self requires you to say.

Try being authentic and spontaneous, or what some call a "divine fool." Then you will not manipulate for outside power and recognition, you will not seduce for sex, and you will not work solely for money. Instead, you will be driven by a higher vision.

One of the joys of being authentic is that you never have to worry about being politically correct and saying just the right thing. You are who you are and it's the world's loss if it can't handle you. Of course, you might stumble occasionally, but just pick yourself up and say, "If it was easy, everyone would be doing it."

Some friends will fall away because they can't handle who you're becoming. This is inevitable, because one of the bases of friendship is shared or similar worldviews. But you no longer want to wallow in their limitations, denials and victimhood, and opt out of their little games. However, you will begin to attract new people into your life with whom you resonate.

The mindsets you begin to reevaluate in this step revolve around survival. In order to survive, I must:

- Do it all myself, otherwise I will be hurt and let down, even though it means never stepping beyond my own limitations.

- Make people like me, so I will sublimate my needs to theirs, even though I hate doing that.

- Present myself well to others at all times, so that I am upbeat, attractive and positive. Even if I'm having a bad day, I will wear a cheerful face, even though I don't feel cheerful.

- Work hard and earn my right to stay in the rat race even though I hate it.

- Get my share of the spoils, more if possible, because there's only so much to go round, and when it's gone, it's gone.

- Take responsibility for the happiness and well-being of everyone I meet. And always follow through on my commitments even at great personal cost.

- Strive to be the fittest and most powerful because only they survive in this dog-eat-dog world.

- Follow the "rules" because they define what power is, who has it and who doesn't.

These mindsets lead only to self-loathing and you *must* let them go, maybe slowly, or maybe all at once by some life-changing wake-up call such as an accident or severe illness. However, your Middle Self may scream, "Are you crazy? The world will reject you, and you'll starve and die." You, the authentic self, simply replies, "As of now, I am in this world but not of it."

The catch here is to make peace with Middle Self and Ego as soon as possible. Make friends with them because they are an important part of your team.

Here is a test you can use to gauge progress. Your survival self's greatest fear is of physical death, and when you can calmly contemplate that event without denial, your survival self will have been placed in the archives for safe storage and your authentic self will have been reborn will emerge.

You, your authentic self, will no longer grasp on to anything, because you no longer fear its loss. You know all will be well. The rigidity in your personality will give way to a new fluidity. You will give yourself permission to be wrong and to fail because you see "failure" as only an arbitrary measure anyway. The purpose of Earth plane existence is to explore, to research, to see what works and what doesn't, so you can't possibly fail. Each time Thomas Edison discarded another substance as unsuitable for an electric light filament (and he tested thousands), he didn't see it as a failure but as one step closer to success. The only time you fail is the last time you try. And successful people fail more frequently than failures.

As an authentic self, you can relax into the flow of life, no longer a rock in a river against which the current smashes, but like the water itself flowing around obstacles. As you align with the rhythms of your life, you find yourself moving to a higher octave of happiness, security, joy, and love. And life becomes an ally rather than an enemy waiting to "get you."

In due course, you will see that the old survival self was based on the *fear* of being found out, but you, the authentic self, acts from the *joy* of being found out and the love that this will bring. Also, you will enjoy interacting with others—mate, lover, boss, friends—with gusto and exuberance for the sheer thrill of *really* relating, out in the open and not from behind the cardboard cut-out and its carefully planned, politically correct responses.

You have started the journey "home." You don't have to wait until death frees you from the clutches of false personality. You are free now, and much happier. And wasn't happiness the original intent of getting on the path to begin with?

You will find the peace that comes with knowing and being who you *really* are, and realize that your survival self limited you to just that—survival. Now you can begin to enjoy *living* as a whole human being, rather than just surviving. Thus the next step in enlightenment is accomplished.

Avoiding the Guru Trap

There is a danger in this initiation of putting some guru or other teacher on a pedestal. A guru who lets you do this feeds off your energy and steals your power, so you must consciously resist the temptation. The only possible outcome of this is that when you realize what's happening, you will resent the guru and kick yourself for having been duped and wasted time.

In later initiations, others may try to put you on *their* pedestal. Unless you want to end up despised because you can't live up to their idealized image of whom they think you are, resist the temptation by gently refusing to accept their power. The bright side of this, of course, is that it starkly reveals a weakness in your would-be followers that they can then heal.

The saying, "If you meet the Buddha on the road, kill him," warns you not to project your own power and divinity on to anything outside yourself, for the true Buddha (and the true Christ) lie within you.

Taking Your Power Back

This is the key to passing the second initiation. Since we first banded together in caves, some people have always tried to steal the power of others. This eventually became institutionalized by the Church—the ultimate power-thieves. Amassing power, however, never makes people happy but only makes them want more.

Ask yourself three questions:
- Is my life one long compromise, as I try to make people feel okay at my expense?
- Is my life filled with activities that do not bring me joy?
- Am I possessed by my possessions?

If the honest answer to any of these is yes, you have some serious reevaluation ahead. Fortunately, you have plenty of resources.

If you think that reclaiming your power is selfish, think again. Giving to everyone except yourself is called *martyrdom* and has no place on the path because of the resentment you will eventually feel towards those you sacrifice for, or you will deplete yourself and be useless to everyone. The trick is to balance service to others with service to self.

The remaining initiations systematically examine these blocks, exposing them for what they are, thereby allowing you to see and dispel them. By step 5, you will be ready to widen your love experience to pure, unconditional love.

Second Initiation Meditation

Use this visualization for opening the door and going through the second initiation:

See yourself in a meadow with soft green grass. Smell the freshness of the air with the wind blowing around you. Realize that this initiation is about letting go of your old self and attachments to the past. You are going to let your old self die and lock all the records up in the history section of your mind. Reaffirm that you can do this by saying, "I am committing myself to change and am letting my old self die. I am locking up all the programs in the history section now."

Now that you are ready to transcend the past and let it go, you can walk down the path to a new life and rebirth. Walking along the path through the meadow, you see a mountain ahead in the distance. On the side of the mountain sits a small cabin nestling in the trees. As you come closer you can see the cabin more clearly.

Approaching the cabin, you can see it clearly. You climb the steps to the front door, knowing with each step you take that you are giving up the past and letting the old self die. It will pass away as you go through the door.

You approach the door and pull it open. All you can see inside is inky blackness. You pull the door wide open and enter in complete trust that you will be safe and secure in the darkness.

You leave your old self outside the cabin and close the door behind you. Now you are standing in pitch darkness, not knowing where you are. You affirm that you are ready for this new experience and to be reborn into a new life.

Off to your left, you notice the first light of the new dawn beginning to filter in through the window. The light begins to light you up and everything begins to sparkle.

The flowers, shrubs and trees outside the window begin to light up with their colors. The fragrances of the flowers and trees become intense as the wind blows them in toward you. The cabin dissolves and you are standing in a garden.

You walk further into this garden, smelling all the fragrances of the flowers and the trees. You realize this is unconditional love, for nature just gives them to you without any withholds. You breathe them in deeply and fill all of the places in your body that once held pain, anger, fear and resentment. Fill your body from the top of your head to the tips of your toes. Breathe the fragrances in all the way down to your toes and let them fill all the cracks, crevices and crannies that once held rejection and not feeling all right. The flowers and trees totally accept you. They have nothing to give but love. They don't ask you whether you want their love; it's just there for the taking. Let the colors of flowers and the trees fill your body with radiance.

You see a bench, surrounded by flowers that glow. You sit down and bathe yourself in the colors of love, filling your body all the way to the top of your head.

When you feel that you are complete with this rebirth experience and are ready to come back into the world, get up and walk along the path back into this new world, filled with new expectations and realizations. As you walk, remember that you are now the power in your life and can make any decision you wish. You are not controlled by the views of others about who you should be. You are now on the path to enlightenment and you accept the responsibility for disciplining yourself to follow the path.

Coming back into present time and space, you now know you have been reborn. Smile at someone.

Going through this affirmation will not guarantee that you will stay here. Enlightenment is yours in return for the necessary vigilance, discipline and work.

3

The Third Initiation:
Understanding Spiritual Principles
and Universal Laws

The third door is a relatively easy initiation but it creates a challenge with which you will have to deal for the rest of your life. Getting through the door is easy once you understand universal laws and spiritual principles, some of which are presented below. Others, more advanced, are revealed in later steps. These laws are based on the physics of energy and operate at the cosmic level. They are vast impersonal principles that you go up against at your peril. You can use them without love and compassion in your heart, but they work much more effectively when applied with loving intent.

You must also understand and be able to use unconditional love even though you might not be able to live in that state for long periods. It is also important to overcome procrastination and indecision, and drop any denial of emotions and justifying situations.

Once you choose the ascension path, you must follow universal laws and spiritual principles, so let's take a look at these important rules for living. The difference between those on the path and those not on the path is that the former base their lives on the laws in this chapter.

The Law of Resonance

This law states that any energy magnetically attracts similar energy, and that the stronger the energy (especially emotional), the stronger the attraction. So you get what you focus on, regardless of whether your thoughts and emotions are joyful or fearful. And the stronger you *feel* about your thoughts, the more quickly they will manifest in your reality. In other words, thoughts are "sticky" and, simply by having one, you attract similar thoughts into your aura and life.

We live in a huge ocean of every kind of energy imaginable, and it's all available to us, whether love, fear, pain, joy, abundance, lack, etc., and your thoughts and feelings determine what kind of energy, and in what quantity, comes your way. Under this law, the energy matrix simply reflects your choices back to you in the form of the events, situations and people in your life.

To have this law work *for* you rather *against* you, monitor your thoughts, for each one is a magnet. The odd stray thought is not a problem but habitual negative thoughts, especially if reinforced with emotion, amalgamate into beliefs that most certainly program your reality. The solution? Become aware of your thoughts and beliefs, decide to change them, and substitute different thoughts and beliefs; they're only electromagnetic patterns, not cast in concrete, so you can change them very easily once you're aware of them and *once you know you can.*

Suppose you're paying your bills, your bank balance is getting low, and you get a knot of fear in your belly. That thought, backed by fear, instantly informs the Universe about your emotional attachment to unpaid bills, which will guarantee that it will deliver more of them. STOP RIGHT THERE! Replace those thoughts and feelings with the joy you feel when you make a large bank deposit. Savor completing the deposit slip and handing it to the teller. See his or her smile when you slide the check or cash across the counter. Enjoy the glow in your belly. Then get up and move around to shake off any residual energy. As you do, repeat out loud an affirmation such as, "I am in the flow. Money flows to me effortlessly so that I can pay my bills. I will always have enough."

Another angle is to give gratitude for whatever goods or services prompted the bill. As you pay your utilities, thank the universe for the benefits of electricity, water, gas, etc. in your life.

An important implication of this law is: "you get more of whatever you focus on." So if you run around fighting "evil" in the world, the universe will ensure that there's always a plentiful supply of evil in your life to keep you happy and busy. Hence the biblical advice, "Resist not evil." Rather than focus on what you *don't* want, such as war, gang violence, or high crime rates, focus instead on what you *do* want in your life, such as peace, love, harmony and joy.

Become aware of your thoughts 24/7 and whenever a negative comes up, let it go and replace it with a positive. A lifetime of focusing on lack and limitation is a strong habit, and breaking yourself of it will take time, effort and persistence but, if you start right now, there will come a time when you'll be coasting the downgrade. Then you'll be glad you went to all the trouble.

If you find a limiting pattern, don't beat yourself up for having it, for you're telling the Universe that you're focusing on your limitations, so you'll just get more to work with. Instead, ask your guides, angels, or whoever, to remove it.

The Law of Duality

On the physical plane, everything has its opposite: good/bad, right/wrong, etc., and your job is to navigate a path through the hundreds of choices you make every day. If you had to make all those choices consciously, you'd be exhausted. As we've just seen, you make most of them unconsciously based on your beliefs, thus letting autopilot fly your life for you.

A belief that the world is a hostile place, that it's "dog eat dog," will deliver that reality to you. So why not believe that the world is benevolent, supportive, and abundant? It is! However, you might watch the evening TV news and say, "Safe and benevolent! You've got to be kidding." But which comes first? The murders, muggings, shootings and rapes, or people's belief that the world is a violent and unsafe place?

Those who would control humanity have been instilling those beliefs for centuries in order to justify increased control over us. Ostensibly this is intended to protect us, but its real purpose is to progressively erode our freedom, as we're seeing in the wake of the WTC terrorist attacks.

We all live, work and play as nodes within an unimaginably huge, intelligent, and infinitely loving matrix, formed from Creator energy, that makes up All That Is. Energetically, the matrix is *everything* and can deliver every shade of reality to you, from supremely blissful to beyond horrendous. So the matrix examines your beliefs to figure out what kind of reality you want to experience in your life. It does this by noting *where* you put your energy, not the *kind* of energy you put there. Whether you wrap your thoughts in ecstatic joy or sheer panic doesn't matter. If you're walking down a dark city street, repeating, "I don't want to get mugged. I don't want to get mugged," all the matrix detects is a focus on getting mugged, and will conspire to deliver that reality.

Another useful mindset to have in order to automatically make many of the duality choices is, "My life is about learning, growing, moving forward, serving others and having fun." Therefore, spend time every day focusing on these life qualities, so that they guide your choices.

The Law of Intent

Intent is organized, coherent purpose to achieve a specific goal. Compared with the diffuse glow of general wants and desires, intent is a focused laser beam shooting out into the universe. Of course, this takes more work on your part, but well-formed intent is unstoppable. For example, you could set your intent to have only growth-promoting and fun events, situations and people in your life. However, be sure your intent is "karma-free," otherwise you'll tangle with the next law. Before forming any intent, I always check with my guides that it's consistent with the highest and best interests of all concerned.

The Law of Detachment

Ironically, once you've set your intent, you must detach from the outcome. Worrying or fussing over it muddies the energetic waters because attachment to an outcome emphasizes to the Universe the current *lack* of that outcome, its absence in your life. Infatuation with *getting* equals a state of *not having*.

By all means, spend a few minutes a day using the Law of Intent to reinforce your desires, needs and intention, keeping them consistent from day-to-day, but don't keep "mussing their hair." Let the Universe deliver the outcome in its own way, how and when it deems appropriate. You've been heard; now get out of the way and expect a miracle. Once an archer has loosed an arrow, does he focus his will on directing it toward the target? No, his work has been done, and now it's up to the laws of physics to take over and deliver a bull's eye.

Detachment applies across the board: material things, how others behave toward you, outcomes to situations, and world events. Be willing, eager even, to operate in uncertainty, because that leaves room for miracles to happen for, as a friend of mine says, "God loves to surprise us."

The Law of Synchronicity

When miracles do happen in your life, gratefully accept them as the universe's way of guiding you along your path, or onto it. Do not write them off as luck or coincidence; they are the result of your guides and teachers painstakingly pulling off a masterpiece in logistics, so thank them and ask what they plan for an encore. By virtue of your incarnating here, you are entitled to miracles in your life, so constantly be on the lookout for synchronicities, large and small, as help along the way.

An excellent example is another friend who had set his intent to relocate from San Francisco to southern California but had no idea how to go about finding a place to live from 400 miles away, made even more difficult by his having two large dogs. The next day, he met someone at a party who owned a house in the very same town he wanted to move to, and needed to find a trustworthy renter because they in turn wanted to move to Arizona for a year. The deal was done that evening and both moves occurred within the month—coincidence or a perfect example of their guides pulling strings in the background?

When the year was up, a house came on the market that was a VA repo, which he bought for a song. It doubled in value in three years, when he sold it in order to move 300 miles to Nevada. This too would call for long-distance house-hunting, except that a friend of a friend of his owned a rental property in the city he planned to move to. The tenants had just vacated the house in a hurry, so she needed a new tenant quickly. It was a perfect match. As for the dogs, his landlady also had a dog but couldn't walk it, so once a week, my friend walks all three dogs. It seems that my friend's guides also make excellent realtors, too.

The Law of Asking

Your spirit guides, guardian angels, and many other higher-dimensional beings are eager to partner you on your path, and arrange for the miracles you've just read about. However, there is one catch … they can't interfere. To elicit their assistance, *YOU MUST ASK!*

We are surrounded by nonphysical assistance, but they can't just barge into your life and rearrange everything to make things peachy. That would violate your free will and whisk away your lessons, hence the need to ask. Ask in general terms, however, because you do not know enough to make a detailed request—let your guides attend to the details. Just tell them the effect you want something to have in your life. Suppose you get a job in another town and try to buy a house in that town, but keep hitting obstacles. However, several people offer you rental situations, so you decide to rent instead. Then, six months later, your new employer downsizes but your old employer wants you back so you need to return to the first city. Renting makes leaving town a snap but, if you'd bought a house, you'd be faced with selling, possibly in a depressed real estate market and might have lost a great deal of money—something your guides knew in advance. So, rather than say, "I need help in buying a house," say, "I need help finding a place to live in a way that's in the highest and best interest of all involved." That could even allow your guides to bring you a six-month, rent-free housesitting arrangement!

It's that simple. Just ask. Ask aloud, ask quietly in your heart, *BUT ASK*. Your request need not be elaborate and no grand ceremony is required although, if you feel that this shows due reverence, then go ahead, but realize that it's more for your benefit than theirs. I use the Kahuna Prayer (see *Becoming a Spiritual Being in a Physical Body*) while Tony, my editor, prefers the Superconscious Technique* given by a group (now disbanded) called Earth Mission:

"Superconscious, by the force of Grace, will you manifest the performance, the effect and embodiment of the highest possibility of _____, so that the power of that can be manifested fully in my life. And so it is."

Notice how this request is couched in the most general terms, and focuses just on the end result. If even this seems to be too much trouble, a heart-felt cry of "Help" is enough; your guides know *exactly* what's bothering you without you having to spell it out, and will come flocking to your aid.

Do not worry that, by asking, you're bothering busy entities who have better things to do. First, they are not bound by time and can accomplish a great deal in the spacious present. Second, helping you *is their job*, and they need to help you as part of *their* evolution and service. And besides, they get a kick out of the expression on your face when they pull off a juicy synchronicity in your life.

Stories from the Mystery Schools

The ascension program I follow is based on the ancient mystery schools and their processes that have been proven over thousands of years. Many people try to make up new rules based on things they assume will happen because of what some channeled information has revealed. My feedback from the GOD Source is that the processes have not changed at all over millennia; they're still the same as in ancient times.

---

* The term "Superconscious" refers to your higher self in concert with the higher realms in their entirety, and calls on anyone and everyone there, not just a being whom you name. After all, you don't necessarily know the best being to call on.

Many valuable transformational tools are available to us at this time, and we just need to find how to work with them. This book presents a protocol of specific steps that I have found works well. Some may not agree with the steps or sequence, but it's a starting point so let's go back to the beginning and find out what the early mystery school writers had to say on the subject. Many ancient texts and teachings provide clues as to how to open up the treasure chest of our life. They all have the same general requirement: let go of control and take responsibility.

During the time of Atlantis, people were much more knowledgeable and technologically advanced than we are now, and mystery schools were considered a normal part of life. In anticipation of the destruction, however, many groups left Atlantis and settled in other parts of the world, such as South America and Egypt, mixing with the indigenous populations. At that time, the mystery schools became hidden, as they are today. Greek, Egyptian and other mystery school traditions were established, but initiation was by invitation only; you couldn't just "apply" as if going to college. The traditions have always emphasized discipline, commitment and personal responsibility as their major underlying principles. Without these, your past simply becomes your future.

Denial and illusion are the most serious impediments to these principles, even though you may not recognize them at work in your life. The history of your life up to the present, and how you plan to achieve your goals for the future, will foretell how successful you are in handling your life.

From written material on ascension, our responsibility is clear: we must understand the spiritual principles and universal laws that govern life and ascension, laws that the Source has revealed to me over the past 20 years. Contacting GOD Source is not a phenomenon reserved for just a few. We all have the ability and just need proper training, commitment, concentration, and discipline. The records are available; everything is known, and we must simply discipline ourselves to ask questions and listen to the GOD Source. But first we must learn to quiet the self-talk. (For more information, my book *Opening Communication With GOD Source* provides the methods.)

My first direct contact with a person who had mystery school experience was Paul Solomon. He was a fifth generation Baptist minister who awoke with a start when his wife suddenly divorced him. All the metaphysical material he then encountered was totally new to him but he dove into it as fast as he could. A few of the highlights of his life illustrate what making the shift in consciousness takes.

We often get off track in our journey, as Paul did in the beginning. Since he'd had no experience with alcohol or drugs, he got lost in that detour for a few years. Then he had another spiritual awakening and found that he could talk to GOD Source and receive valuable answers. (As a minister, he'd never had that ability.) In the early 1970s, he gravitated to Virginia Beach and began giving the same type of readings that Edgar Cayce had given.

Solomon's driving force was to find a mystery school in which to study, so he began practicing out-of-body travel. On one of his out-of-body trips, he finally contacted a mystery school but it was a scary experience for he was told that he had not been invited and could not enter. One day, he met a man who ran a mystery school using *bonsai* (Japanese miniature tree cultivation) as a teaching tool, but again was told, "You are not allowed to seek out a mystery school. They will contact you when they feel you are ready for initiation."

At a lecture he was giving, Paul was curious about an older Japanese man sitting in the back of the room, who just observed and left before Paul could talk with him. He asked a friend, "Is my teacher ever going to contact me?"

The friend replied, "He already has. Many times."

"When and where? Was he the older Japanese man who came to my lecture two weeks ago?"

"Yes, he was," came the reply.

"And I missed him," Paul said, dejectedly.

The friend replied, "He has been observing you for the last six months. He is very methodical and moves slowly in the matter of choosing new students."

Paul was disappointed and wondered how he could contact the old man. Again, the friend advised, "You cannot. He will contact you."

Of course, Paul was anxious and lost a lot of sleep until contact came two months later.

In Paul's first interview with the teacher, he was surprised at the requirements to enter the training program. The first was that he would need to give up all outside commitments and live in the teacher's home and take care of his house for thirty days. That meant cleaning house, doing dishes, washing clothes, cooking, and any other chores the teacher assigned.

The teacher told him to think about this requirement and let him know, and then just walked away. Paul did not know whether to follow him or just leave and call back. He decided to wait until the following day to call him back. He went home deeply puzzled by the interaction. "What's housework got to do with a mystery school?" he asked himself. "And why did the teacher say nothing at all about the school?"

(Paul would eventually discover that all mystery schools operate on a similar basis of a period of residence, with mundane chores as the first lesson in the curriculum.)

When Paul called the old man to say that he would accept the 30-day condition, the student currently keeping house answered the phone. The teacher returned the call and invited Paul to start in two weeks, reminding him to bring everything he needed for a three-month stay, as students were not allowed to leave during their 90-day internship program. So even though he would have to give up his work giving psychic readings and lectures, Paul was willing to do anything to get into the program.

During induction, the teacher took Paul out to the greenhouse and showed him a bonsai tree that he'd been working with while observing Paul to see if he could enter the school. He described how the bonsai resisted training and needed wire to force its branches into the desired shape. He described Paul's behavior accurately as he talked about the little bonsai, and Paul was surprised that the teacher could observe him through the little tree.

Paul's experience at the mystery school was well-rounded as he found that his teacher did not say much but was very forceful in the way he taught. He noticed that when people would get angry, the teacher would send them to the greenhouse to mix potting compost to get work out their anger. After they'd calmed down, he would spend individual time with them, going over their feelings and the cause of them. Paul began to notice that often, the teacher would not say anything, most of the communication being intuitive, and was impressed by how the teacher could project a vision to get his point across.

After leaving the program, Paul asked his teacher if he would give a lecture to his group to see if they could receive a projected visionary experience. To Paul's amazement, the teacher arrived with a bowl, some grass on a cookie sheet, and two bonsai trees. He put water in the bowl and arranged the grass and the trees around the bowl on the cookie sheet. He then began the lecture by asking people to close their eyes and see if they could receive the vision represented by the props. Everyone there saw a lake, a meadow, and two trees around it. He then described his work and how he showed people that intuitive communication was much more accurate that verbal communication.

Paul's next experience was even more baffling. While giving a lecture, he noticed a man sitting in the back of the room as his first teacher had done, only this man seemed to have control over the room. When Paul started to speak, he found that he couldn't say a word, so he said internally, "I'm unable to talk. Okay, God, you'd better start talking because I can't."

He looked at the man, who winked. Paul winked back and began to smile. Suddenly, he was able to speak again. After the lecture, the man came up to him and said, "Very good presentation, Mr. Solomon," and left.

About a month later, a man came in for a reading and asked Paul, "Do you know what the August Body is?"

Paul said, "No, but I'll ask the Source."

The Source revealed the August Body to be an exclusive mystery school that operated secretly on the physical plane. Students were only invited into the school if it was felt that they could handle the curriculum.

Paul's curiosity piqued and he wanted to find out about this mystery school, but the man left with no mention of how Paul could contact them. About a month later, he received a letter with no return address or any indication of who sent it. It simply directed him to go to a particular address in New York City for a 2:00 PM appointment with the man he had met at his lecture. His intuition told him that he must go to this appointment. The letter also told him that the door would only open if he said the words, "I seek to be of service, so that I may enter."

At the appointed hour, he arrived at the address but found the door would not move, no matter how hard he tried to open it. He said the words and it opened immediately. Inside, a woman greeted him by name. Paul met first with the man who'd asked for the reading about a month earlier. He described the curriculum of the school and some past alumni, including Benjamin Franklin, American presidents and other well-known figures. Next he met the man from the back of his lecture, who told him the requirements. These were stiffer than the *bonsai* school. "This is a five-year commitment, to be spent under a vow of silence. All you can bring with you are the clothes you are wearing at the time of entering. If you decide to enter, we will pick you up at a specified location. What we tell you is given in total honesty on the understanding that you tell no one about the curriculum or anything about the school. When you come here, no one must know where you are, and you will have no contact with the outside world for five years. If this meets with your intention, let us know and we will monitor you for a period of time and then let you know where we will pick you up."

Paul agreed to all that and was initiated but, after six months, the teachers told him, "You really do not need to stay any longer because you know everything we can teach you. You have the discipline issue handled so go back out in the world and get on with your mission."

Unfortunately, Paul again allowed his personal life to interfere with his mission and began to experience declining heath in 1994. In 1995, he died from unknown causes.

Paul was an amazing speaker and a bottomless source of knowledge. I have yet to meet a more awesome teacher. He taught without notes or outlines, as if he had a direct line into the spiritual realms that provided him with all he needed to know at the time. However, he was not walking his own talk, and his personal life was in disarray, which led to his demise.

Ronald Beasley, another teacher I worked with, had the same abilities. Tragically, he died in a bus crash in India on a tour he was leading, while the passenger sitting next to him was unhurt. In a dialog I had with him after his death, he told me, "I was not walking my talk, which was why I was taken out. Always walk your talk and never advocate anything that you would not do yourself. Replicate yourself; do not hold anything back. Do not keep secrets about personal or spiritual growth. Teach it all. You will not be threatened by giving away all you know. People will respect your integrity and honesty. Be very ethical and do not deceive. That is the downfall of most teachers. The most important rule is to walk your own talk."

I have tried to practice what Beasley told me to do at all times. Unfortunately, in the early days, I had not overcome my lack of self-esteem and self-worth, shortcomings that soon came home to roost. After teaching everything I knew to a group of people who sponsored locations for me to work and made appointments for me, I lost them all. They no longer needed me and went off on their own, leaving me stranded with no facilitators or places to work. Catching on to what was happening and getting a program going again took me about six months. It was an amazing lesson in stepping forward, self-validation and reestablishing oneself.

In my workshops, I cite the example of Madam Blavatsky and Annie Besant, a more intense version of Paul Solomon's lesson. Annie Besant had agreed to enter Madame Blavatsky's mystery school under the same terms of doing the housework and cooking, only there was no time limit. Each day, Annie tried to hard please her difficult mentor, who always found something to complain about: the toast was dry, the eggs were too hard, there was dust on the bookshelf, the rugs were not straight, the vegetables were overcooked, or the windows had spots on them. Something was always wrong. Annie frequently ended up in tears, but Madam Blavatsky showed her no mercy, even chiding her for crying, which made her cry all the more.

One day, Annie had had enough and decided to not take any more abuse and to leave, school or no school. As Annie delivered her teacher's breakfast, Blavatsky began her usual critical tirade but Annie interrupted, "I'm leaving. It seems that I can't do anything right for you and if this is how you operate your school, I do *not* want to be here."

As she turned to walk out, Blavatsky called after her, "You finally got it. Now you can go onto the next level."

Puzzled, Annie asked, "I got what?"

"You are no longer allowing yourself to be a victim. That's what I've been trying to get across to you all this time, but you must recognize it yourself to make the next step in transformation. Nobody can hurt you unless you let them."

They then sat down for a long discussion and Annie agreed to stay. She went on to become one of Madam Blavatsky's best students and a mystery school teacher in her own right.

I attended two weeklong seminars with Paul Solomon and his staff. They were set up along mystery school lines in that we had a grueling schedule and zero tolerance for victim consciousness. The dropout rate in both seminars was about 25 percent, with only the strong surviving.

Apart from Paul, the teacher who stood out most was Tara Singh, a Sikh from India. He was strict and cut us no slack at all. I continued to study with him after the seminar because he had considerable knowledge to impart. He once told me, "You will never teach anything that you have not had direct experience with."

His remark shocked me because I was not even considering becoming a teacher. What's he talking about, I wondered. As it turns out, he was right; as the years opened up my path, I did become a teacher.

One of the main lessons of the mystery schools appears to be: *take responsibility*. Take your personal power back, for victims do not make it very far in this life. Validate yourself, for no one else will validate you until you do it yourself. Reclaim your self-worth and your self-esteem.

Giving victims what they want creates a weak society that one day will topple. Taking care of people who feel the world owes them is crippling our society. One day, the working population will no longer be able support those who refuse to pull their own weight.

In today's world of instant gratification, discipline goes out the window. Many children in school do the minimum work possible to graduate or even drop out to have children of their own. The drop out rate in some inner city schools is approaching 50 percent, which guarantees another generation of state-supported victims.

In ancient times, mystery schools trained our leaders in discipline, self-reliance and judgment. The result was men such as Washington and Lincoln. Today, our leaders just have to know "how to work the system." History has shown repeatedly that when societies fall out of balance, they inevitably decline and fall. I only hope that America can find a balance before that happens.

Our primary obligation is to our own healing and, to avoid the downward spiral, we must follow the program given to us by the masters so that we can evolve in our enlightenment. The only reason we are here is for soul growth, transformation and returning to the divine spark of Light we were when we were part of the Presence of GOD as co-creators.

The most pernicious part of this whole process is denial of the truth. Many of my clients delude themselves into believing that they are far along in their spiritual journey, not realizing that the journey doesn't start in the spiritual arena at all. It begins by taking responsibility for your mental, emotional and physical needs. You must feed and nurture all levels of your body equally at the same time. Jumping over the physical, mental and emotional levels into the spiritual level just does not work. The stark truth is that you must take responsibility for all aspects of your growth.

Some people cannot see the truth of this until their life review following their crossing over. Viewed from the other side, your mistakes and detours are obvious but this does you no good because, over there, there's nothing you can do about them. Human limitations can only be addressed while in a human body. So you go back to the Lords of Karma for another body and another chance. You will start out exactly where you left off in the last life and hopefully, this time, can continue learning, growing and dissolving those human limitations.

The school of life is a workshop. Once you opt at the soul level for a cycle of lifetimes, you must see it through until you graduate as a co-creator and rejoin GOD Source. Your only choice is how intensively you learn the lessons and how many lifetimes you want to spend in this school while repeating grades.

You can hasten the process by becoming clear and facing the truth. If you follow the path correctly, you will not have to repeat the lesson again. Eventually you will graduate and become a Light Being, joining the teachers in the White Brotherhood and the true Presence of GOD.

An intriguing and relevant dialogue with GOD Source appears in my book *Opening Communication With GOD Source*. I had asked, "You mentioned earlier that we would not always contact the same being each time, since the GOD Source consists of many beings at your level of enlightenment available to consult to us in specific areas with which they've had direct experience. Would you care to comment?"

They replied, "That is true. You could be one of these beings too, as those making up GOD Source have all gone through the 'tribulation,' as the Christians call it. They have become light beings and self-realized sparks of GOD so they are at the same level of enlightenment. As a result, if you choose to use the term, they are in the GOD Source. There is no discrimination in our reality. A being who can go through the lessons and activate the Presence of God within can achieve the transformation that will move him or her through the transfiguration. Them they can become part of the GOD Source."

In reply, I asked, "This is an amazing destiny to strive for. To know that it's available to everyone is even more wonderful. But how do we get on this track to the lofty levels you have described?"

"Why are you asking this question when you know the answer?"

"Because I felt it would give more credence if you answered the question."

"We are not going to answer the question because it will take too much space and you have already written a book with our support on the subject. So we refer you to your book *Journey Into The Light*, which provides the information that we have already given you."

"I was asking this question for benefit of the readers of this book. I can see your reasons for your answer, however."

"This would be a lengthy answer since it encompasses many concepts to do with the spiritual journey."

The GOD Source also gave a considerable discourse on the spiritual journey. In a nutshell, a specific spiritual path may or may not lead to the spiritual journey. Spirituality is a concept and philosophy that we cannot embrace until we enter the spiritual journey and begin to traverse the lesson plan.

The question I posed was, "There's a lot of confusion about the term 'spirituality.' What's the difference between spirituality, spiritual journey and the spiritual path?"

"Yes, there is much confusion about the terms. The difference is that anyone can practice a process or conduct a ritual but that does not mean that the ritual or practice is going to prepare them for attaining spirituality. Spirituality is a state of mind that one attains by clearing all negative habits and the need to control and have power over others. On other end of the spectrum are the codependents who give their power away and feel victimized by others. These people are the followers; they will give their power to any guru, teacher, or shaman who they believe will provide the spirituality for them. Of course this is an illusion that the teacher creates to lure followers. The teacher tells them, 'If you follow this discipline, practice this meditation and other activities, it will put you on the spiritual path.' Yes, it leads to the *spiritual path* but not to *spirituality*. Spirituality is only *your* discipline and only *you* can create that for yourself. The spiritual journey is the all-encompassing path to ascension that starts out with enlightenment, goes through transformation, and ends with transfiguration into light body. Our directions are in your book *Journey into the Light*."

A Word of Caution

The temptation exists at this stage for people to start tripping on their new understanding and feeling superior to those still in average consciousness. Also you may feel the need to "fix" those whom you perceive as "broken" in some way. I did when I first found this new awareness. It was akin to, "Eureka! I have the gold and want to share it with everyone."

Well, in 1979, not many people were ready for this new concept of reality. I thought, "Wow, this is where it is. But why doesn't everyone want to feel this way?" Over the next five years, I discovered that most people wanted to stay right where they are, safe in their comfortable ways.

At first, I found this frustrating because I still needed to get all my validation from outside myself. If I could show people how they could overcome the blocks in their life, then I would be validated as "all right." Fortunately, among the people I worked with, more accepted my ideas and methods than rejected them. I put myself and my reputation on the line because, at the time, I was unaware that what I did for my clients made no difference. I thought I was a healer and that *I* was doing it, but now I know that all healing is accomplished by the individual. As I traversed the path to enlightenment, I discovered that healing was about them, not me. When I began to accept myself as "all right" no matter what happened, my success rate began to go up. I realized that it was up each client's intent to be healed. As a healer, my job was to show the way.

Only if people specifically ask can you intervene and, even then, carefully. Remember, you can't fix other people; only *they* can fix themselves. Trying to fix others is really an attempt to control them, to manipulate them into becoming like us so that we can feel comfortable around them.

Remember also that wherever others are in their path to enlightenment and evolution of self is exactly where they need to be or they, too, would be in a state of flux as are you. Of course, you can share your truths with other people but only as stimulating input for them, and only when asked.

Seventh graders are no better than those in first grade; they've just been in school longer so they are more aware. Similarly, ascended masters are no better than someone living in average consciousness—they have just "been round the block a few more times" so they have more awareness. We all came from the same place and are all on the path back to GOD Source at our own pace ... the expressway or a few detours along winding country roads. You alone choose. Once I stepped onto the path, however, the pace was greased lightning. I could have slowed the pace by asking for a reprieve but I'm glad I stuck with it because I'm over the worst now and everything is "full speed ahead on the road to abundance."

Achieving spirituality involves discipline and consistent effort, not empty rituals or practices. Success involves recognizing the lessons placed before you and letting go of the need for external validation and acceptance. The hardest lesson is accepting yourself the way you are.

Are you ready for the next step in the spiritual journey?

Summary

By the time you go through the third door, you are familiar with many of the universal laws and spiritual principles, such as the Laws of Resonance, Duality, Intent, Detachment, Synchronicity, and Asking. During the Fourth Initiation, you begin to put these laws into practice.

4

The Fourth Initiation: Temptation

The fourth door becomes a challenge. Can you handle the temptations that your teachers are going to place before you? When you claim to the Universe that you understand universal laws and spiritual principles, you will be tested, and this initiation is the express lane to enlightenment. And if you thought the previous lessons were bumpy, get ready for the roller-coaster ride of your life. There are no outs on this one; you're on the main line now.

This could be an easy, joyous ride if you offer no resistance. All it takes to deal with the lessons is discipline and commitment, and the willingness to apply your knowledge. As with any course you take, you must apply what you have already learned to the next step. The spiritual path is no different, except that you do not come into direct contact with those doing the grading. Your only contact will be through your intuitive ability. If you develop that ability now, you will have ongoing dialogues with the White Brotherhood as they want to provide the best guidance available.

All the tests in this step are temptations intended to elicit your response. Each time you're confronted with a situation, you're being tested to see whether you can recognize the lesson and how you will handle it. Will you deal with the situation, person or response without losing your center, giving your power away or becoming a victim? Strive to recognize and deal with the lesson the first time you encounter it, for if you miss it or refuse to deal with it, it will recur but be tougher to deal with. Choosing to detour and refuse to face the lesson will result in sliding back until you face it. (It's possible to slide all the way back down to the bottom of the barrel if you persist in avoiding the lessons but, if you catch yourself on the down-slide, you can recover lost ground quite quickly.)

At this point in enlightenment you have fewer and fewer time-outs. If you have used all your time-outs, then you must be more vigilant so you do not stumble and lose your way.

In this step, the real tests of enlightenment begin. Up until now, you have found there was no need to be a victim, or to function from fear or anger. You now know that there is another way to live—in peace happiness, harmony, joy, abundance, acceptance and with unconditional love. Once I discovered this fundamental spiritual concept, catching on to the program and making it work for me took five more years, and then three more years to lock it in as a "hard-wired" behavioral pattern. ("Hard-wired" indicates that it is your first response rather than second or third response after some thought as to how to deal with a situation.) Thus passing the "no victim" test took eight years.

Now that I understand how the mind works and how easy it is to rewrite the operating system so that we can reclaim our power, I could have accomplished the same task in a much shorter time. I can now share my experience in this book so that readers can do in days what took me years.

You may not recognize or pass all the tests first time around but, once you recognize the lessons, you can move forward. Each lesson you didn't pass will continue to be brought up during steps 5 through 8. (You cannot complete step 8 until you totally master all the lessons.)

Before you can continue to the next step, you must demonstrate mastery of the following:

- *Detachment.* Are you attached, detached or non-attached?

  - Attachment will result in some form of emotional reaction.

  - Detachment allows you to observe or experience the situation with little emotional response.

  - Non-attachment will not cause any reaction or response, as you can recognize the situation before it happens. You recognize that nothing can affect you because it's all an illusion anyway.

- *Being the cause* of your outer world rather than its result and becoming a co-creator of heaven-on-earth with the GOD Source.

- *Letting go* of judgment, authority, control, blame, and manipulation.

- *Emotional mastery.* Does a situation cause anger, fear, hurt, rejection, or emotional upset? In order to protect the vulnerable self in such a situation, do you need to claim or regain control and authority?

- *Releasing victim consciousness* to build your "all right-ness." To graduate this step, you must attain inner serenity, self-esteem, self-worth and self-confidence.

- *Consciously using relationships for growth*, never allowing them to cause you to give your power away to others or situations nor as a means of "stealing" your partner's power.

- *Living in the Now moment.* Releasing the past fully and completely.

The tests will continue, getting progressively more intense during each initiation until the ninth initiation. Lessons will involve unconditional love, rejection, abandonment, fear, anger and all of the 30+ other emotions that can cause you fall back into control or victim consciousness. No matter how hard we try, we seem to fall into the old behavioral ruts until we cover them over and they are no longer available to us. The temptation to fall back into the known stems from its comfort and the lack of effort needed so, each time we succeed and have a win-win outcome in a lesson, we should find a way to fill in the old tracks so that fallback is no longer an option.

Detachment

Emotional and intellectual non-attachment to outcomes of any kind frees you up enormously, and takes you a step beyond your survival self, which needs things to be a certain way in order to feel safe. You begin to realize in this step that, whatever the outcome, it's what your *soul* placed in your original flight plan, which was set up to continue presenting the lesson until you got it. So the outcome was *intended*, otherwise the situation would not have turned out the way it did.

When you finally realize that *no one* can take your power from you unless you give it away, and that you can empower yourself to stand up for yourself, you're on your way to getting the point.

In the same way, you also begin to lose your attachment to beliefs. Once cherished sacred cows, you come to see your beliefs not as truths but as merely *opinions about reality*. And they're not even *your* opinions but other people's hand-me-down opinions that you bought into before the age of seven. Ironically, the way we process thoughts across the crude, limited interface between our minds and brains, and then express them in primitive linear languages, means that there is no way we can *ever* know the truth of reality while in a physical body, yet we go to war and fight about whose opinion is less corrupt.

In this step, as you begin to jam increasingly higher truths into a limited belief system such as Christianity, you will find that it cannot accommodate the new truths, so you must let go of either the new truth or the old belief system. If you let the latter go, your remaining beliefs may then implode on themselves and reform out of the wreckage. This is normal in this step, however, but, until new truths replace old lies, not knowing what you believe can be uncomfortable.

My experience in this initiation proved to me that few people, including many of the so-called masters, have achieved this level of awareness. If you avoid dealing with life and become the no-self, you can *appear* to pass this test, but are you "in the world but not of it"? Are you detached to the point where you can confront the world and live in it, yet not let it affect you, i.e., self-mastery. Are you able to confront every facet of life and handle them all successfully?

This is where the self-made masters emerge, i.e., those who discipline themselves to exercise and feed their bodies a nutritious diet, and walk through life detached from the effects of the world around them. They stand out like torches in the darkness.

Such masters may be average people who stand out from the crowd, such as my friend how recently crossed over because she could not pass the major initiation of realizing that her family could not take her down without her permission. Her family set out to destroy her will to live because she refused to act like an old person and let them take care of her. She was 90 when she left this plane but had the vim and vigor of a 60-year-old, living proof that aging is a state of mind governed by programs that can be rewritten.

Co-creating Heaven-on-Earth

Because you live in the matrix of All That Is and are constantly transmitting into the matrix, your transmitted intent interacts with the intent of others at all levels of your being, and will align with energy of similar intent. To avoid falling under the spell of other people's agendas, first clarify *your* intent.

Second, try to sense the patterns of intent around you so that you can recognize "kindred spirits" when you meet them. You will draw to you those people who embody the lessons you need to learn. No matter how hard you try, you will not be able to avoid the people who bring these lessons to you. Many times, the people who interact with you will not know that they are teaching you a lesson. Of course, the interaction serves both of you. The other people also have their own lessons to learn or they would not be involved. Every lesson is a two-edged sword and will cut both ways depending on the person's awareness. The most important thing here is not to place blame.

The forces of darkness will be vanquished in the end, and people who live in the light can hasten the demise of the Dark by joining as masters and pooling their intent so that Light prevails. When we get to a point where our light shines out, people will see it and be drawn to spend time with you. At first, this may feel good but in the enticement lies a lesson, too. Can you handle being in the limelight without allowing Middle Self to create self-righteous, controlling sub-personalities? Most people cannot handle being famous yet remaining humble, accepting, courteous and honoring towards those who supported their rise to fame in the first place.

Until you got on the path, your survival self looked to the outside world for approval (good) and criticism (bad). In any situation, its first (and often only) question was, "Will this make me look good to other people and hence boost my popularity with them?"

Until now, other people's approval rating of you mattered more than your own and you berated yourself, not because your behavior was out of integrity, but because of how others would judge that behavior. Of course, you were playing the judgment game, too, and kept a running tally of how others compared to you, glorying in their shortcomings because of the breathing room it gave you to have shortcomings.

By this initiation step, however, the only thing that matters to you is whether a situation or event helps or hinders your efforts in co-creating your vision of heaven-on-earth. If it supports the vision, you choose to participate in the activity; otherwise you choose to refrain.

Your vision may involve, say, everyone living their authentic self and honoring universal laws such as "treat your neighbor as you wish to be treated." No armies, police forces or even governments would then be needed because everyone is self-governing and working for the greater good.

Your vision might involve people doing what they love, with the community supporting their expression of spirit and creativity. "Get real," some may say. "That could never happen. It's only a vision." My response is that if enough of us hold that vision and pass it to the next generation, it will be a reality one day. It's already starting to happen in little pockets around the planet, and one day, the "hundredth monkey" break through will happen. When it does, we will have hit critical mass, which will catapult the planet into a quantum leap forward in spiritual expression.

When your soul drops its vision into your awareness, it captivates, haunts and compels you towards it, and you perceive anything else as a trivial pursuit. Whatever your vision is, achieving it begins in this step as you move from being "a human having spiritual experiences" to being "spirit having human experiences."

When this happened to me in 1998, my life had never before felt as good, and I was always waiting for the other shoe to drop, assuming that something this good wouldn't last. Was life really changing so that we wouldn't need to hustle anymore? My experience taught me that reality *is* changing so quickly nowadays that when you do step into the new reality, you may question it and need to allow time for it to sink in.

Using Relationships for Growth

Relationships on the Earth plane are vital dress rehearsals for life on the soul plane, where unity is the name of the game. In cosmic terms, our only true relationship is, "All is one," but our relationships are the greatest teachers of unity we can have. As *A Course in Miracles* says, "Every relationship is a lesson in love."

The Earth plane is the only dimension in which we can experience separation and the consequent blocking of love. This is what makes it the ideal school, for the best way to appreciate something is through its absence. We can see the whole picture when we are on the soul plane and know the reason and intended outcome of each lesson, so where is the value of the lesson? The trick is to remember the contents of your flight plan and make it a reality while on the physical plane. This is what enlightenment is about—making our soul plane plan a reality in the third dimension where we learn the lessons.

~ ~ ~

Conscious relationships are subject to two rules:

1. What happened yesterday is irrelevant, so change your mind and change your relationship. Refuse to repeat old patterns, and choose to respond anew in the now moment.

2. In any relationship, you're not healing the relationship or the other person but *yourself*, for the relationship is only a mirror for you. Change yourself and you will change the relationship. This calls for you to rise above blame and resentment. No matter how dysfunctional the relationship is, there are lessons in it or you would not be in the relationship. Before we depart the situation, we must release and learn the lesson or it will follow us to the next relationship. The temptation here is to run away and stuff our feelings, which will cause us to slide back until you get it.

The most important aspect of relationships is openness to other people, which means living from your authentic self. (When you present your authentic self in a relationship, there's no fear of being "found out.") If you do not set up illusions, there's no need to cover your tracks. The biggest challenge here is be aware of who you are so that temptation does not stalk you.

To align and blend your energy with that of someone else, you must first be aligned with yourself, and this means self-honesty. A prerequisite for having someone else enjoy your company is for you to enjoy your own company and accept your self-worth.

In my work, I find that we make interpretations about what people are thinking about us rather than being honest with ourselves. So we *assume* what others feel rather than asking them. As a result, we avoid relationships with people whom we feel might not accept us. Many times, our assumptions are inaccurate, as we're actually seeing our own mirror of something we reject in ourselves, and projecting it out on to others. So we are reacting from our own delusion, which is inaccurate.

When I first arrived on the path to enlightenment, I was sure that most people did not accept me so I hung back from groups where I didn't know anyone. So I forced myself to attend workshops and lectures because I knew that there was an answer to this feeling. By getting intimately involved with people at these events, I broke through this limitation.

~ ~ ~

There are two important things to remember about relationships:

- A relationship is *not* a security blanket so, except for a prudent eye to the future, do not constantly worry about how long you will be together. Relationships are about *growth* and you can grow greatly in a short but intense relationship. Often this is to prepare you for an upcoming longer relationship. Also, long relationships can become habits in which no growth is happening, and that's not what your soul wants. But it's often hard to be honest about your feelings in a relationship, so you hang in without learning the lesson. A short-lived relationship, therefore, does not mean a failed relationship. And if growth occurred, the relationship certainly did not fail.

- In any meaningful relationship, you are also relating at the soul level, and it's good for both partners to strive to remain aware of the soul component in the relationship, for that dramatically enlarges the Earth plane energies. For example, the partners can align across 12 chakras rather than just the seven in-body chakras, although few couples manage even the latter. Almost all relationships begin in the first (security/survival) or second (sexual) chakras and rarely advance to the third let alone higher to the heart chakra and unconditional love.

Imagine your energies as a 12-rung ladder, with each rung representing a chakra alignment. The 12 chakras are centers for our:

1. Survival/Earth connection
2. Sexual/creative energy
3. Will/power/drive
4. Love/compassion
5. Communication/creative
6. Psychic insight
7. Spirit connection
8. Higher emotional connection
9. Higher mental connection
10. Higher spiritual connection
11. Oversoul (highest source of your being)
12. Direct Connection to the God Head or GOD Source

Self-healing

Relationships between two people both on autopilot can be grim affairs in which both parties try to use the relationship for their own purposes, which usually involve fear and insecurity. Seeing each other as a "need-fulfillment device," both parties judge the actions of the other *only* in terms of how it affects them, i.e., "How can I use you before you use me?" The relationship, therefore, becomes a battleground for control and manipulation, as each tries to steal power, validation, approval and what they perceive as love (although love has no meaning to such people). As a result, much karma is generated on both sides.

People looking to a relationship to heal loneliness and give them whatever is missing in their own inner life overlook a major truth: they're suffering from relationship addiction. *No one can give you what you can't give yourself.* No one can give you love until you can give to yourself. Once at a lecture, I was testing a volunteer for the presence or absence of basic programs. He appeared to test strong for love, indicating that he loved himself, but my intuition told me this was inaccurate. Each time I checked him, he tested strong. I had never questioned this in the past but, this time, I was sure that something was "off key." So I checked each file for glitches in the programs and discovered that he held the belief that he loved himself because he'd been working intensely on self-love for over ten years. In his denial-of-denial files, we found programs holding anger at being rejected. When we brought these to the surface, he checked "weak" for self-love. He had created the illusion of self-love, and was living in a false belief. When I questioned him about relationships, we found that most people did not feel that he was a loving person even though he thought he was.

The antithesis of "autopilot relationships" are "lucid relationships" in which both partners strive for balance, peace, harmony and truth. They see relationships as co-creative ventures between two masters, each with two aims:

1. To learn as much about yourself as possible by having your partner mirror you back to you.

2. To find ways to support the other's growth, such as always listening creatively and not over-talking or interrupting during discussions. You would never put your partner down in order to build yourself up.

~ ~ ~

Such a couple begins by not bringing into the relationship old baggage from previous relationships. Since both parties practice "lucid living," every relationship is healing, and any baggage from one relationship is healed before beginning the next.

The main purpose for a relationship is to serve as a mirror for each other. As we progress on the spiritual path, we need someone to mirror back to us who we are, where we are on the path, and whom we are becoming. Without this, we could slide into self-delusion. In other words, our partner keeps us honest. Of course, we must allow for distortions in the mirror itself, i.e., any personal agenda of our partner. Similarly, we mirror our partner back to him or her as honestly *and* lovingly as possible. In this type of a relationship one should be able to discuss any topic without fear of rejection.

Honesty

Our fear in the past used to be that honesty might hurt our partner or cause us rejection so we would tell people they wanted to hear. But once on the path, honesty is an important part of "the walk." But so is compassion, therefore our honesty also involves kindness and caring. Any expression made in love leads to healing, but avoiding hurting the other person's feeling is a waste of time because you're not being a clear mirror for his or her behavior. On the other hand, many people go on the attack while *claiming* they're just being honest. The way to tell the difference is by whether there is love in their words.

Many people use honesty as a way to "dump" on other people, but it's usually judgmental or resentful, which is not honesty and separates people from each other and from Spirit. Love-based honesty, on the other hand, combines truth and compassion and does not resort to the duality of good/bad or right/wrong. It focuses on *feelings* as the real issue, instead of behavior. Rather than saying, "I get angry when you withhold your feelings from me," love-based honesty says, "I'd love to know how you feel, so could you express that to me?" It honors the self and respects the other person's free will regarding complying with your request.

Another form of dishonesty in relationships is to sublimate your own needs and desires to those of your partner under the guise of love. Such self-abusive sacrifice will inevitably end in one of two ways: progressive death of your spirit (not to be confused with Spirit) or a build-up of resentment on your part that will culminate in an eruption to some minor trigger. This is a codependent pattern to get validation.

If your partner seems to want all the same things as you so, be absolutely sure that he or she is not self-manipulating to please you. In a healthy relationship, each partner *honors* the other's unique expression of Spirit rather than try to imitate it.

Conflict

Another hallmark of lucid relationships is how the partners deal with conflict—openly, honestly and quickly. They do not let resentments fester below the surface but deal with them on the spot for, when the volcano gets full, the inevitable blow-up happens that scoops up all the old buried issues and the eruption is out-of-proportion to the actual trigger. The temptation to avoid here is stuffing feelings rather than dealing with them so, if you know that you can't have an open, detached conversation just then without erupting, defer the discussion to a later time.

Growth

We also have a second responsibility in relationships. Being on the path means exploring your full potential. This obviously means changing, also an integral part of being on the spiritual path. After all, enlightenment is all about being able to shift beliefs as understanding increases, so the partners in a relationship must support each other in developing their potential and in making those shifts. Whereas in autopilot relationships, partners see change in each other as threatening and a cause for fear, in lucid relationships, change is a cause for celebration and each partner encourages the other's changes without resistance.

A prerequisite for a balanced, harmonious relationship is that both partners have balanced, harmonious relationships with themselves. They know that their partner is not responsible for their happiness; they alone are responsible for their *own* happiness. Neither are they there to "fix" each other, but only to support the other in "self-fixing."

Both partners are also whole in themselves and are not searching for "their other half." This means that a man does not look for a woman to "borrow" his inner woman from, and vice versa. His inner woman is alive and healthy, and delights in playing with his partner's feminine energy.

If disagreements come up, both partners know that conflict is merely a call for love. One party isn't trying to harm the other but just trying to get love from the outside. As *A Course in Miracles* tells us, "You can be right or happy, but not both." The only reason we strive to be "right" is because we feel separate and vulnerable, which makes it a high priority to prove the other person wrong. The only way out of this is to recognize what you're doing and stop playing the game.

If a lucid relationship ceases to serve as a clear mirror and platform to explore both partners' potential and growth, they amicably agree to move on with grace and ease, and without recriminations or hard feelings. They know that the only reason to hang on to past limitations is to perpetuate a sense of separation. Relationships are not about two people relating; they're about healing separation and exploring unity. Therefore, there's no room for secrets, withholding or any other form of separation, because this thwarts the goal of healing separation.

Over the years, I have worked with clients who referred their partner to me to settle issues, create a better relationship and improve communication. Sometimes it works miracles, yet many times, dredging up old secrets causes even more problems. Empowerment sometimes breaks relationships up when you tell the truth and one of the partners still wants to cling to the contract from the past.

Emotional Mastery

Until this step, if a situation arose that caused you to feel anger, fear, hurt, rejection or emotional upset, what would you have done? Many people would have striven to protect the vulnerable self by trying to exert control or authority, i.e., by going into fight all out to "win," or flight to get away from the conflict. A third reaction would be to shut down and fade out.

Feeling cut off from their spirit, they feel powerless and manipulate to increase their personal power by "stealing" it from others with whom they relate. They assume that there's only so much power to go around, so they compete with other people for theirs. Due to separation from spirit and each other, they feel insecure and believe that the only way to feel good is a preemptive theft of the other person's power.

Among those on autopilot, human interaction ends in one of two outcomes. One or other parties comes away feeling stronger or weaker depending on what happens. It's human nature to try to control the encounter and prevail, thus getting the psychological boost of winning. Most interactions are based on the need to control and not what the interaction is actually about. The one in control siphons the other's energy, so the first wins at the other's expense. Controllers use many subtle strategies, most of them unconscious, to undermine the other's self-confidence in attempts to steal their power. What they don't realize is that their feeling better means that the other feels weaker, may resent them, and certainly feels separate.

Unfortunately, most relationships end up being power struggles as the couple fights over who controls the relationship. And the loser always pays the price as the winner sucks up the loser's personal power. On this battleground, you either steal power by actively forcing other people to pay attention to you, or by playing the martyr, evoking sympathy or curiosity. However, once you step on the path, this behavior must cease. If you fall back into this trap, you slide back, as you cannot remain on the path and generate karma with people at the same time.

Emotional growth and mastery is about first getting in touch with your feelings and then taking responsibility for them, because you can't change what you don't own, and you can't own what you don't feel. Denial does not work. But why do we suppress our emotions in the first place? Usually to avoid feeling pain during childhood, which may be created by dysfunctional people around us or, in a functional family, we may just find the recent separation from the soul plane to be painful. The problem is, that by withdrawing from your emotions to avoid *unhappiness*, we also close the door on *happiness*. But you will get the former anyway because life without feeling is slow death, and the unfulfilled yearning for closeness with others can result in you blaming *them*. They in turn may reject you.

Your unexpressed emotions are still there, becoming more compacted over the years, and you end up in adulthood sitting on a volcano that some minor incident could trigger, such as a parking lot fender-bender. The eruption can escalate into road rage, often with tragic consequences such as when one driver in California threw the other driver's lapdog into heavy traffic following a slight bumper-to-bumper nudge. The dog was killed and he was sentenced to three years behind bars. Did he know what he was doing when he reacted? Probably not, as he was on autopilot and not in control of his emotions at all.

The best way to deal with the emotional magma is to vent it under controlled conditions rather than in a relationship as many do.

Initially, destructive emotions may have you pummeling a punchbag or screaming until you're hoarse—all healthy forms of release, but it doesn't get to the cause or program. When you release the cause and the catalyst that caused the eruption, you're free to enjoy the constructive feelings, confident in your ability to handle all kinds of emotion *under your control.*

You can still have emotions, of course, until you recognize that emotions are goal-oriented behavior, but now *you control them* rather than them, you. As you begin to detach from outcomes and drop your expectations of the world and people around you, happiness, love, joy and compassion will replace less mature emotions such as anger and jealousy.

You will also stop blaming other people and outside circumstances for your emotional state, and begin taking responsibility for it yourself. Other people cannot make you feel a particular way; only *you* can do that by how you choose to respond.

To avoid creating a new Vesuvius, you begin to express your emotions as they come up, gently, lovingly and honestly. If someone is chattering incessantly and driving you crazy, you say, "No offence intended, but I'm not really interested in this topic." Your time is too important to waste. A good example of this: A few years ago I was at dinner with two friends where we listened to one of them talk for over 45 minutes about topics that were important to her so we allowed her talk on. When she began repeating herself, I finally asked, "Are you interested in what we might have to contribute?"

She said, "Yes," but continued to rattle on unabated. When I finally said, "You've been talking for almost an hour. Would you allow the rest of us to say a few things as well?" she blew up and accused me of commandeering the conversation. In a huff, she walked out and went home. Later, she wrote me a two-page letter detailing how discourteous I was and how she didn't want anything to do with me in the future.

As you traverse the steps to initiation on your path to ascension you will discover that emotions become less intense as you no longer react to situation, people or events. When you reclaim your personal power and take responsibility, becoming anchored in your center, emotions fall away as you're living in peace, happiness, harmony, joy, unconditional love and acceptance, and make forgiveness your way of life. Nobody can rock your boat.

From Victim to Victor

The only way you can be a victim is to believe the lies that others tell you about how powerless you are. These lies include:

- You have limited understanding and will fail.
- The world is inherently hostile and "out to get you."
- You are separate from everyone and everything else.
- You will never amount to anything.
- You were born in sin so you need a savior.
- Not buying into these limitations is a misinterpretation that your mind makes.

The "innately flawed" lie is a marketing ploy on the part of religious brainwashing, which then tries to sell you the "antidote"—eternal salvation if you sign up with them, and eternal damnation if you don't. This lie flies in the face of the truth that you are a vast, multidimensional being, a divine spark of All That Is. Over many years, you talked yourself into believing this lie and, in this step, will need to talk yourself out of it with equal zeal and determination.

The "hostile world" lie originates in people's perception of their own seeming powerlessness. Faced with a daily news diet of war, violence, accidents and natural disasters, most of us assume that we play no role in inviting these things into our lives. The truth is that, at the soul level, you incarnate into a particular country knowing whether you will experience peace or war in that lifetime. Or, say you chose to live in "tornado alley," all the souls involved plan the course of tornadoes, in conjunction with Gaia consciousness. There are no murder victims, only participants in a drama carefully scripted by the spirits of all involved. However, this truth seems to contradict what we observe in the world around us, so debunking this lie takes considerable reflection.

The "separation" lie is a gift from science, which states that if something can't be weighed or measured, then it doesn't exist. The truth is that we all exist as points of consciousness in a living matrix that makes up All That Is. Your consciousness extends far beyond the confines of your physical body and up through countless dimensions. Perceiving the nonphysical matrix requires stepping outside the five senses and believing without seeing, which is why most people live in doubt.

The nature of the matrix is pure love, the "glue" that holds everything together, so we are constantly immersed in a love field. Through the expenditure of enormous energy, most of us manage to keep the love at bay so that we can live in the familiar comfort of fear and ignorance. The temptation here is that if you do not release the programs that justify these beliefs, they will continue until you recognize who you are. This test will be put before you until you get it.

The way from victim to victor involves flipping each of these illusions around: *You are an innately good being, existing as a vast and powerful consciousness, connected to everything else in an inherently benevolent universe.*

The path can be very steep and arduous, and getting from here to there may take much reading, reflection and conversation with people who are already "there," but the rewards make the effort worthwhile. There is a fast-track express line that can cut the time in this initiation by a factor of twenty. So you can accomplish in a year what once took me 20 years.

We can cut the enlightenment path significantly if we can work out each failed test by recognizing each one and releasing it, simply by deleting and erasing the program and/or belief, and establishing a new mindset with a new operating system.

Living in the Now

I am constantly amazed at how children at play can exist in their own fantasy world, where a packing crate becomes a fort and a stick becomes a sword. They are totally there in the fantasy and completely in the *Now*. For them, yesterday has gone, tomorrow is light-years away, and there is only the *Now*. As adults, that's something we've long ago forgotten.

The problem with not being in the *Now* is that this is where inner peace lies, and only there. You can't find peace yesterday or tomorrow, but only in the *Now*. Of course, we've all been hurt in the past—it's part of the human package deal—but stop dragging those heavy suitcases full of pain around with you. Start fresh in each *Now* moment. Just because "Today is the start of the rest of your life" is a cliché doesn't mean that it's untrue. In fact, it's a well-used cliché precisely *because* it is so true! But the temptation is always to fall back into the past the past is all we know and, without trust, living with old pain is more predictable than an uncertain future.

Summary

You will not pass through this initiation until you pass the tests placed before you. The lessons that set you up were temptations to test and show you that you could handle the tests. By the time you pass through the fourth door, you are living lucidly, detached from the melee around you and, in becoming the master of your life, recognizing that emotions are no longer an issue.

When you pass through the fourth door, emotions will be a challenge of the past. You will recognize them as they arise and release them immediately, as you have become the co-creator of your outer world. If you are in a relationship, it is healthy and supports your growth and that of your partner. You are living in the Now, with ever-increasing inner serenity and self-esteem, self-worth and self-confidence. This is the end of this part of the path of enlightenment, as we must now apply what we've learned. We move into the transformation step on the path to ascension.

5

The Fifth Initiation:
Understanding the Power of Your Mind

Transformation begins with this door as this step marks the end of the enlightenment process. In previous steps, you have reviewed the basics in this mystery schools curriculum and now you must apply what you have learned. From now on, *application* is the main trust of this course of action.

The fifth initiation deepens your control over your life. You are now becoming the possible human, ready to master many feats that average humans consider out of their realm. You must begin to detach further from your emotions, although temptations will continue in those areas where you have not fully detached from the emotions that affect you.

The Power of Your Mind

The true story is told of a railroad maintenance worker who was cleaning the inside of a refrigerated boxcar when the door accidentally closed and locked. Because the door could only be opened from the outside, he was trapped. The following day, co-workers found him huddled in a corner beside a message scratched on the wall: "It's freezing cold in here. I'm dying." However, the boxcar was at room temperature because the freezer unit was not working. What really killed him was the thought that it *was* working. This demonstrates the awesome power of the human mind.

We've all seen stage hypnosis in which people exhibit extraordinary strength on command, crow like a rooster or raise blisters on their skin because the hypnotist tells subjects that they've just been burned on the arm. If the mind can raise a blister or even kill you, it can be turned around and heal any illness or disease. *"What you believe Is"*

Why have we let this amazing ability atrophy? Because those who imprint young minds do not know they have the ability, nor their imprinters before them, so the legacy never gets handed down through the generations. How could we have forgotten such powers? Because, throughout history, certain groups have worked consistently to undermine our beliefs in our own powers and abilities so that they can control us. And they have succeeded brilliantly as, today, we operate at only a tiny fraction of our true potential. The intention of this initiation step is to develop our fullest potential as a possible human.

If a doctor said, "You have cancer and will die within six months," those on autopilot faithfully believe him and dutifully oblige, handing their life savings over to the medical profession in the process. Other people—all too few unfortunately—will put their heart and mind into gear and heal themselves. Of course, to do that, you must *believe* that you can do it.

This example from *Becoming a Spiritual Being In a Physical Body* bears repeating as a powerful testament to the power of the human mind:

A man went to his doctor for a check up and discovered he had metastasized cancer throughout his body. The doctor told him he had only weeks to live. He decided to research alternative drugs or methods that might help him, and found a drug under testing named *Kerbotzen*. His doctor obtained the drug and put him in the testing program. Three weeks later, he was cancer-free, with not one trace in his body.

About three months later, the FDA and the drug company released the results of the 18-month testing program. The results were unimpressive and inconclusive, but the company decided to continue the trial for another year. Soon after reading this, the man consulted his doctor about his seeming loss of energy. The cancer was returning so the doctor contacted the drug company to see if they had changed the drug's formulation. They had not, but the doctor decided to try an experiment on his own. He gave the man another injection, telling him that the formula had been improved. In fact, the injection was pure saline water. Two weeks, the cancer was in remission, and stayed that way for the next year until the FDA and the drug company published their final report on *Kerbotzen* and announced that the drug was being dropped as ineffective. According to the man's wife, he read the report and died two days later. The power of his mind that had kept him alive for over a year killed him within days of reading the report.

~ ~ ~

How do you transcend the limiting belief system that prevents you from self-healing? Simply your *imagination*. You use it all the time, usually to imagine negative scenarios with dire consequences—that's called "worrying." Instead, use your imagination to envision positive outcomes and fuel the visions with the glorious feeling that will accompany those outcomes. Your empowered visions will magnetically attract that reality into your life under the Law of Resonance.

The place to start is *you*. You are barely tapping your vast potential, so begin by visualizing that you are starting to unleash some of your hidden, unexplored powers, not all at once, but little-by-little each day throughout this step.

Remember, if you don't use your mind, someone else will. Advertisers, religions, politicians and myriad other groups would love to reprogram your mind with their agendas, and not always to your advantage. Become aware of the insidious messages that bombard you constantly. Even the TV news and newspapers feed you the steady diet that the world is a dangerous place. If you believe what you read, then that is the world you will experience.

Since September 11, people have been affected subconsciously by the terrorist attacks to the point that four out of five people have unknowingly been pushed into a survival mode of operation. When I checked my clients for Instinctual Mind control, most of them are surprised to find that they are in survival mode. Many of these people were well on their way to enlightenment yet the fear took over and slammed them back into survival. Why? If you're not totally in control of your mind, it will be your enemy. It has no intention of doing this, yet this is an automatic knee jerk reaction that occurs if the mind contains any program that allows fear to enter.

Other facets of this initiation are:

- *Emotional mastery.* In exploring the use of the power of your mind, you continue to be tempted by your emotions, only more intensely and must master them in this step before you can go through the sixth door. You have been working to attain emotional mastery and, while in this step, you will not gain total control but at least you do take responsibility for all your actions.

- *Unconditional forgiveness of self and others, demonstrating unconditional love in all situations.* In a situation where you have been wronged, you can choose one from a number of alternative actions. In this initiation, you choose the action where you respond: (1) with love, because you know that we are all one so however you treat another, you similarly treat yourself; (2) with acceptance, because the alternative is resistance and that just gives fuel to whatever you resist; (3) with compassion, because you realize that the other's action was prompted by ignorance, not true malice; and (4) with forgiveness because withholding it triggers resentment in you that robs you of your power and gives to the other person the ability to determine how you feel. If judgment or resentment do come up in you, you can see them for what they are and note their presence. Even though you may not master them at this level, at least you do not let them master you and dictate your choices.

- *Mastery of the Law of Cause-and-Effect.* You accept that *you* create and are responsible for all your reactions and responses. No one does anything to you, you allow it to happen. If your actions adversely impact others by limiting their free will, you will reap the same in return. (The only exception to this is parental guidance, when children may not appreciate all the consequences of fully exercising their free will.)

- *Recognizing fear and anger for what they are.* (Fear creates illness and disease, and is False Evidence Appearing Real.) This includes letting go of "The Big One"—the fear of death. Before beginning on this path, you may have bound your identity to that of your physical body, so the notion of being without that body used to cause you great anxiety. However, you now know that your true identity is a vast, multi-dimensional spiritual entity that takes on a body as a necessary "earth suit" to wear for a few decades while on the physical plane to give it a sense of location and focus during its mission. Once the mission down here is complete, you return to the soul plane to continue your growth there. So now you begin to see death not as a reason to fear the unknown but cause for great celebration as you return "home" after a difficult job well done. Similarly, you treat the death of loved ones not selfishly as *your* loss but unselfishly as *their* gain. Of course, you'll miss them in your daily life, but you know that the gap they leave creates openings for new people and activities.

- *Complete the elimination of irrational victim patterns from your repertoire.* Again, you accept that at some level of your psychic make-up, you script and sculpt your life to bring you lessons for growth and understanding. Any "unpleasantness" that results springs from dysfunctional beliefs, which the universe unerringly reflects in your daily life.

- *Self-confidence from recognizing and knowing your "all right-ness" in the world.* This comes from knowing that you are an important part of All That Is, and a unique expression in time/space of body, mind and spirit that has never occurred before and will never occur again. As a unique part of the Creator's body, through you, the Creator is exploring its own nature via the unique combination of your eyes, your mind, and your body. As such, you must not compare the way you explore to the way others explore, because the Creator needs as many different perspectives as possible. So how can one perspective be more or less worthy than any other? Therefore, your "all right-ness" is guaranteed simply because you exist, busily gathering data for the Creator.

- *Asking for and receiving healing for all past wounds and hurts.* Letting these go becomes easy once you realize that, if others have hurt you, first, you let them hurt you by giving them power to determine how you feel, and second, by taking it personally. They were not striking out at you personally but at what you represented to them. Something about you hit one of their buttons, caused them pain, and they blindly lashed out at the pain. You just happened to be in the way. For example, a father who molests his daughter isn't actually molesting *her* personally but is seeking intimacy in the only way he can—with someone who is more vulnerable than he is because he lacks the emotional maturity to find intimacy with another adult. (This in no way condones such activity, but a civilized culture would treat him rather than imprison him.)

- *Lucid living.* Few people enjoy the gift of lucid dreaming in which they know they're dreaming, and amazingly few of us practice lucid living. Most are content to be swept mindlessly along by life's events and other people's agendas rather than living on purpose—*their purpose.* As you go through life with your eyes wide open, you recognize lessons as they happen, learn what they can teach you, release any fear as soon as it arises, and look for opportunities to serve humanity and your fellow man.

- *Releasing all AKA cords and attachments from self and others, both past and present.* (AKA cords are usually attached to the solar plexus, or third chakra. They can be attached to other points on the body depending on the reason for the attachment. Others use them for control and to drain energy.

- *Demonstrating personal mastery at all levels.* This means mastering stressful and emotional situations by techniques such as energy work to change the mood of a room or crowd, knowing how to respond to physical conditions, and listening to guidance as to how to act.

- *Releasing the need for control and authority.* By this step, you know that exercising control over others generates more karma with them that you will need to deal with and, as a master-in-training, that's the worst thing you can do. Until you can accept that other people are "spirits in earth suits," with the right and obligation to be unique expressions of the Creator, you will not leave this initiation. This also applies to your stewardship of the animal kingdom, nature and the environment in general.

- *Understanding the Law of Communication.* This means using creative listening so that you do not need to control conversations. When others are speaking, you shut up and send them energy to help them clarify the expression of their truth.

During the Golden Age of Teachers over a 1,600-year period, the GOD Source sent a plethora of teachers to different cultures around the world beginning in 1500 BC to around 100 AD. (See timeline in Figure 1.)

Did we learn what these teachers postulated in their teaching? I have my doubts bearing in mind that most of them were murdered, assassinated, crucified, sentenced to death or banished to remote places devoid of followers. After these people met their demise and their universal teachings and spiritual principles were diluted and/or corrupted, humanity has been on a downhill slide.

It is our responsibility today to reactivate and live by the original principles, along the lines given in this and many other books. I know it can be done, as I have been living by these principles for the last 20 years. I have gone through the temptations and initiations specified in

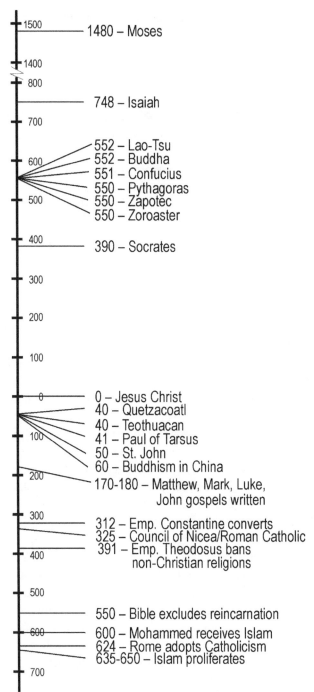

Figure 1: Timeline of World Teachers

this book, which has resulted in a spiritual journey on which everything is falling into place. I do not see this as "miracles" but just synchronicity.

Control and Authority over Others

Doing the work is about lightening our load. About 15 years ago, my friend Tony Stubbs had a vivid dream in which he was on a cruise. Everyone was ashore visiting the port and he'd wandered far from the ship. When its whistle blew to call the passengers back for departure, he realized that he'd never make it back in time because he was lugging around two heavy suitcases. The lesson? Dump the baggage or miss the boat!

Letting go of control is one the toughest lessons to learn. You must first let go of judgment and blame to get to the programs that cause control, manipulation and authority. These are all caused by insecurity and not feeling safe in your own environment. Few people are comfortable in their life, feel confident, or appear actually happy. All you need do is sit in any area where people congregate, and watch them and their body language.

What we humans want more than anything else is to be accepted, acknowledged and recognized, and to feel safe. When we do not feel safe, we will assume people are judging and criticizing us. We create our own hell because our second-guessing other people will sink us. Very seldom are our beliefs and interpretations true renditions of the situation so we live in illusions, trying to control our surroundings in an attempt to feel safe. When we are not in control of the situation, we feel threatened. (Victims are covert active controllers just as much as the overt control freak.) If we *can* have power over people, situations and our environment, then we can feel safe.

As you release all the emotional triggers that trap you in knee-jerk reactions, you begin to loosen the bonds that tie you to limitations. Clearing karmic contracts and agreements further lightens your load. You must also clear any curses and hexes attached to you, such as vows, oaths and allegiances you took in past lives. These are probably still active must be released. They often stem from past life involvement with the Roman Catholic Church, either because the Church killed you for opposing its dogma, or you enforced it on the Church's behalf.

As you work your way up the steps and go through the doors of initiation, your discipline and commitment will be tested. Of course, your teachers in the White Brotherhoods do not want you to stumble or fall, but you must cross the finish line yourself. This individual process could be likened to the 12-step recovery programs such as Alcoholics Anonymous. At some point in these programs, you recognize that you cannot do it alone, so you let go and ask for guidance from a higher power. This works well for many people who use it as a temporary crutch while they take their power back, but others give all their power away to the group and never take it back. The GOD Source, in fact, wants you to empower *yourself*, not them. If you give your power away to a God and that's what you personally need to take the next step in empowering yourself, that's fine but at some point you must take your power back.

When people end up giving their power away to a group, they become codependent on the group. The group is meant as temporary support until you're strong enough to stand on your own feet but many people get trapped in a bind because they feel that the *group* is the source of their power, and to separate from the group is scary because they would then be powerless. Of course, this is exactly how cults work. Initially, cult members are friendly and supportive, but once they've won a target's trust, they deliberately and insidiously cut their targets off from the outside world, develop mistrust regarding that world, and erode personal power so that targets become dependent on the cult for validation. Then leaving is unthinkable, the thought filling them with terror. If the ongoing abuse on the part of the cult leaders eventually causes members to "wake up" and want to leave, horrific sanctions are threatened and often carried out to keep members in line.

Many people in metaphysical movements have allowed some group or other to become their power. A self-proclaimed master teacher, guru, shaman or medicine man leads the group and feeds off its power. As long as members follow the leader's dictates, they are rewarded with little tokens of their own power back. Any dissention that threatens the leader's power results in stern rebuke such as being ostracized, shunned, humiliated, or even ejected. Leaders know that their followers need a leader who is superior to them so that they can feel confident that their guru/leader knows the path for them to follow. Their followers would quickly lose confidence if the leader showed any weakness or vulnerability, so he or she nips insurrection in the bud.

A good example of this is the Alive Polarity organization that insisted on impeccable ethics, honesty and integrity at all times. For example, members had to be married, because living together was seen as immoral. Once an obscure group with a little retreat center on Oracas Island, Washington, it had grown into an internationally recognized organization with chapters all over the world. The group was prospering. For example, they owned a large hot spring resort in Murrieta, California that was doing well financially.

The organization's leader spent six months in Australia visiting groups there. During his stay, he had an affair with a married woman. When word got back to the main group in California, their leader's violation of their most basic tenet brought the whole organization down. The resort closed in turmoil, resulting in many people losing their life savings since they had invested in the group to buy the resort. They had spent many years rebuilding and restoring the multi-million dollar resort and lost everything overnight when the lender repossessed and sold it.

The group's basic teachings were obviously flawed since all their power was vested personally in the leader. When he strayed from the path—a perfectly normal human thing—the organization failed. This indicates faulty teaching and a basic weakness in the members of the organization. (The leader, by the way, stayed in Australia and continued his affair.)

Few people could understand why the organization collapsed. Some tried to save it as a business venture because they realized that the business practices of the group were not responsible but rather the weakness in those who ran it. Unfortunately, they could not get enough support; people were leaving in fear so, when the majority wanted out, the whole organization collapsed. This aptly demonstrates what happens when all a group's power is invested in the leader and not the members.

Also, the organization was based on agreement and not alignment. Had the group been aligned in their vision, it could have survived the upheaval, which, after all was a minor hiccup. But it was based on agreement, and when the leader broke his agreement with the group, it all fell apart.

To understand how this group consciousness functions and how it attracts victims who give their power away to a strong leader, see Eric Hoffer's book *The True Believer*, a classic on mass movements. A champion of taking personal power back and reclaiming personal responsibility, he feels that America is falling backwards and becoming a nation of sheep. Hoffer's basic tenet is, "True believers are not intent on bolstering and advancing the cherished self. They are craving to be rid of the unwanted self. They are followers, not because of a desire for self-control and self-advancement, but because it satisfies their passion for self-renunciation. ... True believers are eternally incomplete and insecure."

Leaders know that if they allow members to come to their full power, their leadership could be threatened because the group no longer needs the leader, so the leader *competes* for power with the members. The real test is whether everyone can *cooperate* so that the group members can be empowered, not the leader. Anyone looking to join a group should ensure that it stresses *self*-empowerment as the main goal rather than competition and leader-empowerment. Many pay lip service to this but do not deliver. Discernment is essential because delusion is rampant.

Many leaders are taken over by the dark forces and can sound inviting and supportive, yet they take your power away without you knowing it. Leaders in illusion will deny that they must have power and do not even realize that they're getting their validation from the group. A true leader does not need followers or a group. Successful groups and their leaders are interdependent; neither needs the other but both benefit from the synergy.

Alignment vs. Agreement

Those who live within the rules strive for *agreement* as a way of eliciting approval, and are terrified of disagreement or conflict. They will manipulate themselves and others to win agreement in the hope of seizing control of at least half the situation.

Survival selves worry about being ostracized from the group if they disagree; authentic selves prefer to honor their truth but will not fight over it, for they know that sometimes "You can be right or happy, but not both." Sometimes you just have to agree to disagree but, if you are *aligned*, disagreement is okay.

Alignment of vision puts us on the same side even if we disagree on the details. Agreement is mental convergence; alignment is spiritual convergence. If the group in the previous story had been spiritually aligned rather than bound by agreement, the leader's infidelity would have been a ripple rather than a tidal wave. Another person could have taken over, upheld the vision, and asked the leader to leave. This could not have happened in this case because all the power was vested in the leader and the followers were unable to elect a new one.

Mind Control

Mind control is big business nowadays. Many government projects are involved with it, and it is now so subtle and insidious that you can be sucked into the process without even knowing it. In fact, the controllers will convince you that they're helping you when, in fact, they are causing you great harm. Since the September 11, 2001 terrorist attacks, people are willing to give up their freedoms for security. This is exactly what our government wants. They already can track us with all the numbers we have with credit cards, etc. The next step is a National ID Card, the absence of which would hinder terrorists (although obtaining a fake card would be the first objective of a terrorist). So in the name of freedom, we are seeing the erosion of freedom.

Our lesson in this is to be discerning in what we accept. The big message is: "Give up. Surrender. It will all be done for you." Groups even come up with phrases such as, "the Holy Mother is now holding you in her prayers," or, "God has given us a special dispensation for a mass clearing of our karma." Such flowery affirmations tell you that the sources are not clear. Your mind is a computer; it does not need flowery phrases to impress it.

I have met many seekers who never find the bliss they're looking for. They will try to convince you that they are seeking their "True Self," yet they never seem to find it, hidden as it is behind layers of illusion and denial. When I question these theories of flowery bliss and, instead, lay out the path logically, avid seekers judge me as "not spiritual enough" and go off to look for their true self with the next dispenser of the panacea of illusion. The direction is within, not outside self, but most people are seeking an easy way so they join groups who will direct their life. (The chapter "Battle for Your Mind" in my book, *2011: The New Millennium Begins* offers more insight on this subject.)

The higher sources are quite aware of our intent. They monitor us and watch us walk down dead end roads. They also watch the teachers, shamans and gurus. If we have taken on the mantle to be world servers and changers, they are monitoring us all the time. Any false claims and illusionary teachings are noted in your file in the Akashic Record.

The Law of Cause and Effect

A physical plane law states, "For every action, there is an equal and opposite reaction." Energetically, the Law of Resonance means that the Universe responds to whatever you send out, with equal and *like* energy. Generosity brings generosity back to you; hostility brings hostility.

Historically, this law was often hidden because of an inbuilt delay that dampened the response and maybe even pushed it back into a later lifetime. Nowadays, this is not so; the response comes much faster and with more intensity.

Obviously, the broader the cause, the broader the effect. If your cause ripples out and impacts a large number of people, either positively or negatively, so will the effect. Once you know about this law and how to use it for the good of all, you can "take the brakes off" and be assertive with your reality creation, for the greater the cause, the greater the effect. Don't worry about "shouting at God." You're actually just interacting with a principle that's as impersonal as the Law of Gravity. It doesn't care about your cause; its only job is to deliver the effect. So how you use this law is *entirely up to you.*

The Law of Karma

Definitions of karma abound. *Karma* is a Sanskrit word meaning simply "action," but Indian culture has made karma very complex. They have many forms and definitions of specific types of karma. My research suggests that karma is created where a prior interaction with a person in a previous lifetime did not end on a happy or constructive note. Obviously, the extreme case is where you caused a person's death in a past life.

Another school of thought suggests that karma is generated whenever you curtail another person's free will. Obviously, murder will do that, but so will manipulation, control or even unwarranted criticism that changes how the other person acts or feels. You cannot do anything that demeans another person without having to deal with the resulting outcome of that action. Even if no one else knows about it, it is recorded in your own Subconscious Mind. You will then pick the time and place to rectify the situation and the person or activity to work it out with. Nothing is ever erased until the karma is released and the lesson is learned. The catch is that karma can cause you to feel guilt so that you must rectify the karma with a philanthropic act towards the person when you meet up again.

I have worked with many people who are between a rock and a hard place but cannot find a way out. All we need do is release the karma and the situation goes away. Here are two examples that troubled two people:

One of my clients allowed her brother to move in with her two years ago after he lost his job. His lack of success at finding a job deteriorated to the point of not even looking for a job for over nine months. She asked me, "How do I handle this situation? If I throw him out, he won't have a place to live. He has no money and his unemployment has run out. I feel guilty about the way I am feeling about him."

We found two past lives where her co-incarnations had killed his co-incarnations. We released the past lives and claimed Grace, deleting the programs and locking up the records. Then she went home and told him, "I'm giving you two weeks notice, and then I'm going to put your belongings out on the front lawn. You'd better get yourself a job so you can pay me rent."

His inner mind was taking advantage of her because it knew he could get away with it. She had been ranting about this for a year and he didn't believe her. But without the past life programs controlling her, she stuck to her guns and threw him out.

My younger son got himself hooked up with a codependent from a past life that he could not shake. Every time he said he was ready to end the relationship, she claimed that, if he broke up with her, she would commit suicide. The same pattern was here, too. He felt guilty so she used it to hold onto him. When we cleared the three past lives, he told her, "It's over. I'm moving to another town to attend college and I will not allow you to follow me."

When she tried her little trick again, he told her, "If it's your choice to end your life, so be it." His Middle Self finally recognized that it could not control him. He has since run into a similar situation with another girl, but this time in reverse. She has been chasing him for three life times, in one of which he jilted her and enraged her family, who had him killed. His fear, therefore, was that if he became involved with her and it didn't work, he might be killed again. We cleared the past lives up and the relationship smoothed out.

Our Subconscious Mind is very literal, as it has no way of differentiating between the past and the present. All it knows is that the program is in the file so it could happen again at any time.

Isaac Newton told us in 1687: "Whenever one object exerts a force on anotherobject, the second object exerts an equal and opposite force on the first." So, we interact with each other not knowing that we're reacting to karmic lessons that our Middle Self is picking up. The lessons are quite apparent to our Inner Selves yet we are not aware of the karmic reaction. We interpret it as anger or fear when, if we could decipher the lesson, we could release it.

Before I was aware of the full impact of karma, I used to notice a weird, disturbing feeling as if electricity was sparking when, on first meeting, I would look into a person's eyes. I now know that this meant I had some intense lessons coming up with this person. If I had known this back then, I would have cleared the lesson rather than go through a painful experience. Whenever a lesson does come along, you can choose between:

1. Going through the experience and suffering the pain or possible serious consequences, or

2. Gaining the understanding without the pain and claiming Grace, thereby letting go of the lesson.

Option 1 is for people on autopilot. Karma is intended to reveal something in you that needs healing and, if pain is the only way to get your attention, that is what your guides and teachers will use. No teacher has ever advocated this option, however. Those on autopilot cannot see the big picture wherein life is a series of learning experiences designed to bring wisdom, love, understanding and growth, so they just stumble from one drama to the next, probably learning little as they do, akin to a log floating down a river, hitting anything the water pushes it into. When people go from one disastrous relationship to another, they are not stopping to think, "Is another abusive relationship in my highest and best interest and, if not, what can I do to avoid the next painful learning experience?"

Option 2 is for those who *can* see the big picture and say, "Ah, here comes a lesson. Let's see what I can learn from it before it gets painful." This doesn't mean dodging the lesson, just the pain, so you probe it for meaning while it's still only a feather touch and not a two-by-four on the side of the head.

Begin by taking responsibility for the lesson. The Universe isn't doing it to you; *you* are doing it to you, so love yourself for setting up a wonderful potential growth experience.

How do masters-in-training deal with karmic lessons? First, they practice "lucid living," which means they go through life paying attention to people, events and situations, and noticing subtle changes in them. When something interesting or unusual does happen, they pounce cat-like on it, asking, "What does this mean? How do I handle this now?" As a master-in-training, it's your call.

To divine the meaning, they may meditate, run a Tarot spread, dowse with a pendulum, or just plain "figure it out." Once they have the meaning, they ask, "How do I choose to respond? I can retaliate, generate more karma and stay on the wheel for a few more lifetimes. Or I can pour love into this situation and heal it."

(Useful in knowing where you are is to know where you've been, and the best tool to track these lessons is a journal. See my book *Becoming a Spiritual Being In A physical Body* for information on the journaling process.)

The Law of Karma simply means that a soul usually needs to experience both sides of a situation for its complete growth and understanding. So, if one incarnation, you take action X, then the same or another incarnation, your soul must experience being on the receiving end of action X so that it can fully understand the energy of the interaction. Of course, if the soul can get an incarnation to come to that understanding *without* experiencing the action, you can transcend this law.

In the past, karma often took a long time to rebound because we were the only person who could deal with and clear our own karma. Nowadays, we have a little help to clear it as soon as possible, so karma can be almost immediate.

Ignorance is no excuse. Being unaware that your action creates karma makes no difference. A karmic record is created each time you enter into an agreement that you do not fulfill. You choose every action you take or enter into at any time. There is a reason and a payoff for every action we take. It may be only a lesson to wake us up to what we're doing. Suppose you're on autopilot, blindly follow someone's advice and get into a situation in which others are harmed or their free will curtailed. You still made a choice and created karma. The lesson here is to not blindly follow without knowing where you're going. (The surest way to avoid creating new karma is to test an anticipated action against the Golden Rule before acting.)

Many people will justify their behavior as to why they took a certain action or no action, as their justifier sub-personalities try to evade responsibility. Once an action is taken, however, it has an opposite reaction. As Newton also told us, "An object in motion will continue in motion until another equal and opposite force stops it." Karma will continue until you reverse the effect that it created. If you do not get the drift of the lesson, it will pick up more force and intensify the energy behind it until you do get it.

One of the best examples of this is a person who asked me to find out why his friend stuttered. I used Kinesiology (muscle testing) and asked the friend when the stuttering started. He replied that it began fifteen years earlier. My next question was, "Did something traumatic happen just before it started?"

"Yes, my house burned down," he told me.

This gave us a direction to take, so I asked his body, "Is the house fire connected with the stuttering?"

YES.

"Is the root cause in this life?"

NO.

"From a past life?"

YES.

At that point, I had him do an affirmation to bring up the past life record so I could look at it. The affirmation brought up the record as if it were being accessed on a computer. In a past life, I saw the house and barn that he had burned down. That was original cause. His house burning down in the current lifetime resurrected the core issue. Since he was not getting the lesson, the catalyst—his stuttering—continued to affect his life because he could not function in his job very well. In twenty minutes, we had released the karma and his stuttering stopped. That was four years ago.

He said, "I have a hard time believing something in a past life was causing my stuttering."

I explained, "The stuttering isn't caused by the past life in any way. It's the catalyst in *this* lifetime that reminds you about the lesson since you didn't get it when your house burned down. When you don't recognize the lesson, it gets more intense each time. In your case, you didn't get it from the fire so your mind is creating a lasting reaction to keep reminding you. You're now on the two-yard line with no more time outs left. If you hadn't met me and cleared the lesson, it would have intensified. More than likely, you wouldn't have gotten it during this lifetime, so it would be re-filed as a failed lesson. Next time, it would come up again only more intensely."

~ ~ ~

Today, karma rebounds much more quickly and with much heavier impact. Most people do not see that actions they take can have immediate and serious effects. A major source of karma today involves money. People assume that if they do not want to pay for something they can return it, put a stop order on a check or file a charge back on a credit card. Also financial scams are at an all-time high, in which people are conned into investing in some phony program or project and they lose their money. On a larger scale, recent years have seen many Saving & Loan and junk bond scams. Regardless of how much or how little, it still creates karma. The Golden Rule—do unto others as you would have them do unto you—means that you cannot take advantage of anyone in any way and get away with it. Even if you don't end up in jail, it's all being logged in the Akashic Record and you will have to deal with it sooner or later.

Many times, we feel that we did not receive the services or work that was agreed upon and refuse to pay or stop payment on the check or credit card. If the services were rendered as agreed upon before the project began, then payment is due. Unless you can prove that the agreement was breached, then your objection does not hold up and you cannot take advantage of that person. You can make up all kinds of stories in your head to justify your actions but, if you have taken advantage of anyone's time or services that are due, you have created karma.

For example, a friend ran up $50,000 in credit card debt and got many of the credit card companies to settle for twenty cents on the dollar as an alternative to her filing bankruptcy, in which case they would have received nothing. A few years later, she has more credit cards and is running up debt again, with the intent of filing bankruptcy this time. All along, she is living in survival with lessons flying in all different directions, yet she cannot see anything wrong with her behavior. In the midst of a downward spiral, she still works hard to justify her actions.

By the same token, presenting a service or program in a way that misleads gullible people is just as serious a breach of spiritual principles and universal laws. Granted, people should use discernment in their dealings but that does not excuse intentional misrepresentation or fraud. Worse, being in denial of what you're doing compounds the karma. This also applies to spiritual teachers, "pseudo" shamans and self-styled medicine people who present programs that do not deliver on their promises. Presenters who do not walk their talk face serious consequences; karma is not selective. We cannot take advantage of anyone, no matter whether we're in denial, illusion or not.

The more evolution your soul accomplished in past lives, the farther along you begin with your initiation in this lifetime. In her book, *It's All Right*, Isobel Hickey wrote in the mid-1960s that the positive actions and service you performed in past lives put points in the "love bank." Even if you participate in negative activities in this life, you can draw on your bank balance in the love bank to negate some of those activities. Of course, you will still need to deal with that karma at some point, but it buys you a reprieve so you can recognize the lesson.

We saw earlier how so very few of us, once we enter this life, remember our flight plan that details all the karmic lessons we'd planned to undertake and how we intended to handle them. However, we are coming to a critical point in our evolution and must switch from going through painful lessons to just getting the understanding. As a species, we are about to reach critical mass. When we do this, our planet will be thrust into the fifth dimension. We have no choice about that. We can, however, choose whether to be on board for the ride or remain on the cycle of return on another planet that is being set up as the next karmic schoolhouse.

The Law of Grace

This is one of the most important Universal Laws of all and could cut lifetimes off your spiritual journey. You can take the "eye for an eye" approach to clearing karma but it can very traumatic and will need many lifetimes. You do not need to die a traumatic death to clear yourself for killing someone in a past life. All you must do is *understand* the lesson, the circumstances and the situation. When you acknowledge the fact of your misdeed and error, you are ready to clear the lesson. All you need do is ask for forgiveness and love, and forgive yourself. Then take the program and lock it up in the archives so it will never affect you again. As you do, make sure you say, "I claim Grace."

Grace is the energy of the fresh start. If you invoke it, you erase the past. Once you are free of karma but understand what it would have taught you, you are free to move on. If you follow your Higher Self, you will create no further karma but, if you follow other people's rules, you will generate self-karma that you must deal with. And every time you suppress a spontaneous impulse because of a "should," you create karma with yourself because you have denied your own free will.

It is vital, therefore, that you are constantly aware of whether you're operating inside or outside the "rules," for within them lie limitation, obligation and authority. Outside the rules lie freedom, sovereignty and following your Spirit.

Unconditional Love

In step 2, you worked on choosing a new set of beliefs based on love rather than fear, and on forgiving yourself for having had fear-based beliefs in the first place. In this step, you work on forgiving everyone who has harmed you in any way. Holding on to old hurts gives power to those who hurt you in the past, and that's a no-no by this step.

Holding on to old grudges and resentments also drives wedges between you and others—another no-no as we strive for unity. It also means that your love is conditional—you love some people and not others, and your loving them depends on how they behave. Unconditional love is especially important in your primary relationships, which you began to work with in the previous step.

There are two ways of looking at the world:

- *Zero-sum view*, which says that there is only so much of any specific thing to go round, so whatever quantity others have leaves less for you.

- *Infinite abundance view*, in which the Universe simply creates more of whatever is in demand, so your particular allotment is just a matter of how much you *allow* yourself to have.

Obviously, Earth masters take the second view, especially when it comes to love, whereas those holding the zero-sum view actually resent people in loving relationships because the love those people share is somehow "taken out of circulation." Instead, they should rejoice over humanity's "love quotient" increase, which makes even more love possible.

By this fifth initiation, you begin to sense the underlying unity of All That Is and realize that when you practice unconditional love, you are actually giving it to yourself through the rebound effect. And the more you love, the more rebounds, and the easier it becomes to love unconditionally.

Before talking about love, however, we must distinguish between:

- *Eros*, the force that initially draws two people together

- *Agape*, the permanent state of unity, often termed *unconditional* love.

Eros comes unbidden and suddenly, like lightning on a sunny day. It cannot be summoned and cannot be ignored. In the absence of sex in a relationship, *Eros* is platonic; mingled with sex, it is a potent binding force, and drives the partners to find out as much as possible about each other.

Eros eventually fizzles out and, if both partners have not built *agape*, their relationship becomes a habit, or one or both partners start looking outside for fulfillment. If *agape* has developed, the relationship deepens to one of affection, companionship, mutual support and respect. Your task in this step is to do just that.

To me, love is a profound commitment to the happiness and well-being of all living beings that does not depend on how they behave or whether they love you in return. (Note that the definition also includes you and even your beloved pets.) By definition, love *is* unconditional. If it isn't, then it's not love but some need in you that other people fill, and you in them, i.e., a barter. The implications of love being unconditional are:

- Sometimes love needs to be "tough," as with an errant child or an adult bent on self-destruction.

- Our love must be balanced between self and others, so that one does not eclipse the other. "Me first" or "me last" are not love in balance.

- Love not only allows change and growth in the partners actively supports and encourages them. Love in relationship knows that the purpose of the relationship is not just to experience relating, but the growth that it brings. Therefore, love never fears positive change, even if it distances two people, because love recognizes that they are just moving in different directions. Love trusts that things will work out for the best in the long run under spirit's guidance.

- Until you first extend your love to yourself, you cannot extend it to others or receive the love of others. So, we need to be able to give it to ourselves first.

- Love does not need to be reciprocated in order to be effective.

- Love is not exclusive. You can hold this profound commitment towards everyone on the planet, and it has nothing to do with sex or physical proximity.

- You can be lovingly committed to the well-being of others without necessarily liking them or enjoying their company. Remember, love is unconditional by definition.

- Love forgives, because holding grudges and resentments is a waste of your energy and gives power to others. And you love yourself too much to do that.

- Love is not something you learn or teach, as all of us have it. It was just written over or blocked in childhood by our negative misinterpretation of who we were or how other people treated us.

- Love is not an emotion. It is a feeling that is a positive response in all situations.

The Risk of Loving

A famous aphorism tells us, "Love like you'll never be hurt," referring to the obvious risks in opening yourself up to others. Of course, there are risks, but what are they?

One risk is that someone will take advantage of you. Remember the old Arab saying, "Trust in Allah but tether your camel." Be careful. Loving the fox doesn't mean you must let him guard your chickens. Trust must be earned.

Another risk is that you will make a profound commitment to someone who then leaves, and your heart is broken. So what? It will mend again. Tell yourself, "Okay, if being alone is what my spirit has planned for me now, then that is what I will do ... with gusto!"

I have found that many people who were abused as children have fear of intimacy and commitment. These fears then manifest partners who validate the fear because they're in that rut of proving to themselves that this fear is true. Even when you recognize the fear and try to pull out of it, it will still haunt you until the programs driving it are released and rewritten. The following client story is an excellent example:

He was well-qualified in his field of work yet his personal life did not work. He would go out with his friends to places to meet women and have a good time but was unable to fit in, always feeling "out of the loop." The only women who would talk with him were the occasional controllers who had to monopolize the conversation. The few women he had got close to seemed as if they always wanted to control him, so their behavior seemed to confirm his fear of intimacy and commitment.

During one of our sessions, he described his situation. "This has got to stop. I usually get intoxicated to avoid the feeling of rejection but, as you suggested, last time I watched my feelings rather than getting drunk. You describe Meta-Communication as a radar-like broadcast that projects to other people how we feel about ourselves. Well, when I would try to start a conversation with a woman, she would just talk around me as if I didn't even exist. Staying with my feeling of rejection and not running for the bottle was tough."

On further probing, we found a childhood pattern in which his sister was an only child until she was six. When he was born, she resented him and didn't disguise it. She abused him both verbally and physically. His mother did nothing except mildly scold the sister, so the abuse continued until she left home. When he went to school, he was afraid of girls and stayed away from them. This loner behavior became entrenched so he was unable to have any girl friends through high school. At age 36, he ready to give it up.

In one session, we released all these programs and rewrote the script. When he arrived for his next session, he looked as if he'd walked in from a different planet. The women now included him in their conversations and he'd ended up dating a few of them, with great success.

What was he suddenly doing that was different? He was the same person with the same people, except for one thing: He was no longer broadcasting his "I'm afraid of women" program and was willing to risk and trust that women would respond differently to him. And they did.

Another problem is not so much how others behave but the expectations you place on their behavior. No one can hurt you unless you let them. For example, one evening my wife and I were attending a party to mark the end of the soccer season. I was tired as I'd worked hard all day so my wife, who loves to dance, took to the dance floor with a variety of partners. A man asked me, "Why are you letting Susie dance with all these men?"

In amazement, I asked him, "Why are you asking me that question?"

His reply revealed that he had major issues with trust, rejection and ownership. "I would never let my wife do that. What if she got involved with one of them and took off with him?"

My response shook his tree a bit. " If she were to take off with somebody, I would rather know about it now rather than later. Besides, I don't own her and she can do whatever she wishes. We're here to be happy and enjoy ourselves, and that's exactly what she's doing by dancing."

I could see that he was upset because he couldn't win the confrontation. I was not taking his bait, so he parted with, "And what about you? Are you just going to sit there with nobody to talk to?"

I simply replied, "I don't need to be involved all the time."

My isolation was obviously confronting his fear of it happening to him. And more than likely, he was a counter-dependent who had a need to be right.

You may be thinking at this point that all this sounds hopelessly naïve, and that life is about grabbing as many experiences and as much pleasure as you can, while you can. The sad part of this is that, at the end of the day, you always come away empty, and must rush on to the next experience. Fun and pleasurable moments may be exhilarating for a while but rarely bring long-term fulfillment or meaning to life. However, giving the gift of yourself to others and self *does* leave you with the deep, abiding satisfaction of doing something meaningful.

Love doesn't just happen. You have already been working to eliminate the blocks and fears you have around the well-being of other people, such as, "Increasing the happiness of others will somehow diminish the happiness available to me."

You must also turn your love on yourself, nurturing your self-esteem because you are "worth" it. (By this stage on the path, you already know enough about who you really are and have no self-worth problems.)

Is there a downside to loving? A personal cost? In *The Prophet*, Kahlil Gibran likens love not to the merging of two islands into one, but both islands retaining their sovereign identities and letting the shared ocean of love wash both their shores. To sacrifice *any* part of who you are is co-dependency.

Love says, "If I love you, I will love you from my own sovereignty and not as someone you can manipulate into being who you want me to be, and I expect the same from you. As sovereign human beings, we are both responsible for our own happiness and self-esteem. I require that you require my respect for *both* our sovereignties, as I require your respect."

Summary on Love

If love has conditions, it is not love but a barter between two people intended to lessen their insecurity. In this step, you're beginning to say, "If I love you, you do not have to pass a test or meet my expectations of how you should behave. You do not have to 'earn' my love, for it is given freely. You can be whoever you want to be and I will strive to support that expression. If I cannot, then we will walk our separate paths, but I will not stop loving you, or reject or invalidate you."

Unconditional love is the *only* medium for human growth and, because you love yourself, you are never not in a loving relationship. "Wherever you go, there you are." Even a castaway on a desert island can be in a loving relationship—with himself.

Love frees people up to be their authentic selves because they know they will not be rejected under any circumstances. Gone is the fear of: "If people knew who I really was, they would not love me." You do not have to entertain that fear anymore as you know who you are and you accept that you are lovable. Other people's behavior will validate that for you.

There is a "Catch-22" here that you may not recognize, as it can be an illusion and be stuffed into denial. If any feeling of rejection or not being accepted comes up, you have not completed the step to unconditional love. If you exhibit any codependent behavior by being in a needy state, you have not crossed the bridge yet. You will not pass this initiation until you get through the door of unconditional love. And remember that each major initiation has a number of minor initiations contained within it, and that they are harder to accomplish than the major initiation.

Unconditional Forgiveness

In the Introduction to *Opening Communication with GOD Source*, I tell of how, in 1987, I was almost forced into bankruptcy when a group I trusted embezzled $30,000 from the Wellness Institute, the bookstore and counseling center that my wife and I had started. When the group's attempt to take it over and push me out didn't work, they stole an $8,000 check that had been donated to the Institute to pay off some of the debts that they had incurred. As a result, we had to close the doors and go out of business, and we also lost our house and a car. So deep was the betrayal I felt that forgiving those people took a while. First I had to own the fact that I had called that lesson in for my own growth, and that they had played their parts brilliantly, just as we'd all planned before incarnating.

Central to my forgiveness of those people was the realization that, although they had tried to harm my family and me, in the process they had harmed themselves irreparably. At least I can go to sleep at night with a clear conscience. I have met some of them in the past few years and note that karma has taken its toll on them. Their lives are not working very well and many negative events have befallen them.

The danger with forgiving others is the temptation to see yourself as better than or as morally superior to them, which is, of course, judgment—another no-no by step 5. If this comes up, you will need to get to the catalyst that caused it to come up and reprogram the file.

The Law of Communication Revisited

The Law of Communication admonishes us to never *react* in an argument or participate in one. Instead, let the confronter talk out his or her anger or anxiety. Respond from an objective observer stance with questions, and do not add your own commentary. Be a creative listener and reiterate the other person's argument, as in "What I'm hearing is _____. Does it make you happy to say what you just said?"

While the other person is speaking, avoid the annoying habit of thinking about what you're going to say when he or she gives you an opening, and then impatiently waiting for it. You can be a creative communicator without having to focus on your response while the other person is talking.

If the other person rattles on incessantly, set a time frame and then ask the other person if it would be okay for you to comment. If he or she reacts defensively or negatively to what you say, do not react in the same manner. Explain that you would like it to be a two-way conversation. If the person is a controller, you may find that this will end the conversation. If so, let it go; do not give your power away or let the person manipulate you. But try to end the conversation on a positive note. Quite often, when you ask people, "Did saying what you just did make you happy?" it may stop the conversation and make them think. If it does, you can often process out the comments and finish up with a win-win situation.

An example: One of my clients who we will call Jim had a supervisor who would just jump on someone in the office about three out of five mornings a week. One day, he came and began to jump on Jim, who just listened to his boss until he was done. Then Jim asked him, "Are you happy with what you just said?"

This question caused the boss to stop and think. Finally, he responded with, "Not really."

As the dialogue continued, Jim said, "Most of us in the office are upset when you come in with this chip on your shoulder. If you would like to find out why you do this, would you be willing to see my therapist?"

The boss protested with, "Why should I see a therapist? There's nothing wrong with me."

Jim then asked, "Well, would you be willing to discuss why you're so upset some mornings?"

Jim had worked with me for some time, and was able to discover that the boss gave his power away to his wife when she jumped all over him before he left for work, and the boss took out his frustration on his staff. Once Jim had worked with his boss to empower himself to stand up for himself, the boss' behavior changed, which told the wife that he was not going to play into her confrontations anymore. He was able to create a win-win situation with his wife, so the ripple effect worked its way three levels out from me.

Releasing Judgment

One of the affirmations that Reiki initiates learn is: "Just for today, I will not judge," and many of them are surprised at how hard that is. Most of us make hundreds of judgments a day, all of them invalid because we do not know the whole story—the waitress who's crabby because her feet hurt, or the snappy checkout clerk whose beloved dog has just died. To paraphrase Native American wisdom, "Do not judge a man until you've walked a day in his moccasins."

Furthermore, we are only able to see a "fault" in others when we, too, suffer from that same condition, so who are we to judge?

The opposite of judgment is unconditional acceptance, which says, "I fully accept you as you are and your right to be that way, and I love you unconditionally." This doesn't necessarily mean that you *like* the person, and may prefer that he or she were on a different planet.

Of course, the most destructive aspect of judgment is that we often turn it inward and give ourselves a thorough verbal trashing many times a day. This leads to guilt over what we do and shame over who we are—two very heavy suitcases to lug around all day.

Begin each day with the Reiki affirmation and carefully monitor your thoughts and "self-talk," and, after a few weeks, you will find that non-judgment has crept up on you and is now a habit.

Judgment is an illusive habit that hides itself deep in denial. If it becomes a pattern in your life, Middle Self will create a judgment sub-personality that operates outside of your awareness, as we see in the following example:

In 1982, for reasons outside this story, I was 100 percent stone deaf and could not hear a thing. While driving, I stopped at a red light and a huge Ford Bronco monster truck pulled up beside me. I looked at the driver and a judgment came up that said, "Look at Mr. Macho redneck in his big rig with his cowboy hat on." I had no conscious thought of this, yet my mind created this opinion. How many times does our mind set us up and we don't even know it? Well, this judgment was recorded in our database even though we didn't consciously establish it.

Letting Go of Fear

Fear is a mental projection into the future of something negative happening to you, coupled with all the negative emotions that would accompany that event, be it fear of flying, spiders, snakes, being mugged or raped, or even killed. A major problem is that your Subconscious Mind cannot distinguish between a real or imagined event, and treats them all as real.

As we saw in the previous chapter, thoughts are "sticky" and a fearful thought will attract other thoughts of similar frequency. So, if you're walking down a dark street at night, worried about being mugged, you're transmitting a sticky thought-form that attracts every mugger in a ten-block radius who is seeking a target.

What can you do instead? Surround yourself with white light and banish negative thoughts. Then you won't even be a blip on a mugger's inner radar screen and he'll go find someone else who *is* transmitting victim thoughts. In the 1970s, New York University conducted a study involving three groups of people: 50 convicted criminals, 25 people who had been mugged, raped, or robbed, and 25 people who exuded high self-esteem and self-confidence. The criminals formed the audience in a darkened theater while the people in the other two groups walked across the stage holding cards bearing numbers. The convicts were asked to choose the people who they would select as targets for their criminal activities. Not one of those in the positive group was chosen. Of those in the "victim" group, the more often people had been victims of crime, the more the convicts chose them as likely targets. This study reveals that we send out a fear message that draws the person to us. Therefore, in a sense, criminals teach us a lesson in reality creation. There are no victims; we create it all. This may be hard for some to accept, but I have found it to be true.

You cannot graduate to the next step until you apply all you have learned up to this point. I spent many years in this initiation getting repeatedly tested until I finally got it that I create it all. Nobody does it to you. There is no one to blame. You create all the lessons and draw them to you. Your outer reality begins as an inside job, and no one can learn that for you.

6

The Sixth Initiation: Transmutation

Going through the sixth door involves the ability to claim and demonstrate power over your mind and body. This is another difficult transition because you can longer base your self-worth on who you think you are as a human. You must transcend emotions to pass this initiation.

You continue taking total control of your life. As a master-in-training, you can choose to experience pain if you wish but you can also choose increasing control over every facet of your life, too, although you may occasionally stumble. As in previous steps, temptations of emotion and sickness will come up but, because you have increasing control over your body/mind, they will not have any long-term effects.

Other aspects of your life in this initiation are:

- Abundance as a way of life in all areas. (You may not have totally mastered lack and limitation but at least you must understand them and begin to release them.)

- Understanding your soul level lessons.

- Beginning self-mastery.

- Moving from belief to faith to knowing.

- Becoming one with the Presence of God. Unconditional love is your will. Demonstrating miracles begins, but for its own sake and not to show off your spiritual power, as in, "See how enlightened I am." Self-aggrandizement and arrogance are no longer issues in the sixth initiation.

Soul Lessons

Many books about the soul erroneously talk about what it has to learn when, in fact, your soul knows everything about you and your path, and has nothing to learn. It is your contact with the GOD source.

We are dealing here with a hierarchical order (even though I do not like hierarchies). In this hierarchy, Holographic Mind is the soul level of mind, with its operating system sitting alongside the Ego. Holographic Mind is the Program Manager that reprograms all the files in the database. It also down loads information from Higher Self. The soul works through Higher Self to download information from your flight plan, the God Source and the White Brotherhood. We must use Holographic Mind's abilities to remove defective programs and rewrite the files. Ego is the file manager that moves data from the Conscious Mind and Middle Self to and from Subconscious Mind.

If you have not developed a direct relationship with Higher Self, you must finish up this task now because you cannot graduate from the sixth initiation until you do. At this point, you begin to develop direct contact with Source on demand and no longer need to meditate to make this connection. You can ask a question and the answers will be downloaded immediately. You must begin this by the time you go through the second initiation as it takes considerable practice to develop this connection. To get on the fast track, set up daily sessions where you meditate with the intention of developing this connection. (So that you can monitor your progress and keep track of the lessons that are presented each day, keep a journal. See *Becoming a Spiritual Being in a Physical Body* for more in-depth information on this process.)

Abundance

In this step, your attitude begins to change around abundance, especially financial prosperity. Until now, whenever you received money or goods from others, complementary power dynamics were at work: "I have it, and you want it," and, "You have it, and I want it."

Wants begin to disappear as you now know you can have what ever you ask for. As you move further on this journey of transformation, all you need do is think about what you would like to have and it will manifest. In the beginning of my spiritual journey, each time I needed a parking spot, I made a practice of asking for one. Now, I no longer need to ask as one just manifests when I arrive at my destination.

One might describe this as "miracles on demand" but it is really a manifested physical effect that happens when you align yourself with the universe.

In this step, you begin to realize that every cent you have ever received and will ever receive is orchestrated by your Higher Self. You have your job or the clients you serve because your Spirit arranges it that way and, in the same way, you could lose it all if that would serve your flight plan. Stray too far from this and a sharp course correction may be necessary.

If you are doing Spirit's work, however, resources should flow readily to you unless you take some vow to the contrary. (Believe it or not, some people still think that poverty is somehow more "spiritual" than abundance.) There is no need to take a vow of poverty to pass the test of enlightenment. In fact, take a vow of abundance because the universe is ready to provide anything you desire when you are aligned with Law of Abundance.

By the Law of Resonance, the universe gives you more of whatever you focus on, so you begin to realize that *gratitude* is the key to abundance. Once the universe sees that you are fascinated with all the blessings in your life, it will send you more ... and more. Success is a highly controversial subject. Some people connect it with money only. When you realize that money is merely a tool that you must learn to use, it will come effortlessly. If you are attached to it, however, then you may lose it until you recognize the significance of money. Those who inherit a considerable sum of money could very well lose it all no matter how hard they work to retain it if they do not understand the laws of money.

In 1987, Susie and I lost all our life savings no matter how hard we tried to control matters, and understanding the law of money took us over ten years. Today, everything flows to us because we know that we're entitled to it. This will not come to pass, however, until you step out of the fear of lack. When you know that you can risk and trust without any negative results, you go through the minor initiation with money.

The other side of the gratitude coin is *generosity*, or sharing your blessings with others, for that puts you in the flow. If you hang on to your abundance, it will stagnate and, like water, it's only pure when it's flowing. If you treat your wealth as if it were a pond with no water flowing in or out, it will become dank and a breeding ground for mosquitoes. As long as you covet your wealth, the mosquitoes will bite you to remind you that you're not in line with universal law. Many people are in such fear of loss that they never achieve and financial success. Gratitude for what you already have is one thing; giving thanks for what you do not *yet* have is another, but equally as important. The best way to get somewhere is to visualize yourself, with gratitude, already there. This programs the great cosmic computer with the outcome you desire. But be warned: This is impersonal and you can create karma if the outcome is not in someone's best interest. Always include the phrase, "in the highest and best interest of all involved."

Remember, too, that a vital part of abundance is your willingness to receive. Masters feel worthy of the blessings in their lives and accept them gratefully. Those with low self-esteem may want things but do not feel worthy of actually having them. The level of lack will indicate your ability to accept and receive abundance.

A common phenomenon is what I call "the leap of faith." If your Higher Self is pushing you to do something such as publishing a book but the resources are not there, figure out a way to do it anyway, such as getting a loan or putting it on a credit card. Invariably the resources follow once you make your move of power, for they are yours by divine right. As a master, you must claim them, however. It's a "Catch 22" in which many people say, "I will follow Spirit once I have the money" but, in truth, you will only have the money when you follow Spirit, which brings us to the next topic.

I waited for six years, wishing and hoping for a publisher to come into my life to help me publish my books. None showed up. In fact all I received were rejection slips. So in 1998, I decided that I had to find a way to do it myself. I had no idea how I was going to accomplish this task as I knew nothing about publishing. We refinanced our home to get the money and every aspect of publishing my books fell into place without a hitch. If you *wish*, you get nothing, but when you *know*, you can have everything. Walking boldly into a new venture without any experience would appear as a leap of faith, but it is not when you know that it will manifest successfully.

Understanding Soul-level Lessons

How do you know when you *are* following Spirit? Or tracking to your flight plan? Discerning the urging of your Higher Self from the needs of personality is not always easy. One test is that the former leads to inner peace and fulfillment, while the latter does not.

Two of the main lessons you tackle in this step are:

- Allowing your spirit and soul to guide you in the knowledge that it is who you *really* are. Before you do, however, you must know who you are allowing to set up the path, so that means becoming able to straddle the paradox of your own divinity *and* mortality.

- Integrating power and compassion in a way that reveals to you the perfect harmony in everything that happens, even the seeming cruelty of the world around you.

Until now, you have worked from the personality self, which is a manifestation of your Middle Self. It operates from sub-personalities, controlling your life through autopilot. At this level, you transcend personality self and eliminate autopilot. However, sub-personalities will try to stop your transformation because they operate on fear, lack, anxiety, avoidance, judgment, frustration, indecision, procrastination, lack of self-worth and fear of trusting or risking.

One of the mistakes most people make is that they just assume they have spirit guides ready to direct their life, or that spirit will guide them to the desired Shangri-La. There are two basic mistakes here. First, most beings that we think are spirit guides are nothing more than people who have crossed over to the astral plane and are still earth-bound. Of course, they have better vision than we have because no physical body limits their abilities. They may not be as enlightened as we are but we give our power away to them, anyway.

The next mistake we make is in believing that spirit will direct our spiritual journey when we see spirit as being outside ourselves. Quite often, Middle Self will masquerade as spirit in order to misdirect us. When we get to the point in our enlightenment where we have made contact with Spirit, we can work with it. Spirit is our connection that works within the hierarchy of the mind-soul connection.

Another mistake that initiates on the path make is to surrender themselves to various beliefs and concepts. Using the word "surrender" is the best way to stop yourself. Your mind interprets that word as meaning "giving up power and freedom" as did Jim Jones' followers, who ended up in a mass suicide because the leader told them that "the authorities" were coming for them. And the Heaven's Gate leader, Applegate, said that suicide was the way to heaven.

To surrender in the context of war means laying down your weapons and submitting to your enemy. Many people on the path to enlightenment feel that this is a noble and proper gesture, yet it gives away your personal power. The true path to transformation requires you to *reclaim* your personal power, not give it away. All my books stress taking responsibility for your life, not submitting to others. You are the power in your life, and every process must focus on taking control rather than surrendering.

The control issue is one of the toughest initiations to pass. Even though it is a minor initiation, it can have major consequences. Everyone has control issues at some level in one way or another. Your mind does not have any problem with the phrase "letting go or releasing control" but *surrendering* control brings up fear. Most of us have been persecuted, abused or tortured in past lives for our beliefs. Many times you were forced to follow a path that you did not want to follow or you were incarcerated, tortured or killed for those beliefs. Or if you surrendered your beliefs to avoid being hurt, this brought up feelings of loss of freedom. In some traditions, surrendering your beliefs to become enlightened may seem harmless, but most people I have met who do so seem to be directionless and have no aliveness about them. On the other hand, the controller sub-personality may seem alive and active but they are operating from fear. It may seem odd but victims are controllers, too, and strive to get people to feel sorry for them or have pity on them.

In this initiation, you come to a point where nothing can shake your tree. The only person you want to control is yourself. Again, this can be a Catch-22 if you are afraid to speak your truth. People will control themselves by telling others what they want to hear in exchange for attention and validation. Ideally, you are able to say what you wish to say within reason and not allow others to manipulate you, to be able to stand your position yet not try to influence anyone to accept your belief. When you reach the point of independence, you can begin work with *interdependence* and build a network of independent people who can rely on each other to provide help when needed, but not in a codependent fashion. Then, in the process of letting go of neediness, you will go through another minor initiation—that of becoming self-reliant.

One of the best examples of this was a client who always gave away his power to women who wanted help. A rescuer sub-personality controlled his life. After a few sessions with me, he was confronted by a situation where he had to take control and not allow himself to be manipulated. A girl friend called him up at work and asked him to take her to an auto store to get a new battery because she could not start her car. (He had jump-started her car the previous week and advised her to replace the battery.) Since he planned to attend to my workshop that evening, he did not have time to take care of her and arrive on time. When he told her he couldn't help, he feared that she would reject him and he would lose her as a friend. His desire to prove to himself he could stand up for what was right for him won out, even though he felt a pang of guilt when he hung the phone up. She was the victim trying to control.

In the past, he would have succumbed to her plea of, "George, you've always been there for me when I needed help. How can you do this to me?"

This time, he responded, "I'm not doing this to you. I told you to get a new battery last week. It's not my fault that you didn't follow my advice."

She again tried to lasso him. "But, George, I have to visit my mother tonight and won't be able to make it. I don't want to disappoint her."

His final remark was, "Look, you knew the car problem would happen again. I just don't have time to help you tonight. I'm sure someone at work can take you. Maybe you should join Triple-A because I can't always be at your beck and call when you need help."

As soon as we started the workshop, he asked the group, "Did I do it right because I was feeling guilty all the way over here? I'm wondering if she's going to snub me next time I call her."

George did not pass the test because he was feeling guilty but at least he'd taken the first step. He will be tested again to see if he can stand up for himself next time without feeling guilty or rejected. His girl friend victim, however, will have a much more difficult time getting through this lesson.

A book by Terry Cole Whittaker is entitled appropriately: *What You Think Of Me Is None Of My Business*. We pass the test for this lesson when we can choose to do what we want without being sucked into other people's need.

Belief to Faith to Knowing

The Piscean Age was about blind belief. Life was simpler and people were not as sophisticated in how they acquired beliefs and their content. In the Dark Ages, the Church was a major controlling influence on people. When the priest told you something, you had to believe it because disputing the Church's teachings was heresy. At best you were excommunicated; at worst, you faced a fiery death.

As science made inroads into planetary cultures, people became more questioning and wanted to figure out things for themselves. As a result, we moved from belief, which is *hope* that something is true, to faith, which is *trust* that it is true. Both of these are controlled by fear because you do not know if it is true. When you cross the barrier to *knowing*, you have broken through the fear and passed this minor initiation.

In this step, you move to direct knowing because you are tapping into your own personal sources from the White Brotherhood and GOD Source, who will tell you what you need to know in the moment. Just as circus trapeze artists let go of one bar and fly through the air, knowing that the next bar will be there to catch, you leave behind your old life of belief and faith, confident that your new life will be there for you. How can you be sure? Because your Higher Self tells you! When you make this connection and the whole hierarchy is set up on the Akashic Internet, you have made your connection with Source. The initiation is accomplished.

Becoming One with the Presence of God

Can you look yourself in the eye in the mirror and say, "Be still and know that you are god"? If not, why not, because it is true? Eons ago, your soul split off from the Source and volunteered to be a probe, going down through the dimensions to learn all that it could and report back. You knew coming down that the trip would be turbulent but, "What the heck, it's only for a few million years. How hard can that be?"

Turbulent it has been. You have lived hundreds of lifetimes and have died in every conceivable manner. In every incarnation, you forgot that you were "god-stuff" because that's one of the conditions of incarnating. In several of those incarnations, you remembered being god-stuff and maybe even got to *feel* what that was like. In this step, you are about to again.

When you do, you will experience the unity and connectedness of everything, which is currently just a concept to you. Moving from idea to reality will also reveal that everyone else is god-stuff, too, and connected with you in the same huge, living matrix of All That Is. There is no separation other that what we create, and we are about to break that block open.

So, go back to your mirror, look yourself in the eye and say, "Be still and know that you are God." If you are caught up in the belief that God is out there somewhere and can judge you, you may find that statement blasphemous. You may challenge me with, "How do you know that we're God? How can you say that?" My answer: Because the GOD SOURCE told me so.

Inner Peace

The Presence of God, or the awareness of your god-self, brings the descent of great inner peace. We all crave inner peace but we in the West fill our lives with so much that brings the absolute opposite—inner turmoil, strife, conflict and stress.

Inner peace means that, even though the outside world is going crazy, you are an oasis of calm. Many people run all over the world looking for this oasis but they need not bother. It is not to be found in the pyramids of Egypt, an Indian ashram, out in the forest or some isolated place where you think you can get away from the turmoil and stress. That divine spark is right inside you. In this step, you realize that it is within you and has been all this time but you were not looking for it with the right eyes, so you could not experience it. There are no stressful situations, only stressful people who experience stress because they cannot find the peace inside themselves.

How do you find peace? Simple. *You choose it in every moment!* Peace is simply a state of mind that you choose. Until this step, peace is a hit-and-miss affair—it comes and goes, seemingly of its own volition—but now it becomes your normal waking state, regardless of outer circumstances. For good examples, read the autobiographies of Mahatma Gandhi and Nelson Mandela.

In the midst of chaos, you radiate an aura of peace and calm, something that will either drive others crazy or will be extremely attractive to them. But you don't care which; you just say, "I choose peace." One of the best examples of this was in the movie *Ghandi* where he was walking down the sidewalk and passed a group of beggars. The western minister walking with him said, "Those beggars should not be doing this. They are blocking our way. Why should we have to walk out into the street and endanger ourselves?"

Ghandi's replied, "Turn the other cheek. You are not at risk," and walked around them, in contrast to the minister, who tried to force his way through them.

Ghandi then asked, "Was it worth the effort to force your way through the group?"

The minister retorted, "I have the right to walk on the sidewalk."

Do you have a right to remain calm when everyone else is losing it? Of course you do. It's your birthright. Not only can you choose peace, you *must* choose peace as part of this initiation. But can you still function in the craziness of the outside world? Of course you can, and much better. Whether you want to is another matter. If you're in a high-stress occupation but have a creative hobby in which you perform well, you might be thinking of a career change in this intiation.

Because simply choosing inner peace seems such an impossible goal in the early steps, you may wonder how you will ever arrive at this state. However, it is very straightforward. You have free choice to choose to feel any way you wish and you mastered your emotions in the previous step, so why not? You are living consciously, you see the big picture, and you know you are god-stuff, so living in peace is now natural. You cannot go through this initiation until you master your emotions and find the inner peace of happiness, harmony and joy in your life. As long as someone or some situation can set you off, cause you to retreat or feel rejected, you will be tested until you let go.

Achieving Unity

The spiritual path leads to the I AM presence and a state of unity, but what exactly is that?

When you incarnated as a seemingly separate being as a platform for Spirit to interact with physical reality, you did not and could not relinquish your connectedness with the matrix of All That Is. So you do not have to achieve unity—*you never lost it*. What you do need to do is regain your conscious awareness of it. The two main connections to become increasingly aware of are:

1. Up through the dimensions of your own being, progressively you work through more refined layers of spirit, culminating in the Godhead.

2. Horizontally, as you transmit your thoughts and emotions consciously and unconsciously for others to pick up, you receive the transmissions of others and discern how you are going to work through each test of your ability to maintain your center and remain at peace no matter what the situation is.

Improving your soul connection has the obvious rewards of a relationship with an infinitely loving being—your own soul—and tapping into extremely wise guidance. My other books, especially *Opening Communication with GOD Source*, offer practical advice on developing your awareness of this connection.

Many of us need to "clean up our act" regarding the second connection and what we transmit and receive. My other books also cover this topic, so here I just stress the importance of discovering what you are actually transmitting to the world. Is it loving expansive energy or fear-based contraction? Your contribution to the "energy soup" we all live in is very real and very important, so be part of the solution and not the problem. Transmit only the highest and best frequencies you can to the rest of us.

In terms of receiving, discernment is essential since so many other people pollute the energy soup with toxic garbage. For your own psychic well-being, learn to shield against this and periodically "clean" your aura of any stuck energy, both yours and other people's.

Summary

As you leave this step, you are living with the Presence of God in your life, and with whatever level of abundance you deem appropriate for your purposes. You must become unshakable and achieve inner peace to pass this major initiation. Abundance begins to come to you with no effort at every level. You will be tested on all these lessons in the future and, as you prove your ability to handle them with no effort, the universe and your teachers will check them off as complete in your Akashic Record.

7

The Seventh Initiation:
Moving Into Your True Place in Life,
Locating Your Dharma

At the seventh door, you are moving out of the mundane world of the average human and becoming the possible human. To get into this initiation, you must totally let go of the personality self, as it is attached to emotions as a way of living. As the Presence of God is installed in your body, mind and spirit, emotions become a thing of the past and you begin to demonstrate miracles on demand. The most difficult challenge in this initiation is stepping above the survival-based Instinctual Mind and continuing to build the control over your body/mind that you started in the fifth step. The temptation to indulge in emotional behavior will continue to confront you, as your teachers will test your resistance to backsliding.

Many people fail at this point due to the inability to overcome lower physical/mental temptations such as control, self-righteousness, manipulation, authority, judgment, resentment, frustration, disorientation, avoidance, procrastination, anger/fear, alcohol abuse and other addictions, and codependency. At this door, many fall away because they cannot resist the temptations that are presented as lessons. You will continue to confront temptations as your teachers test your ability to maintain your balance and detachment. From this point on you must maintain your center. There is no room for negative thoughts or actions as they will throw you back to the fifth level or further, depending on whether you give your power away. I spent three and half years getting into this initiation.

Other hallmarks of this step include:
- Recognizing your *dharma*, or mission in life, and beginning the path to world service.

- Recognizing the true place of your three Inner Selves as supporters and getting them to integrate and work with you.

- Mastery of unconditional love and forgiveness. You will be presented with lessons that will determine whether you're ready to detach and work with forgiveness to continue on the path to ascension.

    One of the most difficult concepts from which to detach is that sex is love. If you get your validation from sexuality, this can seem as if you're being asked to become celibate. This is far from the truth, as sex is an integral part of life but must not be a focus in life. As you move up through the steps of transformation, you will recognize that it has a place but not at the forefront. As you transform your life, you will find that the desire for sex will diminish somewhat.

    The requirements are fewer but the path becomes narrower and steeper as the discipline becomes more intense. If you lose your intention, you slide back as there is no room for justification, rationalization or mistakes. You must walk your talk, as all illusions are being stripped away.

You are ready yourself to enter the "online Mystery School" as you work through the issues in your life. This book is not about just reading and saying to yourself, "I know that. Been there done that." You must follow the steps and practice the process to achieve enlightenment and transformation. Up to this initiation, you have had control of your reality as you were able to make your choices as to what you wanted to accomplish and how you chose to handle the lessons. You can read this chapter and think you that you have accomplished or can accomplish these lessons, but it will not happen unless you have finished the foundation work required to get to this initiation. From now on, the grading and testing is not up to you. Your teachers from the White Brotherhood will let know how you are progressing on the path.

    The next steps will test your ability to discipline yourself to follow through with the lessons that are placed before you. To advance through this door you must master the minor initiations discussed below.

Dharma

The Law of Dharma has three parts:

1. Discovering the truth of who you are and your personal uniqueness
2. Living that truth and walking your talk through expression of your uniqueness
3. Applying your truth in the form of service.

By now, you have a pretty good handle on your truth. You are in the process of embodying ever-higher aspects of your divinity and have completely ceased operating from Middle Self. You are also realizing that you have unique gifts and creativity to offer the world. And you have a handle on the big picture and can see where you fit in.

So delighted are you in the new self you have discovered that you live it to the full in every moment. You revel in your newfound creativity, playing there as much as other commitments allow. People around you watch your creative expression in awe and are swept along by your sheer enthusiasm, happiness, joy and gusto. Synchronicity becomes the way of life. You do not have to ask for situations to manifest; they just happen as a way of life. I have already mentioned the example of parking places. Once I was driving into a parking lot and my passenger said, "You'd better take this spot because there are none up front."

We were in a remote corner, so I just kept driving, knowing a spot would open up as we arrived in front of our destination. As I rounded the final corner, a car backed out right in front of me. My passenger asked, "How does this happen to you all the time? It never happens for me."

As your life comes into alignment with spirit, synchronicity happens all the time to the point where you never question it.

You also begin to look for ways in which your creativity can serve humanity, with no thought of how you can profit from your service other than to have your daily needs taken care of. Just exercising your creativity is reward enough.

Inner Support Team

You start developing a true connection with Source as they begin to monitor your daily life. Now that you are a spiritual being in a physical body, tasks that seemed hard to handle in the past are now everyday miracles. There are no conflicts in your mind as every part of your mind has the same goal in alignment. You can get mad if you need to make a point, but it never degenerates into anger as you're in total control of your mind. You will begin to notice that people will show up at the perfect time in your world to help you forward in your journey. Sometimes it will seem as if they received a message to be there for you at an appointed time even though you did not make the appointment.

Discipline becomes easier as you can follow through with commitments without much interference from your Middle Self. Unification of all three selves and alignment of goals at all levels of the mind now begin to come to together so you can focus on peace, happiness, harmony and joy. In the past, you had to focus in and meditate to make contact with your Source. As you work through the following initiations, you will find that you no longer need to meditate to make your connection with Source as you have what amounts to a high-speed Internet hookup with instant contact. It's as if you're tuned in all the time. When this happened to me, it was if I was being monitored. When I would not listen or I would overlook something in a session with a client, they began ringing my ear as if I had a phone line connected all the time. At first, it was irritating to be under such scrutiny all the time, but now it proves to be an asset in my work because I know that if I'm off the mark, I'll get a call offering advice and help.

Mastery of Unconditional Love and Forgiveness

I have talked with many people who feel they have achieved enlightenment, yet they have not worked through their issues on love. You cannot pass this initiation until you have this mastered this minor initiation. We describe it as "minor" as it is within a major initiation, but it's one the most important steps on your spiritual journey. This lesson begins in the first initiation and follows us until we get it. The first step is working out our issues with parents. Very few people have grown to adulthood without issues with parents. We may assume that we survived the growing-up period without many conflicts with our parents because we cannot remember them. That alone is the signal that something happened that you're suppressing.

The less we can remember from our childhood the more that we need to bring the issues up and clear them. I have had many clients describe to me a reasonably good childhood only to find that they had suppressed all the negatives into denial-of-denial in their Subconscious Mind when we begin to access the records from the past.

The most telling indicator is to test people to check if they love themselves and can receive love. In a few seconds, this basic test will reveal all about their childhood. If we test strong on muscle testing (kinesiology), then we love ourself, provided that other conflicts do not misguide the testing. If we test strong to receiving love, then we can receive love. In my practice, only one in 500 people test positive. The problem lies in our ability to understand how our mind interprets sensory input. Our mind will decide how it feels about every input presented to us, no matter how we react or respond consciously. We are not aware that our database is open and receives continuous input from our thoughts, feelings and sensory input that come to us from the physical world or the unseen world of other dimensions. The challenge is to be able to access the level of our Subconscious Mind that holds the denial and denial-of-denial files. There are also are past and future time-line files that hold accumulated information. Your mind backs up its operating files when you are sleeping everyday. If we could listen to all the feedback from every level of our being, we could explain why each incident happens to us.

To illustrate this point, we must go back to the words of Lao-tse. In this paradox, he explains why we get lost in our comprehension of basic ideology. "Gravity is the root of lightness; stillness is the ruler of movement. The Tao in its regular course does nothing and so there is nothing which it does not do. My words are easy to know, and very easy to practice; but there is no one in the world able to know and able to practice them."

As with Socratic thinking, in Taoist thought, the highest step to which thought can lead to is to know that we do not know. "To know and yet [to accept] that we do not know is the highest attainment. Not to know [and yet think] that we know is a disease."

How true this is and yet we live in a self-righteous controlling mindset, thinking we know all about ourselves when we haven't even "popped the hood" on our mind. As Lao-tse puts it, "The Tao that can be trodden is not the enduring and unchanging Tao. The name that can be named is not the enduring and unchanging name. We look at it and we do not see it and we name it 'Equitable.' We listen to it, and we do not hear it, and we name it 'Inaudible.' We try to grasp it, and do not get a hold of it and we name it 'Subtle.' With these three qualities, it cannot be made the subject of description; hence we blend them together and obtain 'The One.' "

The final statement on knowing by Lao-tse is, "He who knows does not [care to] speak [about it]. He who [wants to] speak about it does not know it."

Harking back to the example of Hari-Kan-Baba, he would not let people follow him nor would he offer any basic comments about his philosophy unless asked. He did not preach nor did he try to save people from themselves. He said, "It is up to you to recognize and understand your path in life. I may have the path for you to follow but you have to do the work. I cannot do it for you."

This brings us to the dualistic western philosophy in which we think we know when we don't, yet we trudge forward in life, bumping into obstacles on our path (lessons), yet we blame our missteps on others. We create it all yet we do not accept it, so we project it on someone else so that we can avoid taking responsibility. We think we are enlightened, yet when we must pass the basic tests of enlightenment, we are unable to. We will not pass this initiation until we come to the point of knowing that we are responsible for everything. The more we think we know, the less we really know.

Taking the "love test" is based on a simple process described in Eric Fromm's book *The Art Of Loving: An Inquiry Into The Nature Of Love.* Written in 1956, it's small in size and only 133 pages. Back in 1956, it was a breakthrough book that so impressed me that in 1962 I wrote a college term paper on it. Fromm wrote: "Love is the answer to the problem of human existence because it has disintegrated in western contemporary society." I quickly assimilated his premise but the word "love" brought up fear in me and I could not understand why. Understanding the concepts did not help me because something in me was blocking my ability to love myself or express love. The book explained what I did not understand about love, yet I was unable to put what he said into actual use until 1979. Then making the whole concept of love a functional aspect of my life took another ten years.

Try this simple test of your ability to be with yourself and not let other processes to block your ability to allow feelings and thoughts to rise. For a period of one hour, let anything that comes to you open up, without blocking it in any way. Find a room with as few distractions as possible. Make sure there is no outside interference, such as a radio, TV, CD player, or pictures on the wall that could take your attention off of yourself. Do not meditate or allow yourself to go to sleep even if your Middle Self suggests this to you. Sit in this room on the floor or in a chair for at least one hour. If you can sit still with yourself for a full hour and allow any feeling or thoughts to come up without any outside distractions you are beginning to learn how to love yourself.

Although Fromm was born in 1900, he had a very workable view that would apply to our society today. In 1956 when his book was written, the world was relatively peaceful, with much fewer fear-based distractions than we have now. Fromm wrote that, "We fill ourselves with so many distractions we do not know who we are. We have lost ourselves."

The way to find ourselves is through unconditional love and forgiveness, as Fromm wrote almost fifty years ago. Fromm wrote three other best sellers that also had an impact on me: *The Sane Society*, *Man For Himself* and *Escape from Freedom*. In addition to being a psychologist, he was quite a philosopher, with a vast knowledge of the philosophers of every culture. If people could have followed his recommendations, we might live in a different world today. But, having ignored the prophets of the past, why should we listen to those of today?

There are more people on the path to enlightenment today than there were in 1950s and more information about transformation is being written today than in the 1950s but, for some reason, we are still in a downward spiral of devolvement. Why? We continue to be caught up in control, competition, manipulation, blame, resentment, avoidance, and illusion. Most of the world continues to believe in wars of liberation that are nothing short of blatant acts of aggression and control, made more palatable by a steady diet of violence in TV programs and movies. We are simply not facing the situations that are continually placed before us and not learning from the lessons they bring. This cuts across the board, from personal relationships, to terrorism, to love and to forgiveness.

If a cross-section of the population were asked, "Do you love yourself and are you able to express that love?" most would probably say yes, but is that true? Almost always not true. Why? Because most people *want* to believe that they are capable of loving and being loved, but usually they're incapable of neither. In the last 20 years of working with thousands of clients and attendees at my workshops and seminars, I have found less than 25 who are able to love themselves. (This not a percentage, but an actual number).

Tragically, most people have their belief about love in denial so they do not recognize who or where they are on their life's path. Most people do not know if they were wanted as babies or how they were treated as a child because that information is locked up. Very few have dealt with the issues of their life when they were growing up. Some people do not even feel they have any issues to deal with since all these issues are suppressed and stuffed into denial. Accessing the files for these people is very hard because they cannot conceive what could be missing, having no concept what is in denial-of-denial. To bring up these denial issues would create fear as long-term avoidance is the only way these people can keep their life balanced. If we were to rock the boat, they would see themselves as failures, so to avoid feeling vulnerable, we must keep the past suppressed and can avoid having to face the fear of not being accepted.

Such an honest accurate evaluation may take a practitioner adept at accessing the files that are locked up in denial. Hypnosis may work, and readings by psychics may reveal them. Psychotherapy can possibly bring it up, but what do we do with it once we find out what it is? My other books also examine the same concepts, and in view of their importance, we review the process again here so that we can get to the goal of loving ourselves, and giving and receiving love. The central point of recovering your self-worth and self-esteem is *forgiveness*. Resentment and anger will block your ability to love yourself and any-one else. I call the self-qualities of self-esteem, self-worth and self-confidence "cluster qualities" as you will never achieve one of them alone. They always travel together.

You never lost these qualities; they were simply written over by your primary caregivers during your childhood. Once we release the feelings and programs from childhood, we can rewrite your life script. Quite often, when the truth of your childhood is released, this revelation will bring an emotional release. Many of my clients went through childhood never having received love and acceptance, nor had a model that would show them what unconditional love is. As a result, they have no love program in their data base. Without that in their memory, they cannot express love or feel love, so they will go from relationship to relationship, chasing after this elusive quality without even knowing it, and certainly never finding it.

Fromm's theory was as valid then as it is today. "Love requires knowledge and effort. It is not a sensation that one 'falls into' even though most believe this premise. People are starved for love and all have seen the people who watch endless movies about love stories and listen to trashy songs about love."

The only difference today is that the addiction has turned to violence, an out-picturing that plunges our culture into further degradation. Fromm felt that our culture's challenge was to change its views about love: "Hardly anyone believes that they have anything to learn about *how to love*. Most people see the problem as one of *being loved*, of cultivating qualities that will attract love and help one to be lovable. They follow several paths, such as becoming successful, acquiring money and wealth, and building social position. The next focus is becoming desirable to the opposite sex by cultivating one's body and dress. Many will build their manners and ability to be conversational and inoffensive. As one can see, this concept of love then is a false assumption, the challenge being to find the object rather than build the faculty. People think that to love is simple, but that finding the right object to love—or be loved by—is difficult. In the 20th century, the romantic love object became a concept to pursue. In the past, relationships were set up almost as a contractual agreement between families. Very little thought was given to a person's desires."

Fromm's third assumption was again that people assume they have nothing to learn about love because of their initial experience of *falling in love* and the state of being in love: "The first intimacy will lead to a most exhilarating experience when one lets down the walls between them break down, especially to the isolated person who has never felt closeness and oneness of another person. This intimacy usually leads to sexual contact that people describe as making love. These relationships do not build lasting qualities as the object concept does not build lasting relationships.

"This attitude that there is nothing to learn about love leads to the belief that there is nothing easier than to love, and continues to be the prevalent concept about love in spite of the overwhelming evidence to the contrary. There is hardly any enterprise, activity, business, or endeavor that begins with such tremendous hopes and expectation, and yet fails. If this were the case in any other activity, we would be eager to find and investigate the causes for the failure, yet very little is done. In most situations, we would give up the process and find another method to do it better. In the case of love, we have not done either as it is impossible. There have been very few studies to investigate and study the failures to find an adequate method to avoid the breakdowns.

"The only way to change the path is to study the meaning of love. Living is an art, and love is part of that art. If one is to learn and become proficient at the art, one has to study the process. It is divided into two parts; mastery of the theory and then mastery of the practice. How does one become proficient at any craft or profession? You can study the theory, facets, methods and practices before you enter and begin your work in the field of your choice but will that lead to success? The third requirement to become successful in any endeavor is your devotion to it. You can learn the theoretical concepts but it is your *intent to succeed* in the practice of your choice that governs your success. These concepts are very important in every aspect of life so we teach people how to become successful in every aspect of life except love."

Fromm's main contention was that people do not understand self and are willing to follow the philosophies, religions and beliefs of others without validating whether they will work for them. He chronicles how religious dogmas were created and how they affect cultures in the present. He even quoted Karl Marx: "The philosophers have interpreted the world in different ways. The task is to transform it."

Western religion developed dogma rather than the tolerance that the philosophers were writing about. They set out endless arguments about dogmatic formulations and intolerance of the nonbeliever or heretic. This led to the concept of *believing in God* as the main aim of religious concepts rather than *knowing God*. Then they introduced a savior who, they claimed, would absolve them of their sins. This illusion led us away from the concept of transformation so that we can aspire to accept the presence God within, and instead placed the hierarchy of the church between man and God. Noted philosopher Karl Jung stated in 1925 that he did not *believe* in God because he knew God as a working force in his life. His claim that the presence of God was within shocked many religious writers of his day.

In Chinese religious development, the God-within concept was to lead to tolerance: "If the right thought is not the ultimate truth and not the path to salvation, there is no reason to fight others whose thinking has arrived at different formulations."

Eastern and mystical thought focused on transforming man to a more loving, tolerant being and deepening one's knowledge of self, whereas Western religion was about developing separation, with its dogma and intolerance.

Since we are on this path back to the Godhead, where did we go astray and lose our love and forgiveness? As conquerors have tried to control and take over weaker cultures, this malaise has spread throughout the planet. Even Eastern thought is often eschewed in the very cultures that gave birth to it. in Every culture on the planet now suffers from devolution. Again, what happened to love, forgiveness and tolerance? Since GOD is love, where did we lose the basic appreciation of this? And would people today even be willing to spend the time to study love, forgiveness and tolerance so they could become more successful in relationships and other areas of life?

Where does that put humanity on the path to transformation, evolvement and enlightenment? Our first lesson is working on our own misdirection and clearing our issues on love, forgiveness and tolerance so that we can find the path. We have arrived at this step by working through the lessons, but we will not graduate from this initiation until we pass the minor initiations on love, forgiveness and tolerance.

People seem very attached to their romantic concepts about love even though they are not workable. Romantic love is not love at all, but relationship addiction. As Fromm stated: "[What people call] love is looking for the object to love or be loved by."

Popularly, it is trying to find the object who will give us attention and validate our existence. When that other person ceases to excite us and provide the attention, validation and acceptance we need, we dump them and try to find another exciting romantic relationship that provides the acceptance, sex and attention that we need. On the other hand, those suffering from fear of intimacy will keep everyone at arm's length as they fear closeness. In most cases, such people had overpowering parents who abused them and denied them intimacy.

Working with love, forgiveness, tolerance has formed the basis of my practice over the last two decades. I recently replayed a tape from a 1979 Paul Solomon workshop I attended, on which he said: "Love is the X-factor in healing."

In his recent book and tape set, *Spiritual Solutions For Every Problem*, Wayne Dyer says exactly the same thing that Paul Solomon did 20 years ago and that I have been teaching for over 15 years. I hope that with Dyer's recognition, this point will reach into the mainstream.

To recover self-love and allow yourself to be open to love takes courage, especially if you have never experienced true love or developed fear of commitment and intimacy. In my practice, I have found that there are four types of relationships:

1. *Relationships of convenience.* This is the largest grouping, in which the couple has little in common except agreement that this seems the right thing to do. This is an acceptable way around the taboo on casual sex. Both partners want a roommate or someone to be with. This may actually work if they discover what love is and can grow into it. Some will migrate to group four after working out their issues. (In our case, we took over twenty years to enter group four and could easily have ended up in divorce three times. We chose to work out the issues rather than run away from them. We were aware that if you run, the same lesson will confront you, only in a new relationship. You cannot escape the lessons as they will haunt you until you get them, understand then and clear the issues.)

2. *Unfinished lessons with parents.* In this next largest group, couples seek out people who fit their needs to work out unresolved issues with parents. If we do not recognize why we are in such a relationship, it will be full of conflict. When the unresolved conflicts get out of hand, the couple often ends up in separation. (We moved into this group when we started to understand the lessons we were facing in our relationship.)

3. *Karmic relationships.* A flash or the spark will draw this couple together. I discovered this when I once saw a spark in someone's eyes that seemed to draw me in. A reading on the effect revealed that past life karma was drawing me to that person. Such attractions, compulsions even, may seem magical but, if you do not understand the karmic aspect, they will result in disaster unless the karma is cleared. In my work with clients, I have found that once we clear the karma, the other person drops out of the client's life about 85 percent of the time because they had been drawn together purely to resolve the karma. These relationships usually end up in separation as the spark turns into a roaring conflagration.

4. *Relationships based on common goals and ideals.* This group comprises about 5 percent of all relationships. They do not involve taking from each other, as neither partner has any needs to fill. They complement each other as they support each other with an interdependent relationship.

I urge my client couples to evaluate which group they operate from and then work to clear the issues so that they can graduate to group four, the only group that has successful relationships, the other three being dysfunctional. If you were one of the fortunate children from a functional family, stepping through the sequence will be easy as you have the required data in your file. (Make your evaluation honest. Do not try to delude yourself, as only one person in a thousand is from a functional family).

The process of building a solid foundation for transformation can take many years, depending on your willingness and the resistance your mind has to the process:

1. The first step is to set your desire and intent to succeed in this process.

2. The next step is opening to an awareness that what happened in the past can be brought up without fear or vulnerability and released.

3. We must recognize our parents did their best, no matter how we were treated. We must not hold onto resentment, judgment or anger toward them, as this is the first essential step in releasing ourselves from the past. If we have an illusion that we were treated acceptably and we were not, then we must come to understand this and face it. The only way we can recover our lost self is come to the truth of who we are and release all of our caregivers, and love and forgive them no matter what they did to us.

4. To build a solid foundation to launch your spiritual journey, you must release the programs that have been locked into your body, as all the traumatic childhood programs will be locked into cellular memory. Almost all beliefs about emotional trauma that are held in our mind for more than six months will turn into programs that are locked into cellular memory. (My book *Your Body Is Talking; Are You Listening?* describes the process to take care of this.)

5. Along with releasing with programs from cellular memory, we must also clear the sub-personalities from Middle Self. At the same time, we must reclaim our power by taking responsibility for all our actions. We then can delete and erase autopilot. (This minor initiation should have been handled in the fifth step but, if you continue to recreate emotions and sub-personalities, then you will get stuck in this initiation until you clear them permanently.

6. When all the minds become aligned in purpose and goals, High Self, Middle Self, and Low Self start to align also.

7. If we allow ourselves to dwell on any negative thoughts or feelings, and let people throw us off our center, then we still have
work to do. We have not yet passed the tests on clarity of mind
and serenity. We can go no further until we do. The temptations
on these issues will continue to confront us until we can pass.

8. This is a pass/fail initiation. There is no room for justification or
rationalization. You either pass the test or go back and try again
until you *do* get it.

8

The Eighth Initiation: The First Step Into Earth Mastery

The eighth door will not open until you have overcome the lower nature temptations of the previous step. In a prior initiation, we began our transition into "the possible human." In this initiation, we enter the realm of the *meta-human*, or one who lives by spiritual principles.

To those on the third dimension, it seems that the feats performed by meta-humans are miraculous but, when we enter the fifth dimension and release ourselves from 3-D duality, everything will become accepted as a mechanical effect. We know that we can put the appropriate causes in motion and what the effect will be before it happens.

Other characteristics of the eighth initiation are:

- You knowingly allow the universe and Christ Consciousness to express through you. You do not have to be aware of it; you *are* it. We must be clear that we are not referring to Jesus Christ of the Christian faith. *Christos* is a Greek word that was applied to people in mystery schools who had attained a certain level of competence and exhibited knowledge of the course of study. This term was used long before Christians applied it to their teacher.

- You do not need to be in a special place, dress in special clothes or demonstrate your powers. You have no need to impress people with who you are and what you can do. You are just who you are, and your personal power, happiness, joy and enthusiasm are obvious to observers.

- As the final door of temptation, this step presents opportunities to experience and check your level of inner peace, joy, happiness, self worth, "alrightness," abundance, self-love, self-approval, and

127

self-esteem, and the absence of fear and negative emotions. Until you have mastered all your emotions, and the need for control, judgment, justification, conditional love and validation, you will remain in this step. Outside validation is not required.

- Miracles are mechanical effects that happen without concentration. Everything in your life begins to fall into place with very little effort. In the beginning, accepting that everything happening to me in this step proved difficult. I kept questioning if this was going to continue. When it did continue for over a year, I finally accepted that I was in the right place.

- When you complete the eighth initiation, you, the meta-human, emerges. At this point, what appears to be miracles becomes a way of life. The flow of your life sets up a pattern where you need do nothing yet things still happen. You just seem to be in the right place at the right time for every event in your life.

Working with Christed Energies

Christ Consciousness is a particular frequency of unity within the matrix of All That Is. Because your energy exists at all dimensions up to the Godhead, you exist at the Christed level and, at that level, you are fully aware of your connection. In this step, you bring that awareness to conscious mind.

You have *always* been a Christed being; now it's time to take your conscious awareness up to that level. By now, you've transmuted the dark, dense energy of the lower personality, so it's time to rise like an untethered balloon.

As you become your Christed Self, the first things you notice are an expanded *knowing*, and the brilliance of your own light and love going out in all directions through the matrix.

How will you act in this state? Your every action will be of perfect love and power. You will immediately note any limitation and transcend it. You will dissolve any conflict with the light of your love, and dissolve any disease with the light of your truth to reveal the underlying thought or emotion. Your words will be loving and compassionate. They will never undermine the Divinity of yourself or others. Your words are always uplifting, supporting and inspiring, and always the truth of things.

Expecting Miracles

By this step, you are living your authentic self wholly, enjoying each moment and fully in the Now. You recognize the limitations of the narrow Western rational approach of "I'll believe it when I see it" that locks people into the five senses and intellectual and emotional responses to the outside world.

You realize that daily life emerges from a far richer and deeper inner reality, which you begin to work with directly, letting your intent program your life before it confronts you. In other words, you expect miracles in your life.

You rely more on your intuition and less on your senses and intellect to solve problems and let you know what is true. Clairvoyance and clairsentience become more highly tuned and precognition delivers data about what will happen in the future. Based on this, your choices may *seem* irrational but events reveal them to be wise choices. More and more, you trust and expect that data to be there for you, and you skillfully interweave it with data that is received by more rational means. You recognize that intuitive prophecy is for the time and situation of that particular day. Depending the circumstances around the issue or situation, it may change the following day. The main issue is that you do not have to be right about any situation. All you need do is report what you receive.

You also learn that dreams are a window into the inner reality from which daily life springs, and use them to program that reality. You can change the scenario you receive with lucid dreaming by reprogramming the future reality by visualizing a new picture of reality. What other people call "coincidence," you call *synchronicity* and delight in how your teachers, angels, soul and GOD Source arrange things with your spirit to work for your advantage. However, some people may resent or be envious of your seeming success with everything.

The Meta-human

As a meta-human, you easily perform feats that normal people consider miraculous. However, you do not advertise or demonstrate your skills just to impress or be recognized. Your abilities are obvious to observers, who are attracted to you for what you radiate, yet you have no need for another's acceptance or validation. Other qualities are:

- *You flow spontaneously.* As your Higher Self unveils its flight plan, you tackle every part of it with enthusiasm, gusto and joy.

- *Mastery of all body functions and emotional responses.* This means that you are in perfect physical health because your auric fields are in perfect health. (It is problems with the aura that allow disease by compromising the body's operation and immune system. Also, dysfunctional thought-forms and beliefs will appear in the aura two weeks before they manifest in body's cellular structure. Negative thought forms contribute to health problems.)

- *Body, mind and spirit act in unison now.* There is no separation in the self, and you experience unity of spirit within, as the Higher Self, Middle Self and Lower Self begin to merge into one and become one with the spiritual self.

- *You live outside the rules.* You follow your spirit and Higher Self exclusively and with every breath. Your only desire is world service through co-creating your vision of heaven-on-earth.

- *All your relationships are lucid, love-based, mutually supportive co-creations.* You accept people as they are. There are no conflicts or confrontations as you recognize other spiritual immaturity. You do not try to control or manipulate others into your viewpoints. You accept their views and choose not to argue about anything.

- *You are authentic in every moment.* You *never* manipulate yourself to win approval. If others object to this, you see it as *their* problem, not yours. You live in freedom, without compromise, saying, "What others think of me is none of my business." You honor their pictures of reality as input to you, accepting that they may be true for them but not necessarily for you.

- *You do only what you love and what brings you joy.* You are supported at whatever level of abundance you choose. You are entitled to wealth and can accumulate it if you choose to. Poverty and survival are not appropriate life styles for a spiritual being.

- *You accept everyone as soul-incarnates.* You treat all as equal but different, here with their piece of the big puzzle. You have no reason to change, fix or heal others, but support them in *their* attempts to change or heal themselves.

- *You revel in the Grand Mystery.* You are comfortable with what you do not know, and confident that all will be revealed on a need-to-know basis. You are open and accepting of other ideas and concepts. You use whatever works for you.

9

The Ninth Initiation: Transfiguration

A t the risk of repetition, you can read the material, practice the exercises and do the meditations and communications, but you do not make the decisions from here on. There is no room for illusion as you have come to a point where you will be provided with accurate effective guidance but, unfortunately, many false prophets and spirit guides masquerade as "the true source" out there in this spiritual jungle so discretion is essential.

Many writers have chronicled the ascended masters of the past and written very complex and esoteric books on ascension that give detailed specifics on what to do, yet I have never met anyone who has achieved ascension based such channeled treatises as the Alice Bailey works. Of course, there are misguided people who will think that they are reaching this level, and there will be misguided spirit guides who will validate that they are at this level, yet the proof is in one's daily service to humanity and the planet. An Earth master's behavior is obvious if you have the eyes to see and ears to hear.

In this initiation, you demonstrate your ability to make the shift to Earth mastery as you have achieved the level of meta-human. Up until now, you have been in your internship as an apprentice Earth master. Once you pass this initiation, you will never slide back. When you get to this step, you have passed all the major lessons; this is the end of your transformation and you are ready for transfiguration, or ascension.

This and next two initiations test your ability to make this shift. Transfiguration is not just a shift in your consciousness but a complete change in your body structure and behavior. Your eating habits and sleeping times will change. You will sleep less and accomplish more in your waking hours. Some people have reported cutting their need for sleep to three to four hours a day, and even only two hours a day for short periods. This is one of the examples of our level in this process of ascension.

You begin to sleep at the delta level (as low as 5Hz) as the pressure, conflict and stress are removed from your life. Aa a meta-human, you are stress-free. Everything just washes over you without sticking to you since you have learned how to function in a stressful environment without becoming part of it.

We must learn to eat lighter because heavy food will increase our body's stress level as it cannot function at a high level of consciousness while digesting low frequency food. The frequency of our consciousness begins to pull that of our physical body to operate at 12 – 20Hz. The challenge is to allow our body to function at it highest effective level. To do so, we will need to focus on a diet that includes as much raw food as possible, and cut primary sugar down to as little as possible, which means no white flour products of any kind.

Red meat also draw the body down as it is hard to digest. Even worse, the adrenaline and fear present at the time of slaughter are embedded in the flesh. Fish can be a staple, but poultry should be limited as much as possible. You are trying to wean your body down to essential food sources in readiness for the twelfth initiation, where you will reduce your consumption to almost one quarter of its level when you started this process.

As our body becomes lighter and lighter, it will rise in frequency, which will cause it to become less dense until it finally becomes transparent as you pass through door twelve. At that point, you will no longer need food as you have ascended into a spirit being.

Your teachers control the ninth to the twelfth doors and coach you at each step of the way, monitor progress, and admonish you to not show off your abilities. Once you pass this first real step in ascension, you will never backslide. Source Self now directs your life, as there is no separation from GOD Source. As a result, you now control your life path and become a "meta-human."

Source-self, or God-self

This is your spiritual essence, and not something you *do* but what you *are* at the highest level of your being. It has no separation from, and is one with, All That Is. It never tries to fix anything, knowing that all is in divine order.

As your Lower Self, Middle Self, and Higher Self blend into your Spirit Self, your soul is now enjoined as part of the whole so that you can now respond as Source Self. Your knowledge is at hand at all times so that you can function at the highest level of consciousness. There are no conflicts as you can resolve everything with no need to control or have authority over it. Everything either works for you or you just let it go by without confrontation.

Your Source-self is whole, complete, and a powerful force on the planet. It knows that its presence alone is enough to change the game. In the three remaining initiations, you become this aspect of yourself but, by then, you won't need a book to tell you how! There will be people who will disagree with you at times, but you do not even respond because "you know that you know."

Working with the Hierarchy

In these final steps, you will be working closely with master teachers, ascended masters and the angelic realm, but your work will be effective only if you do not put them on a pedestal. They are in no way superior to you; they just have broader perspective as they are not in body, as do you during the interval between your incarnations on Earth. Apart from needing Earth plane density for your ongoing evolution, you took physical form down here to earn the right to intervene in earthly matters without worrying about the prime directive against unbidden interference. By incarnating, you've "paid your dues" and can operate directly in matters on the planet. As we have said before, the only reason you are on the physical plane is to clear up and work out your karmic files in the Akashic Record.

Unfortunately we cannot edit our Akashic Record when we are on the spiritual plane and preparing to incarnate, but we can review it with the Lords of Karma and discuss the remaining lessons we must undertake. As spirit/soul (who we are as a being), we choose the lessons and the people appropriate for us to work these lessons out with. The Lords of Karma give us a list of possible matches for parents, and we meet with their High Selves (souls/spirits) and decide who we want to incarnate with. Once we make that decision, our soul/spirit sets up the flight plan and the rest is history.

The challenge we fail to meet is being able to hold onto the directions in our flight plan. Over the thousands of years, we have built in a program that causes us to lose contact with the flight plan, even though it's in our soul/spirit files in our Holographic Mind. On incarnating, most people lose their flight plan before they get in their body. A few get in touch with some of their lessons but very few get to the second initiation.

When you have progressed beyond the second initiation, you become aware that there is a plan for your life but, for most people, life involves struggling with suffering and lack of abundance. When you approach this ninth initiation, you know how to coach people in changing their lives so that they do not have to live in survival. (There is a catch here though: do not mistakenly believe that you can teach them, as this is an inside job. They must be willing to commit and discipline themselves to begin this spiritual journey. You cannot do it for them, but only show them the way and introduce them to the steps.)

As your life becomes focused and you can see your way clearly, you are now ready to become a world teacher. This is still a choice. You are not *required* to do so, as this is an individual process. You may just want to graduate to the Brotherhood of Light as the next step after ascension, and join their internship program. You will need to demonstrate your abilities as a light being as you will be assigned a position similar to the Angelic realm. When you pass this initiation, you will then be able to graduate to master teacher and be assigned students to follow on the physical plane. The beings from the White Brotherhood will be advising you monitoring your work.

10

The Tenth Initiation: Crucifixion

It seems as if you are going through the final temptation, as every one seems to be avoiding you and leaving you alone when you need help. Feeling as if you're failing, you scramble for security, isolated in a vast wasteland, deserted in your quest. You will go through the same initiations that all other masters have done in their ascent into Earth mastery. The test is to see if you can handle the isolation, which can feel like the "forty days in the wilderness."

However, you recognize that you need no one to validate you and you are tested to ensure that you can be a true teacher who can stand on your knowledge and experience. It seems as if you are being persecuted, as everything feels as though it's falling in on you. You will go through the test and the lessons until your teacher is satisfied you have arrived at wholeness and forged the ability to function in this state. It may feel as if you're going through another dark night of the soul, only more intense. The Crucifixion is a major/minor initiation all wrapped up in one continual challenge, in which one test leads into the next:

- Ability to handle all negative emotions, conflicts and confrontations.

- Having financial programs collapse and being able to move forward without fear knowing that this is just a test. The funds or programs will correct themselves when you demonstrate your ability to handle the fear of loss. If funds are lost, they will come back in another form.

- Feeling not accepted, recognized or respected.

- Not being supported, or being taken advantage of.

- Believing in your guidance and finding out you were not clear and were receiving faulty feedback.

- Feeling almost stranded, yet knowing that you will be able to find the way out, such as having vehicles break down, yet knowing this is just a test to check your strength to handle the situation.
- Having people criticize your work or what you're writing or teaching, just to see how you will respond.
- Working very hard to create or make a project happen and then have it fail.
- Various illnesses and diseases that try to bring you down, but you recognize this is just a test of your ability to know that you are not affected by them, so you are able to heal them immediately.

During this initiation, all the above situations happened to me and others I have talked with. It seemed as if it would never end but, once we are able to handle each one without fear or insecurity, the testing magically stops. Our ability to not let the tests rattle us or create fear gives us control of them because that allows us to decide to stop them anytime we wish. Nobody can teach this to you as you must come to peace with yourself knowing that, when you can prove your ability, it will stop. When this is over, then you begin to move out of this initiation. I was in this step for many years, as this is the last step where you release all your karma. It's best, however, to release as much of your karma *before* you get to this step, as karma intensifies the lessons. You cannot go to the next step with any karma in your file, so it will all come up in this initiation.

Other aspects include:
- Personal consciousness disappears as you let go of the physical/personality self (who you have been). This is one of the primary aspects that the master teachers are testing in this initiation. Personality self must be dropped from your consciousness in order to make any further steps.
- The Low Self, Middle Self and High Self complete their unification with spirit/soul.
- Spirit now directs your life as your God Self emerges to take control of your life.

11

The Eleventh Initiation: Resurrection

Your spirit becomes the risen Christ as you recognize that this last initiation is the final initiation to test your ability. You become an Earth Master with the choice of ascension. Graduating to this initiation is a great relief as the pressure is off and you can rest in knowing that you do not have go through the Dark Night of the Soul again to prove your abilities. You now have been accepted as an Earth Master.

You live in the knowing that "God and I are one." The Presence of GOD becomes your moment-by-moment reality as you reach out for the final initiation. The next step in journey is the most difficult one as you recognize who you *really* are. You have no need for followers or supporters, although people naturally support you without you having to ask for anything.

This initiation is a slow maturing, as you must practice all the universal laws that govern ascension until your master teacher feels you have mastered them. This may take many years.

I have been in this initiation for three years now, and was relieved, as getting through the tenth door involved many rigorous tests. My teachers will not give me a time frame for how long this step may take, but I am enjoying it because everything seems to work perfectly as long as I stay on track.

12

The Twelfth Initiation: Ascension

There are no initiations at this door, as you have accomplished all of the initiations by the time you enter. You will have to go before the Brotherhood of Light for an evaluation of your achievements and your level of ability in relation the initiations that you have passed. They will allow you to ascend from the physical plane but, before you return as a teacher, you must past the tests they will place before you. You have achieved the level of an Earth Master at this point. To enter the Ascended Master Mystery School to become a master teacher, you must pass all the tests on detachment from fear and all the other major and minor lessons. This is the next step on the path to the Godhead.

In this step, you will be assigned to help people on the Earth plane from a distance, i.e., you will not have direct contact with them. The next step is becoming a Master Teacher, where you will be assigned students to work with on the earth plane. If the White Brotherhood and the beings from GOD Source feel you have mastered all the universal laws and spiritual principles, they will work with you so that you can return to anywhere in the universe to teach as an ascended master. Then you can dematerialize your physical body to a light body and rematerialize at will.

You will not be allowed to do this, however, in the unlikely event that you use it to attract attention. By the time you reach this door, you will have no need or desire to tell others of your accomplishment; it will just be evident by your actions and behavior. However, some people will recognize who you are, but others will resent you because they see the acceptance you receive.

A Cautionary Tale

When you move from *apprentice* Earth Master to Earth Master, you can move from spirit in a light body to a manifested body on demand. You choose what you do next. For example, you may choose to become a galactic teacher as an ascended being.

Do not to make any steps without confirmation from the teacher. Falling back can be devastating and your teachers will not directly support you until you have gone through the first eight doors. *Do not make any assumptions that you can ascend without confirmation by your teachers. It could cost you your life and put you back on the cycle of return.*

Two of my clients decided that they could ascend by meditation. One of them spent a full day meditating using a technique she'd learned at a weekend Ascension Celebration at Mt. Shasta, California in 1995. She left her body through the solar plexus (third) chakra, which resulted in the death of her body. What she didn't know was that the third chakra is a one-way door, with no way to open it from the outside.

I had heard that the same thing happened to some other people who attended the conference, which gives us some insight to the self-appointed teachers of enlightenment and ascension. Most earth plane teachers do not consider the consequences of their teaching and/or counseling as can see from the prior example. Through their misinformation on ascension, they created karmic contracts with the people who ended up placing themselves back on the reincarnational cycle.

We are responsible for all information and material we teach or provide students. We could evade our responsibility by saying that it's up to them to research and/or evaluate the material they receive, but it doesn't work that way. Most of the time, people accept information at face value, assuming that their teachers are accurate and honest. We are totally responsible for any and all information we provide to people. They are looking to us as authorities on our subject and assume we know what we're talking about, so most people take the information verbatim. We are playing with fire if we put out misinformation that causes misdirection, pain or suffering in people's path to enlightenment. We will create karma with those we interact with if the material affects them adversely.

Afterthoughts: Summary of Ascension

If you have read the book and have decide to start this spiritual journey of enlightenment, transformation, and transfiguration that leads to ascension, you must recognize that this is not a totally self-directed course of study. Yes, you do cause and create your own lessons, but much of your lesson plan is not accessible to you until you're able to access your flight plan.

We do correct our own lesson plans (i.e., karma), but quite often we need help from a person who can read our book more clearly than we can. Programs that are locked into denial and denial-of-denial cannot be accessed very easily. Also, we can have programs locked into past time lines and future time lines.

Hypnosis often will not work to access past life programs if they have attached karmic contracts or karmic agreements. The mind will lock up traumatic experiences. We must go to the Akashic Record and request the files from the record keeper so that they can be read and released. We cannot simply release karma without understanding the lessons behind it. We must also understand that forgiveness is one of the primary keys to releasing karma. When the karma is released, you must also claim Grace so that it will be cleared from the Akashic Record.

Quite often, we find that people deviate from the flight plane they filed and take a detour that avoids their intended lessons. Correcting the course may take some work. If we choose to change our flight plan, we must file another with the Lords of Karma.

Free Will

Another controversy involves the subject of free will. The GOD Sources states there is semantic misinterpretation here. Universal laws and spiritual principles are quite clear and specific, and following them curtails your free will options. Of course, we do have free choice to take any path we wish, at any time we wish, even if it violates our flight plan, but we must be willing to take responsibility for the consequences of that. Unfortunately, if we are unaware of its existence or how to access it, we do not know that we are deviating from our flight plan. Quite often, we are blocked off from effective guidance by inner and outer shadows. Our mind can contain many programs and sub-personalities that will block us from simply remembering who we are or what we're doing, and we must release these as soon as possible.

The Earth plane lessons are before you are to take responsibility and commit to being honest with yourself. The only person you can fool is yourself. The only person who that can direct your life is you. No one is going to provide the path for you. Once you provide the commitment and discipline yourself, your teachers will contact you and provide the guidance.

This is not a complicated process with complex special hierarchical requirements, as some teachers present it. It is very a simple program but it does require willingness to face the issues in your life so that you can get down to the process of transformation.

Use discernment when deciding to follow a teacher or a group, as many impostors masquerade as teachers of ascension but are not walking their own talk. Other teachers are controlled by outside forces or on the wrong track. You can recognize true teachers as they have no need for control or authority. Their lives exemplify their teachings and they walk their talk. Abundance is their right, but they do not charge exorbitant fees, as they know they are provided for and do not need to impress or draw students in to them.

A Cautionary Note

Many people may not want to believe or buy into the following, but it has become a virtual reality in the past year. When Aldous Huxley wrote *Brave New World* 40 years ago, some people called him a visionary, and others called it science fiction. What he described in his book was considered impossible then but it's no longer science fiction as it's happening in the real world today. I added this note to the book as it was going to press as I felt it was important and relevant new information.

I became aware of this material when I was appealing to the White Brotherhood for some protection from an attack by certain alien robot terrorists. Before the September 11 incident, my Harmonizer (see Appendix B) generally protected me from attacks by aliens or the dark forces but, after September 11, I noticed more attacks up to January 2002. After January, however, the intensity and frequency of attacks built up to the point where I was attacked hourly. When I identified the source, I realized we were up against a force that had no fear or concern about human life—soulless robots created by rogue Andromedans. I knew then that we were up against a force of mind controllers and that I needed some help.

My request to the White Brotherhood for help was answered by them assigning guardian angels to me, but without explanation as to what their mission was. I was just glad to get some help and protection so I did not question what they would do for me as long as they could protect me from these alien terrorists. I had an abrupt awakening about a week later when I was again attacked and called on my guardian angels. However, they were not there for me and I had no way to ward off the attack. My head felt as if it was in a vise whose jaws were being tightened. The head pain increased and my solar plexus felt as if it was being pummeled by fists. I had pain in my joints and felt completely lethargic. I was coughing and sneezing, my sinuses were discharging profusely and my vision was affected.

When I finally recognized what was happening, things had advanced so far that I was nonfunctional. I was scheduled on a panel discussion and to present a lecture at a conference later so I called on the Brotherhood of Light to see what had happened. They told me that my guardian angels had become scared and abandoned me, and that no other guardian would volunteer to protect me. I had to go to the White Brotherhood to request another set of guardian angels. This time I asked for an explanation of what happened and whether I should do anything to prevent this in the future? The explanation was totally new information to me.

The White Brotherhood told me this about the Brotherhood of the Light: "Your work is not done when you leave the physical earth plane. You can ascend without passing and detaching from all the small minor initiations. We will allow you to ascend without having mastered fear totally, but that will be your first test when you make the transition to the Brotherhood of the Light. We will interview you and test you to discern whether you have successfully passed all the tests in every initiation. If you have not past all lessons, you will be assigned to "Guardian Angel Remedial School" where you are presented with the lessons and minor initiations that you have not passed in the Apprentice Earth Master Mystery School. You will remain an apprentice Earth Master until you pass all the lessons in this Brotherhood of Light Mystery School.

"The Guardian Angel Remedial School is a residential mystery school where the rules are very strict. You are not allowed the personal freedom to return to the physical plane to teach until you graduate from this school. The main lesson most people do not master on the physical earth plane is fear. You must learn this lesson in order to move from an apprentice Earth Master and graduate to the level of apprentice in the Ascended Master School. You must detach from fear totally so that you can confront it without any withholds. To test this, you are assigned to protect and provide support to an individual on the earth plane. This internship will bring up many lessons you must deal with on your journey."

~ ~ ~

It has been my experience so far that most beings assigned to protect me fail the lesson on fear. Five sets of them have abandoned me without calling on help or informing me what they were going to do despite the requirement that they ask for help or ask the White Brotherhood to be relieved from their assignment so that another set of Guardian Angels can be assigned.

They cannot abandon the person they are assigned to without permission from the White Brotherhood, but my guardians left me open for attack without even letting me know they wanted to leave. The second time it happened, I asked the White Brotherhood, "What can I do to stop this from happening?"

Their response was disconcerting: "These beings are assigned to you randomly. There is no order or special competency test as to who they are. Once they are assigned to you, they must perform the tasks that come before them. When we feel they have learned all the lessons and have passed the tests that are placed before them, they will be allowed to graduate to the next level. At this point, one begins as an apprentice in the Ascended Master Mystery School. After learning the lessons in this school you can ask to return to the earth plane to teach."

My next question was, "What happens to the beings who do not learn the lessons and abandon the person they are assigned to?"

The answer startled me: "As a guardian, when you are assigned to a person and do not finish your assignment, you are given another chance to complete your task. If you fail the test again, you are dropped from the school and returned to the cycle of return."

In other words, we only have two chances to finish our assignment. If we do not complete it, we end up back in the reincarnation cycle and repeat the whole process of transformation. This is a tough school with no room for mistakes. Obviously, the higher you go in the ascension process, the harder it gets to accomplish the final initiation into the White Brotherhood. Ascension is no easy task and few make the grade from what I have observed.

The White Brotherhood's final statement to me was: "When we assign beings to you, we interview them and tell them what they will be expected to do for you. They have the option of refusing the assignment before they begin with you. We assume that if they have made it to this point on the path, they would know what they are up against and whether they want to take the assignment. Passing the final test for initiation into the White Brotherhood is tough so they should know it."

~ ~ ~

This may explain why we have not met up with any teachers from the White Brotherhood. They cannot return to the earth plane until they graduate from the Brotherhood of Light. From what I have been told, less than twenty have made the grade to pass all the tests. Are you ready for this ultimate mystery school?

I have heard some people say, "I have ascended and returned to teach the rest of you." It is obvious that they have not encountered the final lesson with the White Brotherhood, which is to do with walking our talk before making such claims. There are more illusions than there are realities out in the spiritual jungle and many people talk their walk, but can they walk it, too?

Recommended Reading

The books I would recommend reading before beginning this course of study are my books:

>*Your Body Is Talking; Are You Listening?*
>*Becoming a Spiritual Being in a Physical Body*
>*Opening Communication With GOD Source*

Also recommended are books by Wayne Dyer:

>*You'll See it When You Believe it*
>*Real Magic*
>*Spiritual Solutions For Every Problem*

Have a great flight on your Spiritual Journey into the light,
>Art Martin,
>Penryn, CA,
>January 2002

A

The Practice of Neuro/Cellular Repatterning

A Self Healing Process?

We would like to think we can heal ourselves, but after twenty years in the healing field, I know very few who have successfully managed to sidestep the mind's games. Many clients who claim to have cleared these issues themselves have attended a workshop where they learn some self-healing techniques and bingo, they think they can heal themselves. But when we actually access the issues, we find that at a conscious level, they believe they cleared them, but at the reality level, Subconscious Mind disagrees.

Few people listen to their body, or their mind, for that matter. If they did, we would not have so many deranged, dysfunctional, or sick people in our world. If people were aware of what their behavior causes, we would not have so many abused children, crimes and wars.

How about those who have studied alternative healing, are on a path to transformation, and are committed to working out their issues? I have found that more than 50 percent are in denial of many of the issues blocking their progress. What of the many teachers, shamans and therapists who claim to help people out of their past and create a new path to transformation?

All I ask for is documented, pragmatic verification that the process actually works in the longterm. How many people have had life-threatening diseases permanently eliminated from their life? How many people with physical disabilities have been healed so they never have pain again? Did the process help clients to find a long-lasting relationship with a partner? Were clients able to overcome obstacles that blocked financial success? Were they able to overcome fear and anger programs that were causing depression or chronic fatigue?

In the last 20 years, only two practitioners have been willing to give me names of clients I could talk to and verify that they were helped over the long haul. In developing N/CR, I was unable to find a process that would permanently clear my dysfunction. I spent a lot of money on seminars, workshops and therapists who assured me that they could clear my pain. Where does this leave us in our search for the truth in healing?

The human mind in denial is complex and intricate. The programs and sub-personalities deceive us so that they can protect us. Their irrational interpretation makes no sense when looked at logically. After ten years research, I discovered how the mind processes information: it functions as a computer. But how can lay people use this information to heal themselves?

Some clients have been able to make progress once I worked with them to clear the basic programs. Some did not need much help from me because they had been working on themselves for many years and were able to make considerable progress. How did they do it? Willingness to be totally open to change; refusal to blame anyone or anything for the problems that faced them; taking total responsibility for every situation in their life; determination; commitment to their purpose; consistent concentrated effort to follow through with their journey to enlightenment.

Discipline and discernment are the most important qualities in the quest. Denial and illusion will try to trip you up at every turn. Auto-pilot will stop you dead in your tracks by creating the illusion of success.

How much control we have over our lives determines our ability to use self-healing techniques and reclaim our personal power from the Middle Self's sub-personalities that operate auto-pilot. Discernment reveals the many diversions on the path and helps us avoid grasping at anything that looks like it may provide direction. The path is littered with deceivers who genuinely believe that they're providing a service but are so deep in illusion and denial themselves they cannot even see the truth. This is not a judgment; it's an observation based on attending many seminars and workshops, and being a client with many therapists. The key word is discernment: evaluate what the therapist presents and ask many questions. If he or she is defensive, noncommittal or evades your questions, then steer clear. Use your discernment to avoid seeing so-called healers as authority figures because, as such, you may want to believe them. Be skeptical until the proof is before you.

So, can we heal ourselves? Maybe. Often you can get to simple issues that are causing localized pain, but to get to deeply-embedded or locked-in programs that are in denial takes a skilled practitioner. To be able to work on yourself, you must uncover the causes of dysfunction that you want to heal, correct or release. If you are clear on what the issues are, you might be able to access the information with practice. Begin with active meditation that puts you in contact with the Akashic Record.

To use Kinesiology, you must be clear of Middle Self's influence. It always wants to be right and control the process. It will block you from using any technique it cannot control (see below for a clearing process).

Pattern Release Process

This section indicates how to access and release beliefs, programs and sub-personalities:

Symptom: Mental, emotional or physical pain, depression, illness, etc. (obvious or assumed cause)

Record: Base cause, actual interpretation of situation, Subconscious Mind's recording of reaction, activity or situation

Program: Core issue, Subconscious Mind's or Middle Self's sub-personality instructions recorded in computer (how I will handle situation next time).

Pattern: Habitual reaction, the illusion of how I have handled the situation in the past whenever the stimulus arose (addiction, control, justification, denial, authority, distortion, dishonesty, delusion.)

Those who can access this information can work with N/CR themselves, but few people are clear enough to do so. Sometimes, the programs are so strong that they're right on the surface so anyone can recognize them and release them, but most of the time, they're deeply-hidden or in denial, and the deeper they are, the harder it is to locate and access them. Even some clairvoyants and clairaudients cannot read their own book.

Yes, I healed many of my blocks myself, but I could not get to the deeply-buried issues. Ironically, they came up when I was working with my clients and had to deal with them in a session. By putting myself in the affirmation with the client, I was able to release many of my own programs.

You may be able release or relieve a symptom yourself, and achieve remission or release of pain, but this will not cause healing to take place. You are simply manipulating the energy tied up in the neurological pathway, meridian, muscle, organ or tissue. If you do not release the base cause and the core issue, the instructions will eventually cause the pattern to reassert itself when a crisis issue arises in your life.

The Conscious Mind can set up a belief and the soul can understand the process, but if the Subconscious Mind does not release the record from the files and lock up the operating instructions in the archives, the instructions will cause the computer to restore the program. It will continue to do so until the pattern/program/record is recognized, filed and released with love and forgiveness. Then, the original cell imprint can begin operating again, healing all the dysfunctional parts of the cell. The immune system can then regenerate, which allows the T-cells and leukocytes to resume their work. To activate the body's healing ability, the body must be able to access the original blueprint. When the programs are lifted from the cell memory, the body/mind will be able to heal the disease and/or emotional dysfunction.

After twenty years practice with N/CR, I can access almost anything and rewrite the program, thus healing it myself, but with programs and sub-personalities in denial of denial, I still need a practitioner to help me. However, if I cannot locate the cause, I do not get caught up in pride. My desire is to be as clear as quickly as possible, so I am not going to get trapped in the need to be in control or to manipulate the situation so I can look good. I have no need to have someone validate me for how effective I am at healing myself or my clients. Being a know-it-all, being in control, having to be an authority figure, arrogance and resistance do not get us anywhere. I often find these qualities in self-proclaimed "enlightened" people, yet they are unaware of these traits because they are held in denial. True seekers, on the other hand, shine out in their clarity.

The next section provides a format for setting up a session and the use of affirmations. The basis of all this work is to rewrite the software in the mind and redirect the manner in which the mind processes information.

The Neuro/Cellular Repatterning Session

Please note that this brief description does not equip anyone to perform a full treatment session. Neuro-kinesiology is described in sepa-

rate booklet for those who want to study N/CR process in depth. A manual for N/CR is also available for those who plan to take the training. Cost is $95, which will be credited and applied to the cost for a level one workshop.

The basic processes use neuro-kinesiology (muscle testing) and do not require the practitioner to be clairvoyant, but it helps. Later steps do require clairvoyant or clairaudient ability.

The electrical polarity of the client's body must be balanced before we can begin a session. We are an electromagnetic mechanism, and must have our electrical polarity balanced in order to operate effectively. If it is reversed, we cannot get accurate answers. Most people's polarity is out of synch due to the stress and fear prevalent in today's world.

The purpose of N/CR is to remove defective software from the mind by deleting, erasing and destroying it. Once done, we install a new program or reinstate the original program that was blocked out and written over. This is done using an affirmation. The therapist cannot install programs on behalf of clients; clients must install the program themselves by repeating the affirmation after the therapist. This installs the program in the computer. The therapist must be observant and listen carefully when a client is repeating the affirmation so that every word is in the right sequence.

A client who skips a word or phrase indicates resistance, a heavy control program, or a sub-personality blocking the issue. The affirmations are specifically worded so as to release an old program or install a new one. Every word the mind takes in can have an effect on you.

To ask questions accurately, put one hand on the client's forearm and the other hand over the client's solar plexus (third chakra). This accesses the Subconscious Mind rather than the Middle Self.

The Use Of Neuro Kinesiology (Muscle Testing)

Basic Neuro Kinesiology

Two important tools of N/CR are the use of affirmations and Kinesiology. These two modalities give us the means to locate the files in the body/mind.

My original training in Kinesiology was with Dr. John Diamond, the originator of Behavioral Kinesiology (BK). His unique methods reveal what the inner mind is holding. This is how he described BK at the time. "I did not understand in the beginning why, when using Kinesiology, putting my hand over my abdomen gave an answer that always seemed to be more accurate than arm-testing alone."

In my work, I have found this to be true 100 percent of the time, but I narrowed the location down to the solar plexus. I no longer check with the arm only (unless I am demonstrating how the two minds differ in their answers). Why do people who work with muscle testing use a process that is only marginally effective? Because they do not know that there is a more effective way. Diamond clearly knew that we received better answers in 1978. We have proven, without a doubt, that when you do not put your hand on the Solar Plexus when you test, you do not get accurate answers. You will find that you get totally different answers when you use the arm only.

When you find the client's arm is like an iron bar and will not go down with any question or pressure, there is something controlling the client's neurological system. This could turn out to be a contest of wills but, more often, it is the work of controlling sub-personalities or entity/being possession. You will have to clear the entities before you can begin any work.

There are many descriptions of Kinesiology. Everybody seems to put their own prefix on it to describe their individual process. We use "neuro" because we are asking the body to tap into the programs in the mind. It does this through the muscles' response through the neurological system. In actuality, all muscle testing works in this manner no matter what prefix you use. The mind is telling you what its response is through a neuro-synapse reaction. All muscle response is controlled by the mind. When you ask the question, it accesses the computer's database and reveals the answers. If you ask it to check a product to see if the client needs a particular nutrient, the mind will check the body and report back the answers. There are only three ways it can communicate: through intuitive projection, neuro-synapses or neuro-peptides.

I developed this process over the last 15 years. I found that I could pick up the answers without any outside means but many people did not believe what I was telling them so I decided I needed to develop a system to validate more definitively what I was describing. Neuro-Kinesiology is the result. I used my Behavioral Kinesiology training to develop my new method and we found a new avenue to help people answer questions without having to use their intuitive or clairvoyant abilities. We found that if we directed the mind to ask the question of the right source, then we could access anything, including the Akashic Record.

Clarity is of the utmost importance when using muscle testing, and there are many ways to use it. First and foremost, however, the practitioner must be clear.

You can use your mind's awesome abilities to talk to your own body or to God with the Kinesiology process just as easily as with any other technique. You can use any set of muscles that will give you an "up and down" action or an "open/closed" indication. Using fingers, you can hold your thumb and middle finger together and try to pull them apart. Using an arm or a leg, you ask the person to resist your pushing or pulling.

If a sub-personality is in control, you can tap on the thymus gland to regress or progress, or take the client's power down so you can test them. You say verbally, "Reduce available power to 30 percent," while tapping the thymus gland. (The thymus gland is located behind the collarbone just below the V-shaped bone below the neck.) Tap on the thymus gland and say to yourself, "Go back to three o'clock this morning." If that does not work, tap again and say, "Reduce the power down to 30 percent." This should work in a battle with Middle Self. (Remember to return the client to present time and full power before you finish. If you don't, it could cause problems.)

If you are unable to get accurate answers with Kinesiology, find a practitioner experienced in clearing in order to clear the client of outside forces so that you can get accurate answers.

When beginning to work with a client, always set the paradigm so you will know what is "yes" and "no." Generally "yes" is a strong response and "no" is a weak response, but some clients may respond differently. Ask, "Give me a 'yes' and give me a 'no.' " Test twice to make sure you have the right response. If you have been doing muscle testing for many years, you have an indigenous program that sets the basic parameters before you start so you do not have to do any testing. Your basic parameters will followed by the client.

In using Neuro-Kinesiology, you will use both hands. If you ask a question using the arm only, you will be accessing beliefs held in the Conscious Mind, which may not be accurate. Always check to see if the Conscious Mind has a different viewpoint when you begin to do this work so that you can experience the difference. To check Subconscious

Mind, put one hand over the solar plexus or third chakra when testing. This will give the Subconscious Mind's viewpoint on the subject. It is always accurate unless you have outside interference. Most forms of Kinesiology suggest that you use light pressure. This may work most of the time but there are occasions when varying pressure must be used due to control by sub-personalities, attached beings or resistance from some program in the mind. Recognizing all the indications that are presented takes practice.

If you begin to test a client whose the arm will not move with any questions, make sure you are not having a muscle battle with a strong person. Explain, "This is not a contest to see if you can stop me from pushing your arm down."

It may take some practice to find just the right amount of resistance to get the three minds to work with the muscles and give accurate readings. If the arm will not go down under normal pressure, you have outside influence. The attached astral beings must be cleared before continuing or they will continue to disrupt accuracy. You may also notice that, at times, the arm will hold, then break and go down. This indicates that the answer would be positive if the person was clear of intervening influences. Finding the controller may take some work, but it must be found or the answers will not be accurate. Sometimes a sub-personality is the cause but, most of the time, it is a hidden attached being. (My book *2011: The New Millennium Begins* gives the process and methods to clear outside attached forces, astral and alien entities.)

When you are asking questions of the Subconscious Mind, accuracy could be compromised by information suppressed in the time-lines, back-up files, denial or denial-of-denial files. The time-line files are written in the year when a traumatic or negative experience happened, and the mind does not want to deal with it. The mind drops it into denial so you do not have to deal with it again. If a lesson has been brought up to deal with and you refuse to acknowledge the lesson, it will be put in denial-of-denial, locked up and will not come up again. It may also have been linked to an autopilot file. If a controller sub-personality was using the program at the time, when it was suppressed on the denial file, the autopilot was also suppressed with it. These must be removed or they will control a person's life.

When all these tests are made, you can be reasonably sure that you can directly contact Higher Self and the Subconscious Mind. If you want to go on-line with the Akashic Internet, then simply connect the phone lines by asking your Higher Self and the Highest Source of your being to connect you. You then can ask questions that are not body-based.

If you choose to use a pendulum, you may run into interference from astral entities, or from entities within yourself or the client. (They can control pendulums without you even knowing it.) It will appear that the answers are correct, but other forces are actually in control. We have experienced this many times over the past 20 years. Because they are heavier, brass pendulums seem to be influenced less. (There are many excellent books in print on pendulums and dowsing. We recommend David Allen Schultz's *Improve Your Life Through Dowsing*, which is available through Personal Transformation Press.)

As with Kinesiology, we must first establish a protocol as to how the pendulum is going swing. Ask your mind to give you the directions for yes and no. Remember the pendulum is just an extension of your mind, and you are projecting the answer out to the pendulum instead of getting it clairvoyantly or through your intuition. Ask it to indicate a no and a yes. The swing will be your guide. Most people will get different to-and-fro and back-and-forth swings or circles. Practice to see what your "yes" and "no" action will be. As you work with the pendulum, you will find there are more answers in addition to yes and no, such as doubtful, not known, etc.

Neuro-Kinesiology uses the same principle. You are getting the information from the client through a muscle reaction instead of using your own intuition. Quite often when working with a client, you will get more accurate answers with muscle testing because you will not be filtering it through your mind that could color the answers if you have strong beliefs, interpretations or feelings about the subject in question.

When we have cleared all outside forces, we must next set up a reasonable understanding with Middle Self that it is not the Source or the phone operator for the Presence of God. Many sub-personalities would like to be in that position, and may well try to convince you of that. In that case, you will be channeling your Middle Self. This will happen when you do not clear it. When you get Middle Self to understand that you sold your power out to it when you were a child due to the need for survival, it will begin to work with you. If it does *not* want to let go of control, you may need to talk with it to bring it around. It might be that it really likes the fact that it can control your life and it feels threatened because it has to give up control. Control sub-personalities may interpret letting go as giving up their power. You may have able to assure Middle Self that it is not losing anything but gaining a new ally because you are reclaiming your personal power. It may glory in the fact that it can manipulate you. If that happens, then all sub-personalities must be deleted from the file before you can claim control. This takes training and experience, so you will have practice this process.

Unfortunately, eliminating sub-personalities does not mean that they are gone forever, because your Conscious Mind can recreate a new set whenever you do not take responsibility to follow through with the decisions you have decided to take action on. Your mind does not like unfinished answers, sentences, actions or commitments you have made. Do not say you are going to do something unless you intend to follow through. If you do not follow through, your mind will assume you did not want to move forward on the decision you made. If you do not take action, your mind has to close that program, so it creates closure by creating a sub-personality and a program about not wanting to take action on that subject. If it happens often enough, then avoider, confuser, procrastinator, disorientor and disorganizer sub-personalities get installed along with a "not wanting to take responsibility" sub-personality. The list can go on and on if you get into indecision and back away from acting on a choice you have made. Any time you make a commitment and do not follow through, a program is created that is interpreted as "I am not willing to take control of my life." If this happens for a number of years, your Instinctual Self will interpret this as if you want to die.

Your mind cannot leave any loose ends unattended; every thought, statement or action you take must have closure; if you start a sentence, Conscious Mind will complete it for you. So every thought and action you create has to be completed or your mind will finish it and file it. It is a very good housekeeper, but it may not complete the task as you would have done.

A program creates a sub-personality and will drive it to get the desired result. If self-rejection is carried to the final stage, it will create a life-threatening illness. There may be disease-specific sub-personalities that were created with the disease, dysfunctional program or belief. A disease, illness or dysfunction cannot exist in the body without a program to drive it. There must be some activating force to break down the immune system or cause stress on the adrenals or the endocrine system. Any form of negative thought or action will start an immediate breakdown in the immune system and the endocrine system. Receptor sites on the leukocytes are notified by the neuro-peptides in microseconds, which begins a physical deterioration of the immune and endocrine systems, which in turn causes the beginning of illness and disease as the immune system function is compromised and fewer T-cells and leukocytes are produced.

When releasing programs, make sure that you check for the sub-personalities that could be enabling them. Each time you clear a time line or operating file, it may activate another series that has been set up to be restored from a back-up file or a denial file.

When clearing karmic files, you must check for gate-keepers, guards and saboteurs that can be connected with the files. They will try to block release of the files. They can be cleared in the same way as attached astral beings.

If a person degenerates or sets up "I want to die" programs, control of the mind/body shifts to the Instinctual Mind. When this happens, programs can be set up in this mind. If there is a conflict in the mind about "I'm afraid to die" and "I want to die," it will set up sub-personalities in the Survival Self, which is part of the Middle Self. This conflict is the main cause of Alzheimer's disease. The two programs cause an Alzheimer's file to be created. This must be cleared before the person begins the backward slide or it will be difficult to stop.

When clearing, you must clear all denial and denial-of-denial programs and sub-personalities. You can bring them up by asking with Kinesiology, "Is this program a belief?" and, "Is this program a reality?" If both are positive, ask Holographic Mind to go through all the veils, shields and illusions in the back-up files, time-line files, the denial and denial-of-denial files, bringing all the hidden files up to the surface to reveal the truth. If the answers continue to come up positive, you have a program that is locked into the physical body. It the "reality" answer comes up weak, then you have a denial. Check for denials and clear them from all files. In cases where the client has been in traumatic situations, time-lines may be in denial files, also. They can also be in autopilot and in denial or denial-of-denial files.

We must also check for reactivator, recreator and regenerator viruses that will create the same program, again and again. These will be attached to individual programs so you must check each program for this each time you clear the program and sub-personality.

We have recently found another program that can recreate sub-personalities and programs. Similar to a computer virus, this program only functions when activated by a word, an activity, a feeling or an emotion. It will activate a program that will run its course and then close down. If you do not catch it during its operational cycle, it disappears. The results or effects of its activity will remain, but we cannot find out how this situation was created until we ask the proper questions to reveal it. We also found another virus that acts the same as a regenerator, which we term an "activator" virus. It can create or activate an existing program that may be dormant.

Each time you clear the sub-personalities will reveal how clients are doing in taking responsibility for their life. Each time they get into a situation where they do not handle it properly and make it a win-win situation, then Middle Self and Conscious Mind will install controller and many other sub-personalities that apply to the situation where the client lost control or did not take total responsibility.

Our mind will reveal our progress in handling our life path by the number of sub-personalities and programs that reoccur over time. Once we clear all the sub-personalities, some will be recreated depending our ability to handle the situations that come up in our life. When we are able to handle all situations without losing our center, needing to be right, being in power and control, giving our power away, and not following through with all our intentions and commitments, then our mind will not install sub-personalities. Anger or resentment will open emotional doors, allowing programs and sub-personalities to be installed. The ideal is to get to a point where no sub-personalities are reinstalled. When this occurs, you will have 100 percent control over your life.

Each time we conduct a session, the controller sub-personalities must be checked. If they keep reoccurring, then we must find out why clients are not taking full responsibility for their life. You may find that they just do not want to take control or discipline themselves. Very few people are actually in control of their life. Many *claim* to be, based on all the seminars, workshops, and therapies they have taken but, in most cases, little has changed.

Taking responsibility is a key issue in everyone's life. Although we had some answers in the past, we could not actually describe how one actually takes responsibility. Now we can, having found all the programs, beliefs and sub-personalities that block a person's ability.

(One of the major blocks is plain laziness.) Once we have cleared all the blocks, it is then a matter of the client's *desire*, which is controlled by his or her Conscious Mind. With clients who do not want to apply themselves and step in and become self-actualized, there is nothing we can do as practitioners to change that situation.

We do not judge where clients are on their individual path. Their body/mind reveals that to us. N/CR cannot force them to take control over their life.

Steps Practitioners Must Take Before Beginning Sessions

One of the major mistakes practitioners make is to step into the therapy process without clearing themselves. Practitioners who want to sell you supplements, herbs or drugs, or want prove their point that you need what they are demonstrating to you can do this easily because all people have an authority figure program that gives their power away to people who know more than they do about a subject. We will accept their opinion, which they can prove to us with muscle testing. (There is an affirmation to clear the authority program later in this chapter.)

The tester must be clear of Middle Self control and the need to be right. There are many sub-personalities that will control your ability to use any form of a divination process. The main ones are the Controller, Authority and Manipulator. They always want to be right. An authority figure can manipulate the test results by the mere fact that the client will give personal power away to the tester. (This is very common in the medical field.)

If testers are not clear, they will get a desired result to sell the client their process, a product or to validate themselves. Testers driven by a sub-personality will not get accurate results. They must release the controlling sub-personality and reclaim their personal power. Outside forces can also impose controls on the effectiveness of testers. They must be clear of attached beings before beginning sessions or the beings attached to the practitioner will jump over to the client.

In doing this clearing process, testers may run into control or interference by attached beings. If this happens, you must clear the entities before going further. You can also have interference if clients will not identify with the name they are using, and you should test for name recognition. If the arm goes weak on using a particular name, test to see which name is causing the difficulty. Quite often, women will have a negative response to a married name if they are divorced or separated from their husband. Sometimes, clients can have a negative reaction to the family name if they had a traumatic childhood. Choose a name that tests positive before testing and test again.

If after considerable testing for name recognition, the tester is unable to test with muscle testing because the arm will not move, there is either a power struggle with Middle Self's sub-personalities or an outside force. It could be that the client does not know how much resistance to put up during Kinesiology or a control sub-personality is trying to control. Occasionally we find that Instinctual Mind is controlling. Quite often we find a possessive being has stepped in, taken over and is controlling the muscle test. If this is the case, test for entity attachment and clear cords and entities.

We have an indigenous program that gives away our personal power to authority figures. It was an acceptable program during childhood so we would obey our parents, but it has no value as an adult. This must be cleared, too (see Steps in Sessions below).

Steps that must be followed prior to testing

1. *Ground yourself* and *balance polarity*: This needs to be done only once a day and may be done upon awakening in the morning. This can be done with the wrist-holding process as it provides all the that is needed (see Steps in Sessions). *Do not put shields, robes of color or energy around yourself to protect yourself.* If you do, you will reflect back all the energy and anything you have removed from the person, stopping the effect of healing.

2. *Clear yourself of any attached beings* before beginning a session or you will drop them on a client. Conversely, if you are not protected, clients will drop them on you. One of the major problems we have is passing out in a session caused by entities that will use the client's mental power to knock you out.

3. *Set your paradigm:* Mentally ask the client to give you a "yes" and a "no." Most people will respond with a "no" as weak or down. "Yes" will be strong, or up. Using the fingers (client tries to keep thumb and middle finger together), closed fingers is usually "yes" and weak or open is "no." With the finger method, you can test yourself. The tester can set the paradigm in any manner desired; we prefer "yes" as the arm tests strong,

and "no" as the arm cannot resist pressure and becomes weak. Have the client hold the arm up and test to make sure it holds up against resistance. Ask the client to say first and last name while you are holding pressure on it, and have him/her continue saying the name until the arm gets weak and goes down. This tests for control by a control/authority sub-personality. Testers can use this test on either clients or themselves.

The most important person to test is the practitioner who is doing the testing. Many times, the tester has received inaccurate answers from me when muscle testing me and wondered why. It is because I know what I am doing and can control the answers but, if the client's sub-personalities are in control, you will not be able to test very effectively. You may want to wait a few minutes and retest to see if Middle Self was playing games. If it is, the arm will resist again. Retest again until the arm becomes weak. The arm may not go down at all. If this happens, then the person cannot function as a tester and get valid results due to control. You must be in a clear space to do effective muscle testing.

One the most troubling issues we find concerns clients who attend the workshops and then begin practicing on others without first working on their own issues. We cannot avoid our own issues, yet we have found that 50 percent of the attendees will not get into recovery. Therapists must be working on their own issues regularly with another therapist, as practitioners must be in recovery working with their own issues all the time. N/CR brings them up and they will interfere with the process when working with a client. If you do not want to work with your own issues, you will slide the client out of the tight space you put yourself in when they come up. You may even pass out during the session if you do not want to face the issue. This can happen to both the client and the practitioner. Sometimes it can happen simultaneously.

Steps in a Session

The following tests must be done in order:

Step 1. Check for Polarity Reversal

Using NK, check polarity. If the arm goes down, polarity is reversed. If the arm is very strong, check for attached beings. If this test yields "yes," then you need to clear entities before going any further. Show the person how to put the wrists together and hold the arms. If it is reversed, a "no" will record as a "yes" and conversely. Restoring polarity can be done using an ancient Chinese balancing method:

Hold your wrists together, with your fingers pointing toward your elbows one on top and one under (which wrist is on top makes no difference). The wrist bracelets at the base of the palms must be touching flat together, so push the offset steps at the base of each palm together. Then hold your hands with your fingers grasping your forearm, pointing toward your elbows just above the wrists and hold for two to ten minutes. For best results, hold for five to ten minutes a day. You will feel your wrist begin to pulse or become warm. Hold until the pulsing stops.

This practice will balance all your electromagnetic fields, your quadrant energies and the electrical flow in the meridians. It will also balance all your chakras and ground you at the same time. Remember that this will not work if the circulation meridian is not connected. The circulation meridian stops at the end of your third or middle finger. When you connect the meridians by holding them together at the wrist, you complete the circuit so that it creates a circular flow of energy around the body. This must be done each day. It will take two weeks to lock it in. It should be continued at least four times a week.

Everyone should do this exercise before getting out of bed in the morning. It takes about five to ten minutes, and balances all the electromagnetic fields, the meridians, quadrant energies and electrical transmission throughout the body.

Sometimes when we get a reading showing a blowout on one side of the body, we have a polarity reversal caused by a birth trauma or a switch of plans before birth where the soul changes the path and chooses different parents than were originally scheduled. They take over a body that would have been stillborn because the original soul had changed its plans and vacated the body before birth. This can be corrected by using an affirmation asking Holographic Mind to erase and delete the file and install a new file to change the polarity balance.

Step 2. Check to see if the client is in body

Using NK, check to see if the client is in the body. (A strong response indicates yes; weak says no.) To pull the client back in, use the following affirmation, asking the client to repeat after you:

"This is _____ (month, day and year). I am _____ (first and last name), I am in my conscious rational decision-making mind."

This will always pull someone solidly back in. You may have to use this during the session, too. Remind the client to use this affirmation every day while doing the balancing exercise in the morning.

If not successful, use the following procedure:

If you get a mushy response after the affirmation, check to see if the client wants to be in the session. There could be fear of having to deal with issues, which will cause the client to block or "gray out." Check for Instinctual Mind control and release that before going any further. You may have to use the affirmation to get the client back into body again. Always finish by stating the name and "I am in my conscious, rational, decision-making mind."

Nowadays, many people are graying out or browning out but don't know it until they are reminded of how it feels. They can function but only at a survival level, so they need to recognize when they are walking out and use the above affirmation (it may be needed 10 or 20 times a day). During a session, if the mind does not want to deal with an issue, it will black clients out. They may appear as if they are going to sleep, but they are actually passing out due to mind control. You will have to bring them back in to the body. Wake them up and ask Holographic Mind to bring them back into the body. This may need to be done numerous times.

Step 3. Check for attached beings

I tried to avoid any mention of attached beings for five years after my first experience in 1986 but it kept hitting us in the face. We decided in 1991, that we had to face the fact that most people had various forms or beings attached to them. Many people want to believe that they do not exist. At first, even the mention of them scared people. Some people feel if they do not acknowledge these entities, they will not bother them but we have found that this is flat out not true.

We find people describing entities as spooks, boogies, or spirit beings, etc. but it makes no difference what you call them. The further along you go on your spiritual journey, the more you will be waving a red flag because the dark forces are attracted to people who are doing well in their life. They want to sidetrack or stop them and will do anything they can to block progress.

Our process is very simple. You do not have to say anything to remove them. You may have to pull cords before you can continue, as they can lock themselves in with cords and implants. Your fingers have etheric extensions up to 18 inches beyond the end of your physical fingers. Allow your etheric fingers to grab the cord or implant and pull it out.

Study the clearing chapter carefully as there are many forms of entities. The ones we seem to be dealing with are the rebel Andromedans who are aliens that have taken over the fourth-dimensional dark forces, plus occasional resident and inter-dimensional beings.

Ask: *"Are there any entities or attached beings, past, present or future, from this or any other dimension or time frame, in this body under any assumed names, false identities, masquerades or names that are camouflages, such as ego, High Self or sub-personality?"*

This will force them to acknowledge their presence and allow Holographic Mind to identify them and force them out.

In 1991 during a level two workshop, we discovered the way to clear attached inter-dimensional beings. Clap down over the client's body from head to foot, clapping very loud and fast (do not use short little claps). Make five or six loud hard claps then hit the soles of the feet on the bottom (shoes must be off). Move hands up the body to the head making sure you do not lift your hands from the body. Some people may feel uncomfortable using this process with women, but we have found if you lift your hands anytime during the upsweep, the entity will jump back under your hands. Check with NK to make sure they are clear.

The Planetary Commission and Archangel Ariel's angels are assigned the task of acting as the "cosmic cops" to assist all spirit beings to the spiritual plane located on the 5th dimension. Call on them before you do any release process. If you have problems, call on the White Brotherhood and the Brotherhood of Light. Ask them and Ariel's angels to take the entity to the spiritual plane.

This process should not take more than two to five minutes unless you run into some nasty entities. If you do, avoid trying to discover who they are or starting a conversation with them. Just remember that they have no right to attach to a person's body.

Step 4. Check for AKA cords and implants

These generally must be cleared before you can continue with the session as they skew the answers. Many times the cords or implants will disguise attached beings so they must be cleared before you can clear the attached beings. Cords attach most commonly in the third chakra/solar plexus region, the base of the spine, brain stem and third eye/sixth chakra but can also be at other locations. As with implants, the cords can have attached beings connected to them. People in your life who want to control you or leach off your energy can attach cords to you. Quite often, another physical person is cording you in an attempt to drain energy from you. And during times of considerable alien activity, we found many forms of implants.

Regardless of source, pull cords with your etheric fingers as in the previous step.

Step 5. Check for Instinctual Mind programs

In May 2001, in people retreating into survival due to feelings of frustration, indecision, lack of direction and feelings of futility, we discovered that Instinctual Mind was being activated by Instinctual Self even though they did not have life-threatening illnesses. We could understand that people felt insecure due to the fear of downsizing in business and companies going out of business. After September 11, 2001, Instinctual Mind files began to show up in everyone as the levels of stress and fear built up and due to the pressure shifts as time speeds up leading to the critical mass shift. Along with this, we usually also found a "refusal to take responsibility" sub-personality, too, which creates *I want to die* and *fear of dying* programs.

This is one of the most critical dysfunctional programs we are finding now. In the past, I assumed that only people in major traumatic experiences or with serious or life-threatening illnesses had Instinctual Mind activated, and never suspected average people would have them activated. But now it seems as if they are activated in anyone who feels fear or has sub-personalities installed, which is currently four out of five people.

We found that when we cleared the "I want to die" and "fear of dying" programs, uninstalled the Instinctual Mind, and erased the operating system, many of the malfunctions also cleared up. If a client feels futility, frustration, indecision, or loss of direction, the Instinctual Mind program will automatically be installed. Most of the time, *want to die* and *fear of dying* programs will also be installed. If both of them are installed, you should also check for Alzheimer's programs, as they may be installed, too.

We have also discovered that if the Instinctual Mind is able to take 70 percent or more control of the mind, it will begin to block out many other files, such as the love program, file manager, and program manager, and activate many disorientation and confusion sub-personalities. If it gets total control, it blanks out all files, and the person goes into total survival. The more control you give it, the more it takes over. If you do not know that it is activated, it could eventually destroy you by contracting an illness such as Alzheimer's.

Ask:
> *Are any Instinctual Mind files active?*
> *How many "I want to die" programs are active?*
> *How many "fear of dying" programs are active?"*
> *Are any Alzheimer's programs active?*

Using NK, check for the number of each and enter them in the blank spaces in the following affirmations.

Use the following affirmation for the *fear of dying* programs, the *I want to die* programs, and *Alzheimer's* programs:

> I am asking you, Holographic Mind, to access all files, remove the Instinctual Mind program from Conscious Mind's operating files, Middle Self's files, Subconscious Mind's files, back up files, time line, future time line, denial and denial-of-denial files. Delete, erase and destroy all the programs, patterns and records. *Uninstall* the operating system, operating instructions and operating programs. Put them in the archives and lock them up so they will never affect me or be recreated. Remove ____ "I want to die" programs and ____ "fear of dying" programs; put them in the archives. Lock them up in the in the trash bin so they will never again affect me. I thank you for your help.

Use the following affirmation to release Alzheimer's:

> I am asking you, Holographic Mind, to access all files and remove ____ Alzheimer's programs and put them in the archives. Delete, erase and destroy all patterns, programs, records, operating instructions, operating systems, and programs that operate the Alzheimer's programs, and lock them up in the trash bin.

(Note that Instinctual Mind cannot be destroyed as it is an indigenous program.)

Step 6. Make peace with Middle Self and program manager. Make friends with the Ego and File Manager. Reclaim personal power.

Before you can change any programs, you must make peace with Middle Self and take your power back from it. We have to make friends with Ego and forgive ourselves for beating it up. Ask the Middle Self and file manager if they will work with you. Very seldom will we get a "yes" to the question unless the client has done extensive work and has been successful in reprogramming the mind.

Few methods and processes available will be successful in actually reprogramming the mind since they do not first get support from both Middle Self and Ego. Middle Self is the program manager and must work with you to coordinate program installation. In most cases, it was handling writing the programs and installing them. We must take that responsibility back and reclaim our personal power. (This is the primary concept in my books).

Ego is the file manager that files programs in your Subconscious Mind. If it is not working for you, it will not file any programs or affirmations in the Subconscious Mind. The programs must pass through Middle Self's censor program and, if it chooses not to let the file through, affirmations will not work in most cases. If Middle Self is left to run on its own, file manager (Ego) will only install files that Middle Self approves. Middle Self will not give up control since it has been appointed as your protector unless you rewrite its operating system. Ego will not allow programs or files to be installed if it feels that you are attacking it. It is your memory retrieval system so it has to be functioning properly.

Since both program manager and file manager are operating systems, their operating protocol can be rewritten and reinstalled with the proper operating programs. The following affirmations will rewrite the operating systems and the protocol that Middle Self and Ego operate under. They will then cooperate with you and file any program you want them to.

Before beginning any reprogramming, we must use these affirmations:

"I recognize now that I have to make peace with my Middle Self. I know that you are the program manager and you did the best you could with the program you had available at the time. It is my responsibility to reclaim my personal power, and I accept that now. I want you to know, Middle Self, that I am taking my power back now. I am not taking your power. I am only taking back the power that is rightly mine. I have no intention of damaging or destroying you because you are an important part of my team and I need your help. I know I must take my power back and take responsibility for my life now. I let you do that for me in the past. I know that I must be the computer operator and the programmer, and I accept that now. It is my responsibility to install all the program files now. I thank you for your help."

"I want to you to know, Ego, that I have to make friends with you now. I know as the file manager, you did the best you could with the programs you had available to you at the time. Due to false information and a misconception, I felt you were the villain and the enemy. I realize this is a false and erroneous misinterpretation. I know now that you are the file manager, the secretary and the librarian for my Subconscious Mind computers. I recognize my mistake now. I am giving myself 100 percent full permission to forgive myself for any harm and trauma that I may have inflicted on you in the past. I need your help since you are an important part of my team. I am loving you and forgiving you since I know you did the best you could with the programs you had available. I am loving and forgiving myself. I am installing these operating systems in the file now. I thank your for your help. I am loving and forgiving myself and I am doing that now."

Few practitioners understand or know that these files exist. They wonder why their process does not hold very well. So often, I find people will cling onto the Ego as the controller of their lives even after I prove to them who is doing the controlling. Blaming Ego is so ingrained into our minds that we do not want to let go of the old definition. These two files must be reprogrammed and reinstalled or very little will work over the long haul. Even though this is true for most people, I have worked with clients who were so intent with changing their life that they reprogrammed themselves. The power of the mind is awesome when we get in contact with our own power to work with it.

Step 7. Opening all files so they can be accessed
   With this affirmation, we open up all the files so that we can access them. We have often found that the time line files are inaccessible and will not be revealed to us unless we open them before we begin reprogramming.

Use the following affirmation to open the files:

I am asking you, Holographic Mind and Ego, to open all files so we can access them now. I am asking you to open Conscious Mind's operating files, Middle Self's operating files, Subconscious Mind's operating files, back up files, time line, future time lines, denial files and denial-of-denial files. Bring them up to the surface so we can access them now. I thank you for your help.

This opens all files so we do not have to continually check back to see if we are getting all the information from all files.

Step 8. Remove authority figure program

This program gives your power away to authority figures, and is one of the most disconcerting. It was installed as an indigenous program in our mind at birth so we would give allegiance to our parents and follow their guidance as a child. As an adult, it has zero value as it causes us to give our power away to anybody who claims to know more about a subject than we do, be it the plumber, garage mechanic, doctor or lawyer. If a doctor gives us a diagnosis of an illness, even if we do not have it, we will accept the diagnosis and manifest the symptom. We can even pick up something from what we read, hear or see if we give our power away to the authority behind the statement. These all end up as beliefs and will control our life. Quite often, programs that begin to operate from these files can annoy us but we do not know how to change them.

To remove the program, use the following affirmation:

"I am asking you, Holographic Mind, to remove the authority figure program. I realize it had value when I was a child so that I would follow my parents' guidance. As an adult, it has zero value as it causes me to give my power away to any person who I recognize as an authority figure. Take this program out of the files and uninstall the operating system. Delete erase and destroy all the operating instructions, programs, patterns and records and put them in the archives, locking them up so they will never affect me again. Put them in the trash bin permanently. Thank you for your help. I am loving and accepting myself now."

Step 9. Check on receiving love

Seven out ten people are rejected before they are born, so I check so see if clients can receive love and love themselves? I find very few people are able to love themselves so, when checking for these programs, I test to see if their mother wanted children at all and whether the mother wanted them specifically.

Since I have been checking for the love program over the last 20 years, the statistics have changed. At first, I was not going into the files very deeply so my feedback was that two in five were rejected before they were born. In my practice, we can go months at a time before we find someone who actually loves him/herself and it's getting worse, especially with children under the age of ten.

Check for love without putting your hand on the client's solar plexus first in order to test how the Conscious Mind feels about love. Normally, this will test strong. If it tests weak, then there is no love file installed. Sometimes clients may check strong on loving self when it is an illusion because they have been working on themselves for years. They have convinced themselves that, after all their work, they must love themselves, to the point they will test strong for self-love.

If you suspect this, ask Holographic Mind to go to denial files to see if this is a belief or a reality. (You must have all files open to do so.)

Remember that this program will not lock the love affirmation into the file unless you release the actual rejection programs that are located in acupuncture points on the body's left side near the top of the shoulder blade. There, many more rejection, I'm not all right, I don't fit in, nobody wants me, I'm not accepted, nobody loves me programs may be found if the person was rejected before they were born or as a young child.

Use the following Affirmation to reinstall the Love program:

I recognize now that love is my responsibility and I accept that now. I know now that I am entitled to unconditional love and I accept that now. I know that love is kindness and caring, acceptance without judgment and control, acceptance without manipulation and authority. I accept that now. I am removing all overshadows that block me off from God and I am doing that now. I know that I can reestablish the presence of God in my life now. I am doing that now. I am removing all inner shadows that block me off from my Higher Self. I am doing that now. I know now that I am entitled to live in peace, happiness, harmony and joy and I accept that now. I am loving myself and forgiving myself and I am doing that now.

This affirmation will rewrite the program every time. The question is, will it continue? If you do not forgive your parents and remove the program from the body files that are located in the area around the shoulder blade on the left side, the love program will be erased and revert to its rejection program again. Just saying the affirmation will not reprogram the file. After you have rewritten the love program, then you can ask why it was lost. We were born with our love program intact, but the way we interpret how we were treated after we were born dictates what happens to the program. So ask the client:

"Did your mother want children? Did she want you as a child?"

If yes, continue. If no, then ask, "Did she reject you before birth?"

If yes, then ask, "Did she accept you after birth?"

If yes, continue. If no, then ask, "Did she think about or take any action about abortion?"

If yes, then ask, "Did she ever accept you?"

If no, then ask, "Did your father accept you? Were you the right gender for your parents?"

If you come up with "no" to the last two questions, you have major work to do with the client's forgiveness of the parents. This must be done or the client will never get out of the victim consciousness programs. Some people can pull through without help but only a few. People treat you based on what you project about how you feel about yourself. You will keep drawing people into your life to work these love programs out until you forgive your parents.

Step 10. Release, delete and erase sub-personalities

If time is limited, it is very important to clear the four controller sub-personalities. If you have time, clear all the autopilot and the validation sub-personalities. When you clear them all and you are testing the client in the next session, the number of sub-personalities that have gotten back in will indicate how much responsibility the client is taking to handle and control in his or her life.

Go through the list of autopilot and validation sub-personalities and list the number of each type on the checklist (photocopy the page so you can use each time you do clearing). Check for all virus activators with each file. These will recreate the program or sub-personality after it has been removed (unless they are removed and deleted along with the operating file.) Use the first affirmation to remove all of the sub-personalities. The control sub-personalities must be released before you can work effectively, so first remove them as a group because they will try to interfere if not removed. Then go to the second group. They do not have to be released in the first session. When finished, go to the second affirmation to complete the process.

Sub-personalities

You can delete the programs they have created to support themselves but not the sub-personalities because they are indigenous to the mind, in that they cannot be removed. Quite often people want to blame Inner Child for their problems and separate it from themselves, which is not possible. When someone says, "My Inner Child was hurt," they are trying to avoid responsibility. Inner Child can only record a feeling and/or interpret it, as the Inner Child is part of the mind and is who you are. It may have had to take over working through autopilot, but it has no control over your life when you take responsibility for your behavior. It can only operate through programs that it creates through program manager (Middle Self). When you take your power back and reclaim control of our life, Inner Child grows up and drops out.

In May of 2001, we discovered that Instinctual Self was activating Instinctual Mind by feelings of frustration, indecision, futility and lack of direction. Usually the "I refuse to take responsibility" sub-personality was installed, too. They create *I want to die* programs and *fear of dying* programs.

In the past, we found the Instinctual Mind activated only in people with major traumatic experiences and life-threatening illnesses. But as of the fall of 2000, it seems that they are activated in everyone who feels any of the above feelings or has sub-personalities installed. We are finding Instinctual Mind files activated in three out of five people.

Do not be surprised if you find that some of these sub-personalities number in the hundreds of thousands because they are a build up from birth. In one extreme case, I found over three million external controllers. Very few people have accessed sub-personalities in any form of therapy.

The Five Basic Sub-personalities

These sub-personalities cannot be removed as they are indigenous to your mind and are installed at birth in the Subconscious Mind's files. You can remove the programs and sub-personalities they use to support them, such as addictive, self-pity forms, etc. The five are:

- Survival Self
- Instinctual Self
- Inner Child
- Critical Parent
- Inner Adult.

1. Autopilot Sub-personalities

These can be installed in all files and all levels of the mind. Write the number next to each one and release as a group. Release these first as a group:

- Power Controller (wants to have power over people, business activities)
- External Controller (wants to control everything around it for security)
- Internal Controller (control over you for security and safety in denial files)
- Internal Controller (in denial-of-denial files)

2. Controller and Victim Sub-personalities

Do the same with the next group, except that you do not need to use the autopilot affirmation.

Controller	Victim
Self-righteous	Procrastinator
Authority	Confuser
Know it all	Disorientor
Manipulator	Indecision
Judger	Avoider
Controller	Resenter Jealous/Envious Blamer
Ingratitude	Disorganizer
Saboteur	Sufferer/Struggler

3. Programs (not the same as sub-personalities)

Feeling of futility / I am not accepted
Refusal to take responsibility / Anger at not being accepted

Frustration / Anger at not being respected
Energy Blocker / Anger at not being recognized
Mental Blocker (blocks memory) /Anger at being ejected/abandoned
I am not all right

4. External Validation Sub-personalities:

Empathizer	Savior	Father figure
Protector	Rescuer	Mother figure

5. Operational Sub-personalities:

Can be located in Middle Self or Conscious or Subconscious Mind:

Self-pity	Projector	Nobody Cares For Me
Insecurity	Annoyer	Regretful
Nagger	I am unworthy	I am not accepted
I don't fit in	I am not accepted	Feeling sorry for self
Scardy-cat	Liar	Rebel
Lack of trust	Pain addict	Sympathy-puller
God rejects me	Soap opera player	

Wanting other people to make decisions for me
Wanting to be taken care of

6. Rejection and abandonment sub-personalities can take many forms:

People are rejecting what I say
People are rejecting who I am
Rejection from Mother
Rejection from Father
Rejected by others
People do not trust me
People don't accept me

7. Anger programs can be supported by many sub-personalities:

These are some of them. You will find more in the clearing process:

Anger at having to reach out	Refusal to step forward
Refusal to reach out	Anger at having to step forward
Anger at moving forward	

8. Fear can take many forms also:

Fear of being rejected	Fear of reaching out
Fear of venturing forward	Fear of vulnerability

Fear of having to take responsibility   Fear being abandoned
Fear of failure   Feeling inadequate

Use this affirmation to release the following sub-personalities:
1. Sub-personalities:
   "As the Christ Master self that I am, I am asking my Holographic Mind and Ego to remove _____ (exact number) sub-personalities and put them in the archives along with all reactivator, recreator, and regenerator viruses. Put them in the archives. Remove, delete, erase and destroy all the operating instructions, operating systems, programs, patterns and records from the operating files. Lock them up in the trash bin so they will not affect me again."

2. Autopilot:
   "I am asking you to uninstall autopilot's operating system and put it in the archives. Delete, erase and destroy all the operating instructions, programs, patterns and records and the format that controls and operates auto pilot. Put them in the archives and lock them up in the trash bin so they will never affect me again."

3. Finish up all sub-personality clearings with (this must be done at the end of each session):
   "Empty and clear the trash bin and make sure all the sub-personalities are removed from all the files in Conscious Mind's operating files, Middle Self's, and Subconscious Mind's operating files, back-up files, time-line files, denial files and denial-of-denial files. Make sure all files are deleted permanently. I thank you for your help."

The remaining steps 11 – 17 are optional and can be done at anytime.

Step 11. Check for Vows, Oaths, Allegiances.
   Use the following affirmation to release Vows, Oaths, and Allegiances:
   "As the Christ Master self that I am, I am now removing revoking, renouncing, rebuking and releasing all vows, oaths and allegiances. (Use the number of and specific vows if necessary.) I am asking you, Holographic Mind and Ego, to remove all vows, oaths and allegiances, past, present and future, and I am doing that

now. Put them in the archives and delete, erase and destroy all operating instructions, operating systems and programs pattern and records. Lock them up in the trash bin so they will never affect me again. I thank your for your help."

Step 12. Check for thought-forms:
Use the following affirmation to release Negative Thought Forms:
"As the Christ Master self that I am, I am now releasing all negative thought forms that have been inflicted on me by other people now. I am returning them to the originators for their own deposition with kindness and caring and unconditional love. I am releasing all self-inflicted negative thought forms with unconditional love and kindness and caring and I am doing that now. Delete erase and destroy all the operating programs, patterns and records and put them in the trash bin so they will never affect me again. I am loving myself and forgiving myself and releasing myself from this bondage now. Thank you for your help."

Step 13. Check for curses, hexes & spells
Use the following affirmation to release curses, hexes, and spells after first checking for the number of each with NK:
"As the Christ Master Self that I am, I am asking you, Holographic Mind, to remove _____ curses, _____ hexes and _____ spells that are affecting me now. I am doing that now. Put them in the archives now. Delete, erase and destroy all the operating instructions operating systems and operating programs, patterns, programs and records, put them all in the trash bin and lock them up so they will never affect me again. Thank you for your help."

Step 14. Removing the medical model, skeptical and doubter sub-personalities
The average person will accept the medical model as general belief, which governs how one deals with illness, disease and most dysfunctional behavior programs. The more one is caught up in or believes that medical science and its practitioners have the answers to illness and disease, the more skeptical one is of alternative processes. They may doubt anything they do not believe, or have had experiences that created skeptical and doubter sub-personalities. They may accept alternative processes and say that they accept the modality consciously

on the surface but Middle Self must also accept the concept, and there must be no programs or sub-personalities that oppose the concept.

Programs released with a simple affirmation may have opposition, such as allergy programs or illnesses that are caused by a belief in a concept created by an authority figure. If a program has no basis in reality and is released with an affirmation, we must check for the opposition because any attached skeptical or doubter sub-personalities will re-install the program.

Check for medical model, skeptical and doubter sub-personalities. Check for exact numbers and write them in the blanks in the following affirmation to release them:

"I am asking you Holographic mind, to remove ____ medical models and put them in the archives. Remove ____ skeptical sub-personalities and put them in the archives. Remove ____ doubter sub-personalities and put them in the archives. Delete, erase and destroy all operating instructions, operating programs and operating systems. Make sure all programs, patterns and records are deleted, erased and destroyed. Put them in the trash bin so they will not affect me again."

Step 15. Check financial success

To free up clients who feel that they are not entitled to money and wealth:

"I have accepted that I am not entitled to money, I don't deserve money, I am not able to accept wealth, I can't keep money when I receive it and spiritual people are not entitled to money. These are all false, erroneous beliefs and concepts. I am asking you, Holographic Mind, to remove, delete, erase and destroy these false and erroneous programs, patterns, records, beliefs, concepts, attitudes and interpretations. Put them all in the archives deleting, erasing and destroying all the operating instructions, operating systems, operating programs. Remove delete, erase and destroy all reactivator, recreator and regenerator viruses and programs and put them in the archives. Make sure they are all locked up in the trash bin so they will not affect me again. Thank you for your help."

Step 16. Correcting the digestive program

People who carry excess weight are not digesting the food that they eat. The digestive system is extracting simple sugars from all the food intake. If people try to lose weight with a protein diet, they will be hungry all the time. When they eat sugar containing food hunger will be reduced. Before any weight reduction is stated this program must be rewritten. If the lack of love program is not corrected, it will be written over and be blocked. If Instinctual Mind is activated, it will block the digestive program. The above programs must be rewritten before the digestive program can be installed.

Ask: "Is your body living on simple sugars?" If yes, then the program must be erased and a new program installed. Use the following affirmation to correct the digestive program:

"I am asking you, Holographic Mind, to remove this defective malfunctioning digestive program that does not allow me to digest protein, carbohydrates, oils, fruits and vegetables. I recognize that I am not assimilating the nutrients from the food I eat. Uninstall this program delete, erase and destroy all the patterns and records, all the operating instructions, operating systems and operating programs. Put them in the archives and lock the up in the trash bin so they will not function again. I am asking you to install a new digestive program now. I know that I can digest proteins, carbohydrates, oils, vegetable and fruits and assimilate the nutrients for perfect health now. I asking you to install this program in all files now so they will not be tampered with again. Thank you for your help."

Step 17. Clear attached programs or sub-personalities
Using a Pendulum or Kinesiology Check for the following:
1. Access the program. What is the name of the file?

Energy blocker, mental blocker, breathing suppression, allergy, dry throat, chronic fatigue, sneezing, sinus drainage, sinus congestion, coughing and headache programs to simulate attached entities (can be almost anything).
2. Locate the file that the program is locked into:

File names can be tricky as they can be camouflaged under beliefs, concepts or habit patterns. A belief that is held for a week or more can turn into a program.
3. Conscious Mind:

    A. Rational Decision-making Mind
    B. Conscious Mind's operating system
    C. Inner Conscious Mind

4. Middle Self:

Inner Middle Self

5. Subconscious Mind:

A. Subconscious Mind's operating system
a. Denial files, future time lines in denial
b. Denial-of-denial files, future time lines in denial-of-denial
c. Back up files

Check for attached reractivastor, recreator, and regenerator programs that will reinstall files in various operating systems after you have cleared them.

B. Time line files
a. Past time lines files
b. Present time line files
c. Future line files

6. After you identify the file, ask for the number of programs in the files.

7. *Ask Holographic Mind* to do a file search and a files scan for any programs in series or hidden under other formats. If they are located go through the same scanning process above.

8. *Once programs are located* and the number found use this affirmation to release them:

"I am asking you holographic Mind and Ego to remove _____ programs from _____ and put them in the archives. Delete, erase, and destroy all operating instructions, operating systems, and all programs, patterns and records. All beliefs and concepts, attitudes and interpretations and lock them up so they will never affect me again. Put them in the Trash bin now."

9. *At the end of each session* clear and delete all files and empty the trash bin.

B

The Body/Mind Harmonizer:
A New Concept for the New Millennium

The Harmonizer Concept

The physical body matches itself to the frequencies in its environment, whether stressful or not. The Harmonizer counteracts the stress in its immediate vicinity, allowing the body to come into earth resonance, which is the most effective frequency for the endocrine system to balance and regenerate itself. The coil-antennae produces a scalar wave field pulsing on and off to create the effect. Technology for the Harmonizer was developed in the early 1900s by Nikola Tesla, who did considerable research into electromagnetic fields and their generation by special coils. He discovered the so-called *scalar field*, a longitudinal wave field that functions outside the space/time of our third-dimensional world. Since it operates beyond space/time, it is unencumbered by the limitations of conventional physics, and is the most effective way to protect the body from disruptive stress of disharmonic fields or vibrations.

We have also found that earthbound spirits, alien entities and extraterrestrials cannot handle the frequencies, and cannot attach to a person in the Harmonizer's field. The scalar wave radiation also blocks abduction and protects from psychic attack. People who have been harassed by earth-bound spirit beings have reported that they have been free of them as long as they keep the unit on them 24 hours a day. This was primarily why we developed this unit. Now we find that it does much more than we expected.

The Harmonizer causes accelerated healing up to ten times the norm, apparently by activating cellular restructuring in the body. Generating a high-frequency bio-electrical field using Tesla technology, the unit reportedly accelerates healing at the cellular level, balances the endocrine system, supports the immune system, rebuilds bone structure, and heals skins cuts and lesions about ten times faster than normal. It also seems to balance the electrical function in the body, which in turn can balance all electrical aspects of the body including blood pressure and neurological function.

The Harmonizer Theory

When it is in perfect health, every living being resonates at its own characteristic frequency. Each component of that being's body also resonates at a particular frequency, and if subject to higher frequencies from its environment, it tried to match those frequencies, which causes stress, and that particular cell, organ or gland is weakened, making it more prone to disease or illness.

A tuning fork in the field of another matched fork that is struck will vibrate at the same frequency. Your body does the same thing. When you are subject to negative vibrations such as stress, fear, or anger in your environment, you begin to identify with this environment and your body begins to resonate with that vibration.

If you go into flight or fight, your adrenals kick in, causing a strain on the immune and endocrine systems. A strong dose of adrenaline helps you handle the perceived danger. Under normal circumstances, when the danger is over, your body should release a shot of nor-adrenaline as an antidote so you can return to normal energy and frequency level of 12 – 18 Hz. But, if you live in perpetual stress, survival fear or confrontational conditions, your body frequency will rise to 250 – 550 Hz, over *thirty* times higher than it should be. As your body frequency rises, you begin to function on adrenaline alone.

Electronic devices that emit strong fields also interact with the physical body's electric and electromagnetic fields. The body/mind will identify with the frequency that has the strongest effect on it. The Harmonizer creates a 15-foot diameter field of energy around the body that blocks out other frequencies that are stressful to the body. It emits a low frequency— the Earth resonance signal—and a high frequency that is the ideal frequency for the body's functioning.

The brain's chemicals, such as interlukens, seratonin, interferon, etc. operate at the Earth resonance 12 – 15 Hertz. The immune system and the endocrine system work more effectively when there is no load on the adrenal glands. Negative sensory input or negative thoughts and emotions cause the neuropeptides to slow down, compromising the immune and endocrine systems.

The body's natural electrical field (chi, ki or prana) must be strong to ward off disease factors, but as its frequency rises, the electrical and auric fields weaken, and offer less protection. The Harmonizer causes the mind to focus its energy and operate at optimum health. However, the device is only an adjunct to such measures as proper nutrition. You cannot abuse or mistreat your body and expect the Harmonizer to overcome this.

The following is a greatly simplified explanation of the theory behind the Harmonizer. The information that regulates the various parts of the body is carried by the body's neurological network system. The brain serves as a "switching center" that directs the electrical impulse information and neuropeptides through the meridian system network to the appropriate parts of the body.

Each cell is a mini "computer" in this network, and receives its orders from the mind through the neurological system, carried by electrolytes and the neuropeptides. When operating properly, the cells maintain a delicate balance of chemicals. When they go out of balance or get run down, the electromagnetic fields break down or blow out. The cell loses its ability to protect itself properly. The brain/mind's ability to communicate with the cellular computers breaks down and the body becomes subject to attack by diseases, illness and outside forces, and *accelerated aging*—the most damaging effect of increased stress and high frequency.

The results are illness, depression, chronic fatigue, emotional instability and life-threatening disease. Metabolism is affected due to breakdown of the function of the endocrine glands, and the body's absorption of nutrition is impaired.

As the body's internal frequency rises past 50 Hz, the good "happy" brain chemicals shut down and the adrenals kick in larger doses of adrenaline to keep you functioning. The adrenals become over-worked, which leads to adrenal insufficiency. When production drops below 30 percent, normal fatigue sets in, similar to low blood sugar tiredness caused by hypoglycemia.

Continued high frequency interference causes breakdown in all systems of the body, resulting in Chronic Fatigue and Epstein-Bar Syn-dromes, which lead to clinical depression. Many doctor prescribe Prozac, Zolov, Valium or other mind-altering anti-depressants, which can be addictive because they suppress the symptoms and fool the brain into believing that the total body malfunction is a false message.

Low Frequency Operation

The Harmonizer balances electrical, metabolic and electromag-netic system dysfunction by shutting out the disharmonious stress that causes the body to elevate its frequency. It emits a fifth-dimensional etheric scalar field that strengthens all the systems of the body by bringing down the frequency to the optimum level for perfect health.

To be in balance, most devices, plants and animals have clockwise and counterclockwise positive and negative energies. A few plants such as garlic, onion, and some herbs radiate a double-positive field, hence their antibiotic healing qualities. The Harmonizer also radiates a double-positive field, which explains the response it creates.

For more than 200 years of recorded history, the Earth's resonant frequency or Schumann Resonant Factor was 7.83 Hz but, recently, it has risen to 12 – 14 Hz. Our original Harmonizers were built to emit 7.83 Hz, and later models have kept pace with the Schumann frequency. The current 12.5 Hz field helps the adrenals to heal and resume their normal operating level. At this ideal frequency, all organs and endo-crine glands function at their most effective level and your body begins to heal because when the body is in the Harmonizer's 15-foot diameter field for a period of time, it will match the Harmonizer's frequency. This may take up to three days depending on your body, but you will notice your body begin to slow down and relax.

High Frequency Operation

The unit also emits a high frequency of 9.216 MHz. When we began our search for the high frequency that would accomplish our purposes, we checked through hundreds of frequencies. Little did we know that the frequency we finally choose was only 0.02 MHz off the actual frequency of the Ark of the Covenant. Apparently, this is a universal frequency that will activate the body's healing modalities and repel anything or anybody who emits a negative energy.

Initially, we were able to get 9.216 MHz chips because Motorola had over-ordered but we have since found other readily available sources. For the latest model, we redesigned the entire circuitry and coil, and used a slightly larger case to accommodate the rechargeable battery pack. As a result, the unit now has a much lower power requirement and is more effective.

When we discovered that we were getting a scalar wave without the circuitry to produce it, we asked some experts about it. All they could say was, "You're dealing with hyper-dimensional physics and it's over our heads and we can't explain it. This is Tesla and Einstein's realm, and we don't understand what's happening."

We are apparently producing an output that no one understands. Nor has any history of this effect been recorded. Two new research consultants joined our team—a radio frequency engineer and a physicist— and they said, "As far as we can tell, it appears that we're on the threshold of a new discovery in quantum physics. We can't measure the scalar field output because it's outside conventional physics, but the radio frequency seems to be a carrier wave for the scalar field."

Harmonizer History

Our first prototype had a weak field, yet it worked so well that we knew we were on to something so we continued our research. The second generation unit had a 100 millivolt output, and the current production unit puts out 800 millivolts. The first unit of the current (tenth) generation had a metal core coil that was absorbing two thirds of the output, so our engineer suggested using a non-reactive plastic core. When we went to a nylon core, we discovered that power output tripled. The next challenge is to build an even more powerful unit that will not interfere with short wave or TV reception, or we would run into trouble with the FCC.

The device uses a triple-wound bifilar toroidal coil/antenna driven by complex electronics that were not available in Tesla's time. Today's computer chip technology has allowed us to reduce the size of the original prototype by over 90 percent. The first generation prototype had a range 18 inches and a battery life of 80 hours. The second generation had a range of 3 feet and a battery life of 260 hours. Early units used expensive 9-volt batteries, and we switched to AA Nicad rechargeable battery packs that lasted about a year. Today's tenth generation has a range of 15 feet and a nickel hydride battery pack that lasts up to four years.

Warning:
Charge the unit for one hour a month, or four hours if it is fully discharged. This is very important, as we have had people return the unit, complaining that battery would not charge. They had over-charged the battery for many hours.

When you first begin to use the Harmonizer, you may find that it needs to be recharged more often than once a month. If your body energy is low and you have been under considerable stress, this will drain the batteries more quickly as the unit interfaces and responds to your body energy level. We have had reports that people have had to initially charge the battery as often as once a week.

Testimonials

Disclaimer
Due to FDA regulations, we make no claims as to what the Harmonizer can accomplish. However, we can report what users have relayed to us. Many claims have been made by users of the Harmonizer but we can not recommend it for anything as we are not psychiatrists or doctors. We are not allowed by law to diagnose or prescribe.

Here, we relay the experiences of those who have used the Harmonizer. For example, many people have reported that it pulled them out of depression in 5 – 14 days without any drugs, and many have ceased taking prescription antidepressants. Two psychiatrists validated this information from their experience.

In my case, I injured my foot with a chain saw, and the wound was not healing well but, as soon as I began using the new Harmonizer, my foot began to heal at an unprecedented rate. I could actually see it heal from one day to the next. The deep gash closed up and healed over in less than two weeks, and today has left only a faint red mark.

1. "It seems to bring programs to the surface that I had no awareness of. It's the best therapeutic tool I have come in contact with." *B.E., California*
2. "I strapped the Harmonizer over a broken leg on the cast where the break was and the break healed four times faster than normal. The doctor was amazed that we could take the cast off in less than four weeks." *J.S., California*
3. "Chronic Fatigue I'd suffered for years disappeared in less than a week." *J.C., Arizona*
4. "I am feeling general well being and able to handle stress more effectively. I'm not getting angry as quickly as in the past. One day, I left the Harmonizer at home and I noticed my stress level began to rise at work." *C.D., California*
5. "Psychiatrists who have purchased the Harmonizer report that it works with depression very well since it reactivates the brain chemicals and supports the rebuilding of normal production of all the essential brain chemicals, allowing the adrenals to slow down and heal. As a result people seem to pull out of depression." *R.N., Virginia*
6. "I put the Harmonizer on a plant that was dying, and it revived in just one day." *T.K., California*
7. "A burn totally disappeared in three days. This was apparently caused by the activation of the cellular restructuring." *J.T., California*
8. "It apparently has caused my immune system to rebuild because I am recovering from a long term illness. It is feels great to get my stamina back." *W.B., New Mexico*
9. "It activates programs in the mind that have been covered up for years. Apparently denial programs are forced to the surface." *H.M., California*
10. "I am finding I have more energy and I sleep less now that the stress is relieved." *G.B., Colorado*

11. "I have been taking drugs for depression, and low thyroid and adrenal function. I continued to take the drugs until they ran out. I noticed that I was getting the same effect from the Harmonizer so I did not renew my prescriptions. That was three years ago and I have not had any depression since. And the new Harmonizer is even better. Thank you so much." *A.P., California*

12. "I handed the unit to friend of mine and he dropped it immediately, saying he couldn't hold onto it. Once I cleared him of attached entities, he had no problem holding it." *J.O.E., California*

13. "I had been to the doctor for my high blood pressure and he prescribed medication to control my blood pressure because it was 190 over 120. I checked it again a month later and it was still the same. I bought the Harmonizer and started carrying it with me all the time. Less than a month later, I was down to 120 over 70. The doctor could not understand how my blood pressure would come down to normal. 'That just does not happen to someone your age.' I cannot attribute it to anything other than the Harmonizer." *C.S., Arizona*

14. "It is amazing. I felt burned out and the doctor said my adrenals were very low and wanted me to take drugs to build them back up. I told him I did not take drugs of any kind and would find another way. I started using the Harmonizer, and my adrenals recovered in three days. I do not feel as stressed out anymore. This is truly electronic medicine." *K.S., Oregon*

15. "I have had a umbilical hernia for 25 years, and have consistently refused surgery to repair it, instead doing exercises to strengthen the abdominal muscles so it would repair itself. It had been slowing getting smaller, but very slowly. I had the earlier version of the Harmonizer for four years and while it helped in many ways, it had no effect on the hernia. But with the new high frequency unit, in just three months the hernia has reduced to about one quarter of what it was last year." *A.M., California*

16. "My husband had flu twice this winter and I usually get it from him and end up down for a week. This year, no flu or anything. I can only assume the Harmonizer protected me and kept my immune system up to par so I was not affected." *C.H., California*

17. "For me, the Harmonizer is a miracle because I seem to go out of my body quite often and driving is very dangerous when this happens. I have been solidly in my body since I have been using the Harmonizer." *J.S., California*

18. "I have had serious immune system problems for years. It seems that I catch everything that comes along. The Harmonizer has upgraded my immune system to the point that I am now very seldom sick." *C.K., California*

19. "When I called to find out about the unit, I was willing to try anything as my blood pressure was 210 over 120 and I had lung congestion. My legs hurt so much I could not even walk around the grocery store. In five weeks my blood pressure dropped to 130 over 90 and still continues to fall. I have no lung congestion and I can drive trucks again. I have gone back to work full-time."

20. "As a healer, I touch many clients in my work and would frequently have entities attaching to me from my clients. Today, I would not be without my 'boogie buster' because it protects me so well." *J.N., California*

21. "I have had low adrenal function almost all my life. Stress really takes me down to the point where I can't function. With the Harmonizer, I have recovered totally. I have not experienced any depression or lack of energy since I began using it." *C.K., Colorado*

22. "Accelerated healing of burns has been amazing. I spilled boiling water on my face when I dropped a teakettle. The burn marks began clearing up in two weeks. In a month, they were almost gone except for redness on the skin. Today, there is no scarring and all the marks are gone." *M.K., Arizona*

23. "One of the most amazing results I have found from using the Harmonizer is that old burn scars and keeled scars are disappearing, some of which have been on my body for forty years. It is truly amazing." *H.M., California*

24. "After a motorcycle race, I suffered a serious third degree burn on my leg from an exposed exhaust pipe. The burn healed in less than one month, and in six weeks was just a dark spot. In the past, burns like this have taken six months to heal."

Others have reported a much clearer mind and more vivid memory. People have experienced more clear and active meditations. We have found that the Harmonizer causes an accelerated healing of cuts and wounds on the skin. It apparently is activating some cellular response as skin cuts seem to heal in a one quarter or less time than normal. The only negative aspect that we have found is that it pulls up emotional programs that have repressed in the past, and the person has to deal with them.

We hesitate to list many of the other results people have received so as not to create expectations, and we stress that the Harmonizer is only an *adjunct* to your body. You must work with it, and not expect it to do things for you. Please do not put unrealistic expectations on it as it's only a catalyst for your own healing miracles. You still have do your part in releasing the emotional trauma responsible for the health condition.

New Products and Upgrades

The price of the new 800 millivolt 9.216 MHz Body/Mind Harmonizer unit is $295.00 plus shipping. (If you have an old original 12.5 Hz or lower unit, we will exchange it for the 9.126 MHz unit and give you a trade-in value of $50.00.)

A new therapeutic unit is being developed that will have an adjustable power output, from 800-millivolts to 5-volts, *five times* more powerful than the current unit. Projected price is $395.00 or less depending on final cost.

A new "ghost buster" unit will be available soon for clearing buildings and creating an overall balancing/clearing effect in seminar and workshop facilities. Projected price is $450.00 or less depending on final cost.

We are working on a new unit that will operate on 120 volt AC house electricity. It will combine both units plus a programming mode to hook up with a tape recorder or a CD player for use with music and voice tapes for reprogramming the mind. One unit will have a tape recorder built into it. It will use piezo-electric discs similar to earphones to input information through the eighth cranial nerve. In this manner, it bypasses the Middle Self, which cannot then tamper or sabotage the input (all dysfunction of the body is mind controlled). In our tests, deaf people reported being able to hear the input, also. People have reported that they were able to learn a foreign language in as little as two weeks. A teacher reported that learning-disabled students were able to master lessons that they had not been able to in the past. Projected price on this unit is about $795.00 depending on final costs, and will include some programming software.

To order the Body/Mind Harmonizer, or books and tapes, call or write:
The Wellness Institute
8300 Rock Springs Rd.
Penryn, CA 95663
(800) 655-3846 (Orders only—all major credit cards accepted)
Fax: (916) 663-0134
E-mail: artmartin@mindspring.com
Websites: www.medicalelectronics.org
            www.mindbodymedicineconnection.com
            www.personaltransformationpress.com

C

Tapes and Books

The first two books are available in most bookstores in the U.S. and in some countries around the world. The other five are available in spiral bound pre-publication format from publisher, Personal Transformation Press.

2011: The New Millennium Begins
$13.95, ISBN 1-891962-02-7
What can we expect the future to bring? How do we handle the coming changes and what do we look for? Prophesy for future earth changes and new planet Earth as it makes the quantum jump from the third to the fifth dimension.

Becoming a Spiritual Being in a Physical Body
$14.95, ISBN 1-891962-03-5
The "operations manual" for your life. Recreating your life for peace, happiness, harmony, and joy. Changing from being a physical being having transitory spiritual experiences to becoming a spiritual being in a physical body. Letting go of the duality of life.

Your Body Is Talking; Are You Listening?
$14.95, ISBN 1-891962-01-9
The theory and process of miracles. A miracle is choosing to rise above limitation and take responsibility for who you are. When you allow the awesome power of your mind to work its miracles, healing begins. We block miracles by our illusion and doubt, which induce fear. Fear is simply False Evidence Appearing Real, with sickness becoming a defense against the truth. The truth can heal any dysfunction, mental, emotional or physical. All we need know is the original cause, core issue and catalyst that caused the breakdown to manifest. Your body will tell the truth, but are you willing to listen? This book is your "how to" manual.

Recovering Your Lost Self
$14.95, ISBN 1-891962-08-6
The author's journey from victim to cause in his life. How you can find your true self and have abundance in your life. Accepting unconditional love in your life through forgiveness and acceptance. Coming to the point where peace, happiness, harmony and joy are reality, not an illusion.

Pychoneuroimmunology: The Body/Mind Medicine Connection
ISBN 1-891962-07-8
What is psychoneuroimmunolgy and the mind/body medicine connection? An overview of the modalities and processes. Integrating the concepts. Research on the modalities. The mind as network computer. Affirmations, software for the mind. Neuro-Kinesiology. Using muscle testing for clearing beliefs and concepts, programs, patterns and records that are causing allergies, emotional behavior patterns, disease, illness and physical breakdown in the body. Neuro/Cellular Repatterning, a method to access the mind's programs, beliefs and interpretations and release them to heal any disease, illness or dysfunction in the mind/body. Miracle healings on demand with love and forgiveness. Supporting the body with nutritional and herbal products.

Tapes

Tapes are available on the guided imagery to train yourself to access the records and on the process for contacting your teacher and accessing the Hall of Records.

1. The Seven Chakra Guided Imagery:
    Train yourself to step out of the body to enter the Temple and the Hall of Records.

2. Accessing your Akashic Records:
    On the process and the various forms and methods of finding the answers to all your questions.

3. Psycho/Physical Self Regulation:
    Originally a tape for runner and walkers to regulate, flush the body of toxins and burn fat for energy. Can be used to train yourself to eat properly and reduce weight.

About The Author

In today's world, the issue of credibility often comes up. How many degrees do you have? What colleges did you attend? Who did you study with? Who were your teachers? How do you know this works?

When I needed outside validation and acceptance, those were valid questions. Now I do not consider them valid, nor do I care if others reject me because I don't have the credibility they seek. What I learned in college has no relevance to what I do now in my practice. What I know is far more important than my background. Therefore, I am not interested in listing all my credentials.

Neuro/Cellular Repatterning is a process that was developed by myself and three people who worked with me during the research period: Dr. James Dorabiala, Mike Hammer and Bernard Eckes. And new information still pours in even today. This is basically a self-taught process, and everyone who worked with us over the last 20 years are our students and our teachers.

What *is* relevant is that we be open to new ideas. I will attend others' workshops and experience their treatments. Healing is an open-ended and ongoing process in which we need to be open to new ideas. The "sacred cow" syndrome is out-dated and does not work for me.

Someone once attacked me with, "You think you have the whole pie, don't you? You believe that nobody can match up to you."

My response was, " I don't think I have the whole pie, but based on the success of the last 20 years, maybe I have a few more pieces than some other practitioners."

Art was born into a family where his father wanted a child and his mother did not. As an only child, he did not have any sibling interaction, so his only contacts were at school. His dysfunctional family laid down many problems, which he has come a long way in clearing, thanks to discovery of the process he developed—Neuro/Cellular Repatterning—and the people who worked with him over the years.

In 1963, he quit college after five years feeling frustrated with the educational system. He dabbled in real estate, but found that it was not his calling. In 1965, he married Susie, his partner ever since. Their sons, Ross and Ryan, were born in 1971 and 1976.

Very few people in the field of therapy work seem to be able to stay in relationship due to the fact they do not want to deal with their own issues. Art was committed to find himself and went on a path to do so. He stabilized his own relationship by working out his issues.

In 1968, he and Susie found themselves in St. Helena, CA, rebuilding an abandoned winery. To clear the land to plant grapes, Art became a logger. To support his family while the winery was being rehabilitated, he hired out his D8 Caterpillar tractor for land-clearing and vineyard preparation. After seven years, the big money interests were pushing grape prices below what was economically viable for a small winery to stay in business, so he sold the winery.

His next venture was a restaurant which he built himself, but found that the restaurant field is one of the most demanding there are. Despite instant financial success, he sold the restaurant after four months and moved on. However, Art met his first teacher at the restaurant, someone who planted a seed of doubt about his life path. At the time, Art was trying to find himself and was studying extensively and attending self-improvement seminars. After closing time, they would spend many hours talking about their paths.

In 1978, the buyers of the restaurant went bankrupt, so their payments stopped. Art had to return to work and his quest was disrupted. Fortunately, Susie was working full-time, but in 1980, she was laid off and Art, who had a green thumb, worked as a gardener at a senior citizens' complex. Having closely studied the Findhorn community, he took the opportunity to apply what he had learned about the earth spirits. He found, from the plants themselves, that the landscape architect had put many of them in the wrong place. Over the next year, he transformed the barren grounds into magnificent flower gardens, and even built a passive solar greenhouse to grow flowers year around.

By 1982, his healing practice was established so he quit the gardener job and concentrated on researching healing practices.

Art soon found that Santa Rosa, CA did not support the type of work he was doing, and when Joshua Stone invited him to go to Los Angeles to give readings to clients, he jumped at the opportunity. He and Joshua found they worked well together as a team, and Art was able to provide a unique and valuable service to many therapists. However, the traveling almost broke up his family, so they moved to Sacramento, CA, and opened a bookstore and metaphysical center.

While Art received considerable support for this venture, he didn't anticipate that few people had the money to support it financially. Having invested all the family's savings, and refinanced their house, all went well for almost three years until he took on partners in order to expand. However, his partners did not understand the law of cause and effect, and when they embezzled $28,000, the business went under.

Knowing that "What goes around comes around," Art managed to accept what had happened, forgive them and get on with his life. However, trying to understand the lesson in this was hard to accomplish. When you are angry at losing your life savings and 20 years of hard work, the clarity and acceptance that he had set it all up came slowly. Even though he knew this at one level, it was a hard lesson to learn. The lesson was that while he received much verbal validation from those who supported the center, he was paying over half its operational costs.

The failure was a mixed blessing. It put him on a new path, one in which he traveled and spread the word of his work, and really had to get down to business. He did finally recover, even though they lost their house and one of their cars.

Looking back, Art recognizes the many great strides forward that he has made. Today, he travels extensively giving lectures, seminars and workshops on a variety of subjects. He also has a circuit of cities that he visits regularly for individual sessions.

He has set up a publishing company to promote his books (see list in the front of this book), and they are available through the Wellness Institute. Many of them will be in bookstores in 1999.

He can be reached at 1 800- OK LET GO (655-3846)

CPSIA information can be obtained
at www.ICGtesting.com
Printed in the USA
BVHW031731030323
659654BV00016B/100